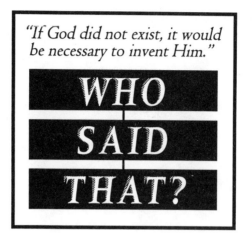

"If God did not exist, it would
be necessary to invent Him."

WHO
SAID
THAT?

. . . .

MORE THAN 2,500 USABLE
QUOTES AND ILLUSTRATIONS

. . . .

GEORGE SWEETING

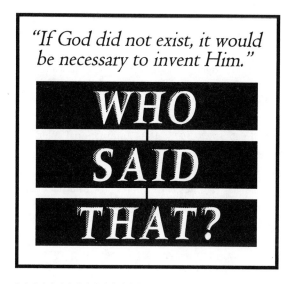

"If God did not exist, it would be necessary to invent Him."

WHO SAID THAT?

. . . .

MORE THAN 2,500 USABLE QUOTES AND ILLUSTRATIONS

. . . .

GEORGE SWEETING

MOODY PRESS
CHICAGO

WHO SAID THAT?
© 1994, 1995 by
GEORGE W. SWEETING

Originally published as *Great Quotes and Illustrations*
Copyright © 1985 by Word, Incorporated. Rights returned to author, 1994.

Unless otherwise marked, all Scripture quotations are from the King James Version.

Scripture quotations marked NIV are from the *Holy Bible: New International Version®*. Copyright © 1973, 1978, 1984 International Bible Society. Used by permission of Zondervan Publishing House. All rights reserved.

The "NIV" and "New International Version" trademarks are registered in the United States Patent and Trademark Office by International Bible Society. Use of either trademark requires permission of the International Bible Society.

Scripture quotations marked NKJV are taken from *The New King James Version*. Copyright © 1979, 1980, 1982, Thomas Nelson, Inc., Publishers. All rights reserved.

Scripture quotations marked NASB are taken from the *New American Standard Bible*, © 1960, 1962, 1963, 1968, 1971, 1972, 1973, 1975, 1977, 1994 by The Lockman Foundation, and are used by permission. All rights reserved.

Scripture quotations marked NEB are taken from *The New English Bible* © 1961, 1970 by the Delegates of the Oxford University Press and the Syndics of the Cambridge University Press. Used by permission.

Verses marked TLB are taken from *The Living Bible*, © 1971. Used by permission of Tyndale House Publishers, Inc., Wheaton, IL 60189. All rights reserved.

The use of selected references from various versions of the Bible in this publication does not necessarily imply publisher endorsement of the versions in their entirety.

ISBN 0-8024-9199-5

7 9 10 8 6

Printed in the United States of America

This volume is affectionately dedicated to my four sons: George David, James Douglas, Donald William, and Robert Bruce. They have been to me an endless source of joy and inspiration.

Special appreciation is offered to Donald William Sweeting for his assistance in compiling this volume.

Also, to my secretary, Joanna Zarriello, for her superb help in preparing the manuscript.

CONTENTS

INTRODUCTION

The right quotation at the right time has explosive power.

Quotations express thought in an unforgettable way, helping the listener to understand faster and remember longer. Supporting a point by quoting Augustine, Luther, John Wesley, D. L. Moody, or Billy Graham aids believability as well as attention, when it's necessary to increase interest.

I have drawn material from a wide source of literature and human experience. It's recommended that the reader, wisely and appropriately, apply the truths *where they fit*. In some cases a quotation may be used to stimulate thought or encourage further exploration.

Early in my ministry I noticed the power and impact of quotations and illustrations. The eloquent Charles Haddon Spurgeon commented, "He who never quotes, is never quoted."

As windows admit light to a house, quotations and illustrations shed clarity to a lesson, sermon, or speech. Even the most academic member of your audience will sit up and listen attentively when you use such a tool.

Abraham Lincoln was a gifted user of stories: "They say I tell many stories; I reckon I do, but I have found in the course of a long experience that common people, take them as they run, are more easily informed through the medium of a broad illustration than in any other way, and as to what the hypercritical few may think, I care not."

Edmund Fuller comments, "Anecdotes are stories with points. They are tools—nail sinkers to drive home arguments firmly. They are the origin of all teaching."

It is my desire that this volume will be helpful, to drive home eternal truths.

Those paragraphs signed "G. S." are my own contributions to the book.

George Sweeting
Chancellor
Moody Bible Institute

GREAT QUOTES AND ILLUSTRATIONS

Great minds ancient and modern have contributed their thoughts to this collection. Here are a few of the contributors:

Konrad Adenauer
Alexander the Great
Augustine
Donald Grey Barnhouse
Joseph Bayly
Julius Caesar
Oswald Chambers
Henry Drummond
Robert Frost
Billy Graham
Richard Halverson
Vance Havner
Victor Hugo
John F. Kennedy
C. S. Lewis
Douglas MacArthur

John Milton
Malcolm Muggeridge
Florence Nightingale
Harold John Ockenga
Blaise Pascal
John D. Rockefeller
Theodore Roosevelt
Lorne Sanny
Francis Schaeffer
C. T. Studd
Alfred, Lord Tennyson
Mark Twain
William Wordsworth
John Wesley
Warren Wiersbe
Thomas Wolfe

AMONG THE SUBJECTS DEALT WITH ARE:

ability
action
adversity
age
angels
Antichrist
atheism
boredom
caring
change
Christian living

Christmas
church
communication
compassion
contentment
courtesy
depression
education
encouragement
giving
God

happiness
heaven
hell
humility
humor*
joy
laziness
love
memory
money

*special section on humorous quotes and stories

ACKNOWLEDGMENTS

Grateful acknowledgment is hereby expressed to the following who have granted permission to include copyrighted materials in this book. Any inadvertent omission of credit will be gladly corrected in future editions.

Joseph Bayly. Materials from *The Gospel Blimp . . . and Other Modern Parables,* © 1983; and *The View from a Hearse,* © 1969, used by permission of Chariot family Publishing.

Harry Blamires. From *The Christian Mind,* © 1963 by Harry Blamires. Used by permission of Servant Publications.

Jerome Carcopino. From *Daily Life in Ancient Rome.* Reprinted by permission of Yale University Press.

B. J. Chitwood. From *A Faith That Works* (Nashville: Broadman Press, 1969). All Rights reserved. Used by permission.

Mrs. Paul A. Ciulhe. Excerpts reprinted with permission from the December 1954 *Reader's Digest.*

Stephen B. Clark. From *Man and Woman in Christ,* © 1980 by Stephen B. Clark. Used by permission of Servant Publications.

Henry Clay. From *Individual Word for Individuals.* Used by permission of YMCA of the USA, Chicago, Illinois.

S. Maxwell Coder. From *God's Will for Your Life.* Copyright © 1946, Moody Bible Institute of Chicago. Moody Press. Used by permission.

Charles W. Colson. Taken from *Loving God* by Charles Colson. Copyright © 1983, 1987 by Charles W. Colson. Used by permission of Zondervan Publishing House.

Jean-Pierre De Caussade. From *Abandonment to Divine Providence* by Jean-Pierre De Caussade, translated by John Beevers. Copyright © 1975 by John Beevers. Reprinted by permission of Doubleday & Company, Inc.

T. S. Eliot. Excerpt from "Choruses from 'The Rock'" in *Collected Poems 1909–1962* by T. S. Eliot, copyright 1936 by Harcourt Brace & Company, copyright © 1964, 1963 by T. S. Eliot; reprinted by permission of Harcourt Brace & Company and Faber & Faber Ltd. (London).

Jacques Ellul. From *The Meaning of the City* by Jacques Ellul, © 1970, Wm. B. Eerdmans Publishing Co.

Billy Graham. From *Day-by-Day with Billy Graham,* compiled and edited by Joan Winmill Brown. Minneapolis: World Wide Publications. Copyright © 1976 by the Billy Graham Evangelistic Association. Used by permission of World Wide Publications.

He who resolves never to ransack any mind but his own will be soon reduced, from mere barrenness, to the poorest of all imitations: he will be obliged to imitate himself.

SIR JOSHUA REYNOLDS
TO THE STUDENTS OF THE ROYAL ACADEMY OF ARTS

ABILITY

When it's a question of God's almighty Spirit, never say, "I can't."
OSWALD CHAMBERS

God does not ask about our ability, but our availability.
UNKNOWN

I can do all things through Christ who strengthens me.
PHILIPPIANS 4:13 NKJV

Knock the "T" off of "can't" and make it "can."
G. S.

I add this also, that rational ability without education has oftener raised man to glory and virtue, than education without natural ability.
CICERO

It is all one to me if a man comes from Sing Sing Prison or Harvard. We hire a man, not his history.
HENRY FORD

Just as ordinary sun rays when focused through a magnifying glass burn holes in the material beneath, so ordinary ability, when focused, excels.
G. S.

When love and skill work together, expect a masterpiece.
JOHN RUSKIN

Ability and learning contrasted. Charles II once expressed his astonishment that such a learned man as Dr. Owen should go so often to hear John Bunyan, the ignorant tinker preacher. "Had I the tinker's ability, your Majesty, I would gladly relinquish my learning."

T. DE WITT TALMAGE

Every man who can be a first-rate something—as every man can be who is a man at all—has no right to be a fifth-rate something; for a fifth-rate something is no better than a first-rate nothing.

J. G. HOLLAND,
PLAIN TALKS ON FAMILIAR SUBJECTS

Ability
1. *Able to save rough fishermen, Peter, Andrew, James, and John:* John 1:35–42, Luke 5:3–11.
2. *Able to save despised tax collectors:* Matthew, Luke 5:27–29; Zacchaeus, Luke 19:1–10.
3. *Able to save a master in Israel, a religious leader and highly moral man, Nicodemus:* John 3.
4. *Able to save a much married and religiously heretical woman:* John 4:7–39.
5. *Able to save a woman taken in adultery:* John 8:1–11.
6. *Able to save a dying thief:* Luke 23:39–43.
7. *Able to save a sorcerer:* Acts 8:9–24.
8. *Able to save the chief of sinners, the leading opponent and persecutor of Christianity, Saul of Tarsus:* Acts 9:1–31; 1 Timothy 1:15.
9. *Able to save a Roman military officer, Cornelius:* Acts 10.
10. *Able to save a business woman, Lydia:* Acts 16:14–15.
11. *Able to save a brutal jailer:* Acts 16:30–34.
12. *Able to save an innumerable multitude out of all tribes and tongues and nations whom John saw already safe in heaven:* Revelation 7:9–17.

F. D. WHITESELL,
EVANGELISTIC ILLUSTRATIONS

The winds and waves are always on the side of the ablest navigators.
EDWARD GIBBON

Do what you can, with what you have, where you are.
THEODORE ROOSEVELT

What we do upon some great occasion will probably depend on what we already are; and what we are, will be the result of previous years of self-discipline.
H. P. LIDDON

Men are often capable of greater things than they perform. They are sent into the world with bills of credit, and seldom draw to their full extent.
HORACE WALPOLE

A genius can't be forced; nor can you make an ape an alderman.
THOMAS SOMERVILLE

When my horse is running good, I don't stop to give him sugar.
WILLIAM FAULKNER

ACTION

And if it seems evil to you to serve the Lord, choose for yourselves this day whom you will serve, whether the gods which your fathers served that were on the other side of the River, or the gods of the Amorites, in whose land you dwell. But as for me and my house, we will serve the Lord.
JOSHUA 24:15 NKJV

The actions of men [are] the best interpreters of their thoughts.
JOHN LOCKE

Eighty percent of success is showing up.
WOODY ALLEN

But be doers of the word, and not hearers only, deceiving your own selves.

JAMES 1:22

When Demosthenes was asked what were the three most important aspects of oratory, he answered, "Action, Action, Action."
PLUTARCH

Dwight L. Moody was a man of action. Once he mentioned a clever promotion idea to a church leader and asked, "What do you think?" "We've been aimin' to do it for two years," the layman replied. "Well, now," Moody retorted, "don't you think it's time to fire?"
G. S.

A dog barks when his master is attacked. I would be a coward if I saw that God's truth is attacked and yet would remain silent.
JOHN CALVIN

Action may not always bring happiness; but there is no happiness without action.
BENJAMIN DISRAELI

Resolved, never to do anything which I should be afraid to do, if it were my last of life.
JONATHAN EDWARDS

My hat's in the ring! The fight is on and I am stripped to the buff!
THEODORE ROOSEVELT

Thou wilt find rest from vain fancies if thou doest every act in life as though it were thy last.
MARCUS AURELIUS

It is difficult to steer a parked car, so get moving.
HENRIETTA MEARS

In the book In Search of Excellence, *Thomas J. Peters and Robert H. Waterman suggest eight qualities that are characteristic of excellent companies in the United States. The first is "a bias for action," which Peters and Waterman describe as a tendency to act rather than to remain passive.*

The authors use phrases like, "do it," "fix it," "try it," and state that "chaotic action is preferable to orderly inaction."

Ludwig van Beethoven arose at daybreak and immediately began composing until 2 P.M. when he would have dinner. He worked in long stretches of unbroken time to allow his thoughts to unfold and flow uninterrupted. He exemplified a bias for action.

John Wesley, the founder of Methodism, traveled more than 250,000 miles on horseback, preaching often fifteen times a week for over fifty years. As an octogenarian, he complained that he found it difficult to work more than fifteen hours a day.

C. T. WINCHESTER

We must not sit still and look for miracles; up and be doing, and the Lord will be with thee. Prayer and pains, through faith in Christ Jesus, will do anything.

JOHN ELIOT

ADVERSITY
· ·

When a man gets to despair he knows that all his thinking will never get him out. He will only get out by the sheer creative effort of God. Consequently he is in the right attitude to receive from God that which he cannot gain for himself. (Acts 12)

OSWALD CHAMBERS

Adversities do not make a man frail. They show what sort of man he is.

THOMAS À KEMPIS

We say, "sorrow, disaster, calamity"; God says, "chastening," and it sounds sweet to Him though it is a discord to our ears. Don't faint when you are rebuked, and don't despise the chastening of the Lord. "In your patience possess ye your souls."

OSWALD CHAMBERS

Sometimes your medicine bottle has on it, "Shake well before using." That is what God has to do with some of His people. He has to shake them well before they are ever usable.

VANCE HAVNER

When I dig another out of trouble, the hole from which I lift him is the place where I bury my own.

ANONYMOUS

We are always on the anvil; by trials God is shaping us for higher things.

HENRY WARD BEECHER

There are three things to remember concerning trials:
  1. *Trials are a common experience of all of us. No one is immune. Trials are a part of living.*
  2. *Trials are transitory. C. B. Williams translates 1 Peter 1:6 this way: "In such a hope keep on rejoicing, although for a little while you must be sorrow-stricken with various trials." Trials, though difficult, are "for a little while."*
  3. *Trials are lessons that shouldn't be wasted. Though not enjoyable or necessarily good in themselves, trials constitute a divine work for our ultimate good. Jesus never promised an easy journey, but He did promise a safe landing.*

G. S.

Pressure produces! As we face the pressures of life, let it not just be a passive acceptance, but rather a positive cooperation with God's purpose for our lives.

G. S.

No author, without a trial, can conceive of the difficulty of writing a romance about a country where there is no shadow, no antiquity, no mystery, no picturesque and gloomy wrong, not anything but a common-place prosperity, in broad and simply daylight, as is happily the case with my dear native land. . . . Romance and poetry, ivy, lichens and wallflowers need rain to make them grow.

NATHANIEL HAWTHORNE,
PREFACE TO *THE MARBLE FAUN*

A young boy was sailing a small sailboat. The string that held his boat snapped, and the little boat was blown farther and farther out on the water. An older boy picked up some stones and began to throw them in the direction of the boat. That infuriated the little boy. But shortly he learned that the older boy's purpose was for his good. Each stone went just beyond the boat, and the resulting waves gently pushed it back to shore.

G. S.

*Sweet are the uses of adversity;
Which, like the toad, ugly and venomous,
Wears yet a precious jewel in his head;
And this our life, exempt from public haunt,
Finds tongues in trees, books in the running brooks,
Sermons in stones, and good in every thing.*

WILLIAM SHAKESPEARE,
AS YOU LIKE IT

ADVERTISING
· ·

Advertising may be described as the science of arresting the human intelligence long enough to get money from it.

STEPHEN LEACOCK

I do not read advertisements — I would spend all my time wanting things.

ARCHBISHOP OF CANTERBURY

The Devil comes along with something the natural man wants, and he paints the town red to let them know he is coming. The church comes along with something the natural man doesn't want, and thousands of pastors seem to think a mere announcement of the project from the pulpit is quite enough.

W. E. BIEDERWOLF

Very old indeed is advertising. The rainbow in the clouds, according to Scripture, was one of the early advertisements. It promised that men should not be destroyed by a flood again. In that advertisement, brilliant in color, magnified in size, Supreme Power announced the fact that that particular flood was to be the last flood.

ARTHUR BRISBANE

ADVICE

In those days he was wiser than he is now — he used frequently to take my advice.

WINSTON CHURCHILL

I not only use all the brains I have but all I can borrow.

WOODROW WILSON

A good scare is worth more to a man than good advice.

E. W. HOWE

It takes a great man to give sound advice tactfully, but a greater to accept it graciously.

J. C. MACAULAY

Don't follow any advice, no matter how good, until you feel as deeply in your spirit as you think in your mind that the counsel is wise.

DAVID SEABURY

In his own gentle, procrastinating way, Dr. George Harris did much as president of Amherst College, but the unpleasant duties of such a post he neglected or ignored. He was not really opposed to work, but I never heard him say much in favor of it. One autumn he rose in chapel to address the students at the first assembly of the year, but after three or four sentences he got tired and, breaking into a happy smile, said: "I intended to give you some advice, but now I remember how much is left over from last year unused." With that he took his hat and walked out.

JOHN ERSKINE,
THE MEMORY OF CERTAIN PERSONS

ADVOCATE

There is an old ploughman in the country I sometimes talk with, and he often says, though in uncouth words, some precious things. He said to me one day, "The other day, sir, the devil was tempting me and I tried to answer him; but I found he was an old lawyer, and understood the law a great deal better than I did, so I gave over, and would not argue with him any more; so I said to him, 'What do you trouble me for?'

"'Why,' said he, 'about your soul.'

"'Oh!' said I, 'that is no business of mine; I have given my soul over into the hand of Christ; I have transferred everything to him; if you want an answer to your doubts and queries, you must apply to my Advocate.'"

CHARLES HADDON SPURGEON

Is Christ thy advocate to plead thy cause?
Art thou His client? Such shall never slide.
He never lost His case. . . .
My case is bad, Lord, be my advocate.
My sin is red: I'm under God's arrest.

EDWARD TAYLOR

*The words the Lord Jesus used when He promised to send the Holy
Spirit leave no room for the idea that He is merely a force or an
impersonal influence. Jesus said, "I will pray the Father, and He
shall give you another Comforter" (John 14:16). The word* another
*in the Greek means "one the same as." The Holy Spirit is the same as
Christ; He is a person. The word* comforter *is from the Greek word*
paraklete, *which means "one called alongside." It is the same word
translated "advocate" in I John 2:1. It is a word that only makes
sense if it is applied to a personal being. The Holy Spirit is our
Paraclete. He is one called to aid us, to instruct us, to intercede for us.
He is a person.*

G. S.

AFFLICTION
·······································

*Nothing can render affliction so insupportable as the load of sin.
Would you then be fitted for afflictions? Be sure to get the burden of
your sins laid aside, and then what affliction soever you may meet
with will be very easy to you.*

JOHN BUNYAN

*If all the skies were sunshine
Our faces would be fain
To feel once more upon them
The cooling splash of rain.*
HENRY VAN DYKE

*God will not permit any troubles to come upon us, unless He has a
specific plan by which great blessing can come out of the difficulty.*
PETER MARSHALL

*Iron till it be thoroughly heated is incapable to be wrought; so God
sees good to cast some men into the furnace of affliction, and then
beats them on his anvil into what frame he pleases.*
ANNE BRADSTREET

The Lord gets his best soldiers out of the highlands of affliction.
CHARLES HADDON SPURGEON

Affliction is not sent in vain, young man,
From that good God, who chastens whom he loves.
ROBERT SOUTHEY

Afflictions are but the shadows of God's wings.
GEORGE MACDONALD

I waited patiently for the Lord; and he inclined unto me, and heard my cry.
PSALM 40:1

Hear my voice, O God, in my prayer: preserve my life from fear of the enemy.
PSALM 64:1

For thou, O God, hast proved us: thou hast tried us, as silver is tried.
PSALM 66:10

It is good for me that I have been afflicted; that I might learn thy statutes.
PSALM 119:71

AGE
· ·

At a church social a visitor asked the pastor to guess her age. When he hesitated, she said, "Oh, you must have some idea."

"I have two ideas," he admitted. "My problem is . . . I can't decide whether to make you ten years younger because of your looks, or ten years older because of your charm."
ANONYMOUS

A stockbroker urged Claude Pepper to buy a stock that would triple in value every year. Pepper told him, "At my age, I don't even buy green bananas."

CLAUDE PEPPER

I wake up every morning at eight and grab for the morning paper. Then I look at the obituary page. If my name is not on it, I get up.

HARRY HERSHFIELD

Every morning a retired gentleman took a short stroll around his yard before starting his customary longer walk around several blocks. He explained to a curious neighbor, "It's the preamble to my constitution."

ANONYMOUS

When Somerset Maugham was recuperating from the flu an admirer called and asked, "Could I send you fruit, or would you prefer flowers?" He was eighty-eight years old. He told her, "It's too late for fruit, too early for flowers."

W. SOMERSET MAUGHAM

How can I die? I'm booked.

GEORGE BURNS

Age doesn't matter, unless you're cheese.

BILL BURKE

WIFE: Will you love me when I'm old and gray and wrinkled? HUSBAND: I do.

ANONYMOUS

Youth is the gift of nature, but age is a work of art.

GARSON KANIN

Getting older is like water skiing, when you slow down, you go down.

G. S.

28

Children are a great help. They are a comfort in your old age. And they help you reach it faster, too.

> *Ashes to ashes, and dust to dust,*
> *If Alzheimer's don't kill ya, then Parkinson's must.*

There are three ages to mankind, youth, middle age, and. . . . My you're looking good.

You can take no credit for beauty at sixteen. But if you are beautiful at sixty, it will be your soul's own doing.
MARIE STOPES

He's so old his blood type was discontinued.
BILL DANA

> *Grow old along with me!*
> *The best is yet to be,*
> *The last of life, for which the first was made:*
> *Our times are in His hand*
> *Who saith: "A whole I planned,*
> *Youth shows but half; trust God: see all, nor be afraid!"*
ROBERT BROWNING, *RABBI BEN EZRA*

Getting older is like riding a bicycle, if you don't keep peddling, you'll fall.
CLAUDE PEPPER

After being defeated in 1945, Winston Churchill was offered a dukedom by the king and the greatly coveted Order of the Garter. He remarked, "Why should I accept the Order of the Garter from His Majesty when the people have just given me the Order of the Boot?"
WINSTON CHURCHILL

Whatever poet, orator or sage may say of it, old age is still old age.
SINCLAIR LEWIS

How to tell you're getting older:
When your knees buckle but your belt won't
When everything hurts and what doesn't hurt, doesn't work.
When you bend over to tie your shoelaces and you think,
Is there anything else I ought to do, while I'm down here?
When, if you're a man, more hair grows out of your ears than on
your head.
When a handsome man or a pretty woman passes by and you don't
notice.
When you have so many liver spots on your hand that they look like
speckled sausage.
And when you pray for a good prune juice harvest.

UNKNOWN

Age-based retirement arbitrarily severs productive persons from their
livelihood, squanders their talents, scars their health, strains an
already overburdened Social Security system, and drives many elderly
people into poverty and despair. Ageism is as odious as racism and
sexism.

CLAUDE PEPPER

Preparation for old age should begin not later than one's teens. A life
which is empty of purpose until 65 will not suddenly become filled on
retirement.

ARTHUR MORGAN

It's not how old you are, but how you are old.

MARIE DRESSLER

When David Ben-Gurion came out of retirement for the ninth time,
he was asked by an American why he bothered to retire. "It's like
those 'going out of business' signs you see along Seventh Avenue — a
chance to unload stock he doesn't want, hire a new staff, and make a
different contract with the union."

DAVID BEN-GURION

Age should not have its face lifted, but it should rather teach the world to admire wrinkles as the etchings of experience and the firm line of character.

RALPH BARTON PERRY

We are happier in many ways when we are old than when we were young. The young sow wild oats. The old grow sage.

WINSTON CHURCHILL

I married an archeologist because the older I grow, the more he appreciates me.

AGATHA CHRISTIE

Growing old isn't so bad when you consider the alternative.

MAURICE CHEVALIER

Life begins at 40—but so do fallen arches, rheumatism, faulty eyesight, and the tendency to tell a story to the same person, three or four times.

BILL FEATHER

Many foxes grow gray but few grow good.

BENJAMIN FRANKLIN

Lord, Thou knowest better than I know myself that I am growing older. Keep me from getting too talkative, and thinking I must say something on every subject and on every occasion. Release me from craving to straighten out everybody's affairs. Teach me the glorious lesson that occasionally it is possible that I may be mistaken. Make me thoughtful, but not moody, helpful, but not bossy; for Thou knowest, Lord, that I want a few friends at the end.

ANONYMOUS

I've never known a person to live to be one hundred and be remarkable for anything else.

JOSH BILLINGS

We have no right to look for a happy old age if in our living we habitually violate physical and spiritual law. The full blessing of length of days comes to those who have known how to live, and the beauty of the years of maturity can be assured only by maintaining high standards of living.

JANET BAIRD

To me—old age is fifteen years older than I am.

BERNARD MANNES BARUCH

If a thing is old, it is a sign that it was fit to live. Old families, old customs, old styles survive because they are fit to survive. The guarantee of continuity is quality. Submerge the good in a flood of the new, and the good will come back to join the good which the new brings with it. Old-fashioned hospitality, old-fashioned politics, old-fashioned honor in business had qualities of survival. These will come back.

ANONYMOUS

Ah, nothing is too late,
Till the tired heart shall cease to palpitate.

HENRY WADSWORTH LONGFELLOW

What if someone had decided that Pablo Picasso, Pablo Casals, or Michelangelo, still producing in their eighties and nineties, had "no future" when they became seventy years old?

MARGARET C. ELWELL

Therefore we do not lose heart. Even though our outward man is perishing, yet the inward man is being renewed day by day.

2 CORINTHIANS 4:16 NKJV

While we look not at the things which are seen, but at the things which are not seen: for the things which are seen are temporal; but the things which are not seen are eternal.

2 CORINTHIANS 4:18

*When a man's friends begin to compliment him about looking young,
he may be sure that they think he is growing old.*
WASHINGTON IRVING

You know you're getting old when the candles cost more than the cake.
BOB HOPE

*Someday you will read in the papers that Moody is dead. Don't you
believe a word of it. At that moment I shall be more alive than I am
now. . . . I was born of the flesh in 1837, I was born of the spirit in
1855. That which is born of the flesh may die. That which is born of
the Spirit shall live forever.*
D. L. MOODY

*So, like a prisoner awaiting his release, like a school boy when the end
of term is near, like a migrant bird ready to fly south, like a patient in
[the] hospital anxiously scanning the doctor's face to see whether a discharge may be expected, I long to be gone. Extricating myself from the
flesh I have too long inhabited, hearing the key turn in the lock of
Time so that the great doors of eternity swing open, disengaging my
tired mind from its interminable conundrums, and my tired ego from
its wearisome insistencies. Such is the prospect of death.*
MALCOLM MUGGERIDGE

*If you draw near the end in somber circumstances, remember that as a
faithful child of God you await promotion. Who knows but that the
brightest jewel in your crown is for that lonely afternoon and night
when all seemed lost but you believed anyway. Remember John the
Baptist in prison and John on Patmos and countless millions who have
been on that road before you. Remember Mr. Fearing in Bunyan's
immortal* Pilgrim's Progress, *who dreaded Jordan all his days. But
when he reached it, the water was at a record low, and he got across
"not much above wet-shod." The last chapter in life can be the best.*
VANCE HAVNER

Crossing the Bar

Sunset and evening star,
　　And one clear call for me!
And may there be no moaning of the bar,
　　When I put out to sea,

But such a tide as moving seems asleep,
　　Too full for sound and foam,
When that which drew from out the boundless deep
　　Turns again home.

Twilight and evening bell,
　　And after that the dark!
And may there be no sadness of farewell,
　　When I embark;

For though from out our bourne of Time and Place
　　The flood may bear me far,
I hope to see my Pilot face to face
　　When I have crossed the bar.

ALFRED, LORD TENNYSON, AT ABOUT EIGHTY

Leaf after leaf drops off, flower after flower,
Some in the chill, some in the warmer hour:
Alike they flourish and alike they fall,
And Earth who nourisheth them receives them all.
Should we, her wiser sons, be less content
To sink into her lap when life is spent?

WALTER SAVAGE LANDOR

Psalm 90

Lord, thou hast been our dwelling place in all generations.

Before the mountains were brought forth, or ever thou hadst formed the earth and the world, even from everlasting to everlasting, thou art God.

Thou turnest man to destruction; and sayest, Return, ye children of men.

For a thousand years in thy sight are but as yesterday when it is past, and as a watch in the night.

Thou carriest them away as with a flood; they are as a sleep: in the morning they are like grass which groweth up.

In the morning it flourisheth, and groweth up; in the evening it is cut down, and withereth.

For we are consumed by thine anger, and by thy wrath are troubled.

Thou has set our iniquities before thee, our secret sins in the light of thy countenance.

For all our days are passed away in thy wrath: we spend our years as a tale that is told.

The days of our years are threescore years and ten; and if by reason of strength they be fourscore years, yet is their strength labor and sorrow; for it is soon cut off, and we fly away.

Who knoweth the power of thine anger? Even according to thy fear, so is thy wrath.

So teach us to number our days, that we may apply our hearts unto wisdom.

Return, O Lord, how long? and let it repent thee concerning thy servants.

O satisfy us early with thy mercy; that we may rejoice and be glad all our days.

Make us glad according to the days wherein thou hast afflicted us, and the years wherin we have seen evil.

Let thy work appear unto thy servants, and thy glory unto their children.

And let the beauty of the Lord our God be upon us; and establish thou the work of our hands upon us; yea, the work of our hands establish thou it.

John Anderson My Jo

John Anderson my jo, John,
 When we were first acquent;
Your locks were like the raven,
 Your bony brow was brent;
But now your brow is beld, John,
 Your locks are like the snaw;
But blessings on your frosty pow,
 John Anderson my Jo.

John Anderson my jo, John,
 We clamb the hill the gither;
And mony a canty day, John,
 We've had wi' ane anither:
Now we maun totter down, John,
 And hand in hand we'll go;
And sleep the gither at the foot,
 John Anderson my Jo.

ROBERT BURNS

AIM
· ·

Brethren, I do not count myself to have apprehended; but one thing I do, forgetting those things which are behind and reaching forward to those things which are ahead, I press toward the goal for the prize of the upward call of God in Christ Jesus.

PHILIPPIANS 3:13–14 NKJV

Blessed are the single-hearted, for they shall enjoy much peace. . . . If you refuse to be hurried and pressed, if you stay your soul on God, nothing can keep you from that clearness of spirit which is life and peace. In that stillness you will know what His will is.

AMY CARMICHAEL

The presence of a long-term, conscious goal has helped me maintain stability through the ubiquitous changes of over half a century.
MARY FRANCIS SHURA CRAIG

Give me a man who says, "This one thing I do," and not, "These fifty things, I dabble in."
D. L. MOODY

To live successfully, everyone needs a purpose.
G. S.

One thing I have desired of the Lord, that will I seek: That I may dwell in the house of the Lord all the days of my life, to behold the beauty of the Lord, and to inquire in His temple.
PSALM 27:4 NKJV

ALCOHOL

Total abstinence is considered Victorian and puritanical. We discuss what to do about alcoholism, but nobody seems to want to do much about alcohol. And that is simply a matter of trying to mop up the floor while you leave the faucet running.
VANCE HAVNER

Good-bye, John. You were God's worst enemy. You were Hell's best friend.
BILLY SUNDAY,
SERMON ON THE BEGINNING OF PROHIBITION
NORFOLK, VIRGINIA 16 JULY 1929
"JOHN" WAS JOHN BARLEYCORN

I'm tired of hearing sin called sickness and alcoholism a disease. It's the only disease I know of that we're spending hundreds of millions of dollars a year to spread.
VANCE HAVNER

I'm tired of hearing about temperance instead of abstinence, in order to please the cocktail crowd in church congregations.
VANCE HAVNER

Some of the most dreadful mischiefs that afflict mankind proceed from wine; it is the cause of disease, quarrels, sedition, idleness, aversion to labor, and every species of domestic accord.
FRANÇOIS FÉNELON

There is a devil in every berry of the grape.
THE QUR'AN

O thou invisible spirit of wine, if thou hast no name to be known by, let us call thee devil!
WILLIAM SHAKESPEARE, *OTHELLO*

AMBITION

Cromwell, I charge thee, fling away ambition:
By that sin fell the angels; how can man, then,
The image of his Maker, hope to win by it?
Love thyself last: cherish those hearts that hate thee;
Corruption wins not more than honesty.
Still in the right hand carry gentle peace,
To silence envious tongues. Be just, fear not. . . .
WILLIAM SHAKESPEARE, *HENRY VIII*

I . . . had ambition not only to go farther than any man had ever been before, but as far as it was possible for a man to go.
CAPTAIN JAMES COOK

Ambition is the germ from which all growth of nobleness proceeds.
T. D. ENGLISH

Keep away from people who try to belittle your ambitions. Small people always do that, but the really great make you feel that you, too, can become great.

MARK TWAIN

Keep your feet on the ground, but let your heart soar as high as it will. Refuse to be average or to surrender to the chill of your spiritual environment.

A. W. TOZER, *THE ROOT OF THE RIGHTEOUS*

AMERICA
· ·

America is a large friendly dog in a small room. Every time it wags its tail, it knocks over a chair.

ARNOLD TOYNBEE

Patriotism is not a short and frenzied outburst of emotion but the tranquil and steady dedication of a lifetime.

ADLAI E. STEVENSON
SPEECH TO AN AMERICAN LEGION CONVENTION
AUGUST 1952

"My country, right or wrong" is a thing no patriot would think of saying except in a desperate case. It is like saying "My mother, drunk or sober."

G. K. CHESTERTON, *THE DEFENDANT*, 1901

Double—no triple—our troubles and we'd still be better off than any other people on earth. . . . It is time that we recognized that ours was, in truth, a noble cause.

RONALD REAGAN

On Thanksgiving Day, all over America, families sit down to dinner at the same moment—halftime.

ANONYMOUS

39

The real democratic American idea is, not that every man shall be on a level with every other man, but that every man shall have liberty to be what God made him, without hindrance.

HENRY WARD BEECHER

Many years ago, Alexis de Tocqueville, the famous French political philosopher, visited America. He came here when this nation was very young to find the secret of our greatness.

He traveled from town to town, talking with people and asking questions. He examined our national government, our schools and centers of business, without finding the reason for our strength.

Not till he visited the churches of America and witnessed the pulpits of this land "aflame with righteousness" did he find the secret of our greatness.

Returning to France, he summarized his findings with this word of warning: "America is great because America is good, and if America ever ceases to be good, America will cease to be great."

G. S.

Having undertaken, for the glorie of God, and advancements of the Christian faith and honour of our king & countrie, a voyage to plant the first colonie in the Northerne parts of Virginia, doe by these presents solemnly & mutualy in the presence of God, and one of another, covenant & combine our selves togeather into a civill body politick; for our better ordering, & preservation & furtherance of the ends aforesaid; and by vertue hearof to eneacts, constitute, and frame such just & equall lawes, ordinances, Act, constitutions, & offices, from time to time, as shall be thought most meete & convenient for the generall good of the Colonie: unto whiche we promise all due submission and obedience.

WILLIAM BRADFORD

No matter how dark and brutish American society may become, it can never extinguish the light of Christlike hearts and homes and churches.

JOSEPH STOWELL

Give me your tired, your poor,
Your huddled masses yearning to breathe free,
The wretched refuse of your teeming shore,
Send these, the homeless, tempest-tossed, to me:
I lift my lamp beside the golden door.

EMMA LAZARUS,
INSCRIPTION ON STATUE OF LIBERTY

Back of every great civilization, behind all the power and wealth, is
something as powerful . . . a set of ideas, attitudes, convictions and the
confidence that those ideas and convictions are viable. No nation can
achieve greatness unless it believes in something—and unless that
something has the moral dimensions to sustain a great civilization.

JOHN W. GARDNER, *NO EASY VICTORS*

In the book The Ugly American *[by William Lederer and Eugene*
Burdick] an Asian journalist writes, "Poor America. It took the
British a hundred years to lose their prestige in Asia. America has
managed to lose hers in ten years." The book in general gives the
impression that we are loud, ostentatious, self-centered, and, worst of
all, proud and haughty.

G. S.

I am well aware of the toil, and blood, and treasure, that it will cost
us to maintain this declaration, and support and defend these States.
Yet through all the gloom, I can see the rays of ravishing light and
glory. . . . The second day of July, 1776, will be the most memorable
epoch in the history of America. I am apt to believe that it will be
celebrated by succeeding generations as the great anniversary festival.
It ought to be commemorated as the day of deliverance, by solemn acts
of devotion to God Almighty. It ought to be solemnized with pomp
and parade, with shows, games, sports, guns, bells, bonfires, and
illuminations, from one end of this continent to the other, from this
time forward forevermore.

JOHN ADAMS,
LETTER TO ABIGAIL ADAMS, 3 JULY 1776

*America—where people do not inquire of a stranger, "What is he?"
but "What can he do?"*

ANONYMOUS

ANCESTORS

*My ancestors didn't come over on the Mayflower, but they were there
to meet the boat.*

WILL ROGERS

Every man is an omnibus in which his ancestors ride.

OLIVER WENDELL HOLMES, SR.

*The kind of ancestors we have had is not as important as the kind of
descendants our ancestors have.*

ANONYMOUS

Whoever serves his country well has no need of ancestors.

VOLTAIRE

He who boasts of his descent, praises the deeds of another.

SENECA

ANGELS

*An angel is a spiritual creature created by God without a body for the
service of Christendom and the church.*

MARTIN LUTHER

*Christians should never fail to sense the operation of an angelic glory.
It forever eclipses the world of demonic powers, as the sun does a
candle's light.*

BILLY GRAHAM

Millions of spiritual creatures walk the earth unseen, both when we sleep and when we awake.

JOHN MILTON

Around our pillows golden ladders rise,
And up and down the skies,
With winged sandals shod,
The angels come, and go, the Messengers of God!
R. H. STODDARD

Do not forget to entertain strangers, for by so doing some have unwittingly entertained angels.

HEBREWS 13:2 NKJV

For if God did not spare the angels who sinned, but cast them down to hell and delivered them into chains of darkness, to be reserved for judgment.

2 PETER 2:4 NKJV

ANGER
. . . .

A soft answer turneth away wrath: but grievous words stir up anger.
PROVERBS 15:1

Anger is a wind
which blows out the
lamp of the mind.
ANONYMOUS

Anger: an acid that can do more harm to the vessel in which it is stored than to anything on which it is poured.
ANONYMOUS

Scornful men bring a city into a snare: but wise men turn away wrath.
PROVERBS 29:8

When you lose your temper—you really lose something. You lose the ability to think sanely and to make balanced decisions.

G. S.

A student said to me, "I lose my temper, but it's all over in a minute." I answered, "And so is the hydrogen bomb. But think of the damage it produces!"

G. S.

Next time you feel the surge of anger, say to yourself, "Is this really worth what it's going to do to me and others emotionally? I will make a fool of myself. I may hurt someone I love, or I might lose a friend." Practice realizing that it is not worth it to get so worked up about things, and always remember Seneca who said, "The greatest cure of anger is delay."

NORMAN VINCENT PEALE

Be not angry that you cannot make others as you wish them to be, since you cannot make yourself as you wish to be.

THOMAS À KEMPIS

Doomed are the hotheads! Unhappy are they who lose their cool and are too proud to say, "I'm sorry."

ROBERT H. SCHULLER

The words of the wicked are to lie in wait for blood: but the mouth of the upright shall deliver them.

PROVERBS 12:6

It is better to dwell in the wilderness, than with a contentious and an angry woman.

PROVERBS 21:19

The sacrifice of the wicked is an abomination to the Lord: but the prayer of the upright is his delight.

PROVERBS 15:8

Legend has it that Jonathan Edwards, third president of Princeton and one of America's great preachers, had a daughter with an uncontrollable temper. As often happens, this fault was not known to many people outside the family. A young man fell in love with this daughter and asked to marry her.

"You can't have her," was the abrupt answer of Jonathan Edwards.

"But I love her," the young man replied.

"You can't have her," repeated Edwards.

"But she loves me," replied the young man.

Again Edwards said, "You can't have her."

"Why?" asked the young man.

"Because she is not worthy of you."

"But," he asked, "she is a Christian, isn't she?"

"Yes, she is a Christian. But the grace of God can live with some people with whom no one else could ever live!"

G. S.

It is the intermittent fever which bespeaks unintermittent disease within; the occasional bubble escaping to the surface which betrays some rottenness underneath; a sample of the most hidden products of the soul dropped involuntarily when off one's guard; in a word, the lightning form of a hundred hideous and unchristian sins. For a want of patience, a want of kindness, a want of generosity, a want of courtesy, a want of unselfishness, are all instantaneously symbolized in one flash of Temper.

Hence it is not enough to deal with the Temper. We must go to the source, and change the inmost nature. . . . Souls are made sweet not by taking the acid fluids out, but by putting something in—a great Love, a new Spirit, the Spirit of Christ. . . . This only can eradicate what is wrong, work a chemical change, renovate . . . the inner man.

HENRY DRUMMOND,
THE GREATEST THING IN THE WORLD

ANTICHRIST
· ·

*Our world is fast becoming a madhouse and the inmates are trying to
run the asylum. It is a strange time when the patients are writing
the prescriptions, the students are threatening to run the schools, the
children to manage the homes, and church members—not the Holy
Spirit—to direct the churches. Such lawlessness always brings a
dictator and the last of the line will be the Antichrist, now in the
offing awaiting his cue.*

VANCE HAVNER

*Little children, it is the last hour; and as you have heard that the
Antichrist is coming, even now many antichrists have come, by which
we know that it is the last hour.*

1 JOHN 2:18 NKJV

*Antichrist's power will extend to every area of life in every part of the
world. His dictatorship will be religious, political, and economic. He will
have supernatural abilities, including the power to counterfeit miracles.*

G. S.

*The word Antichrist means "one who stands against Christ," and he
will do just that. After he has deceived the world into accepting his
rule, he will abuse his power and oppose and exalt himself against
God, even to the point of sitting "in the temple of God, shewing
himself that he is God" (2 Thessalonians 2:4).*

G. S.

*Who is a liar but he who denies that Jesus is the Christ? He is
antichrist who denies the Father and the Son.*

1 JOHN 2:22 NKJV

*Antichrist is so proud as to go before Christ; so humble as to pretend
to come after him; and so audacious as to say that himself is he.*

JOHN BUNYAN

The world is looking for a powerful leader—an international figure to offer practical solutions to the world's problems of war, suffering, hunger, and pestilence. Weary of hollow promises, people want a tried and proven super-leader, a shining knight strong enough to guarantee peace.

In the world today, international leaders change with amazing speed. Looking back over the past ten years, we see that the roster of leaders who were in power ten years ago and still are today is incredibly short. They have been removed from power by resignation, assassination, revolution, and death, and often their power base crumbles with their passing. Those who succeed them often blur their predecessor's achievements and discredit his words; then they fall from power just as quickly.

It is into this kind of political atmosphere that the Antichrist will come. He will offer peace and prosperity, but ultimately he will threaten the very existence of civilization. His power will be so complete and evil that only Jesus Christ will be able to conquer him and free the world from his grip, thereby bringing down the curtain on the present age.

G. S.

APATHY (SEE NEGLECT)

> *Mourn not the dead that in the cool earth lie,*
> *But rather mourn the apathetic throng*
> *The coward and the meek*
> *Who see the world's great anguish and its wrong,*
> *And dare not speak.*

RALPH CHAPLIN

The crime against life, the worst of all crimes, is not to feel. And there was never, perhaps, a civilization in which that crime, the crime of torpor, of lethargy, of apathy, the snake-like sin of coldness-at-the-heart, was commoner than in our technical civilization.

ARCHIBALD MACLEISH

The hottest places in Hell are reserved for those who in time of great moral crisis maintain their neutrality.

DANTE ALIGHIERI

In Germany they came first for the Communists, and I didn't speak up because I wasn't a Communist. Then they came for the Jews, and I didn't speak up because I wasn't a Jew. Then they came for the trade unionists, and I didn't speak up because I wasn't a trade unionist. Then they came for the Catholics, and I didn't speak up because I was a Protestant. Then they came for me, and by that time no one was left to speak up.

MARTIN NIEMÖLLER

APPRECIATION
· ·

A New York school superintendent entered the hospital for an operation. When he came out from under the anesthetic, a telegram was waiting for him. It read: "The school board voted eight to six last night to wish you a speedy recovery."

The class assignment was to write a short paper on "Things I Am Most Thankful For." One fourth-grade boy put first, "My glasses. They keep the boys from punching me and the girls from kissing me."

> *When I'm not thank'd at all, I'm thank'd enough,*
> *I've done my duty, and I've done no more.*
>
> HENRY FIELDING

You can't appreciate home till you've left it, money till it's spent, your wife till she's joined a woman's club, nor Old Glory till you see it hanging on a broomstick of a consul in a foreign town.

O. HENRY

Let never day nor night unhallow'd pass,
But still remember what the Lord hath done.

WILLIAM SHAKESPEARE, *HENRY VI*

ARGUING

·······················

But curb thou the high spirit in thy breast,
For gentle ways are best, and keep aloof
From sharp contentions.

HOMER, *THE ILIAD*

I cannot argue while men die. I do not know who the man on the "Jericho Road" is. I do not know who hit him nor where or why. I only know, there he is! He may not be a member of our tribe, our group, our convention, but he needs my help, and I must help him.

OSCAR JOHNSON

Silence is one of the hardest things to refute.

JOSH BILLINGS

The test of a man or woman's breeding is how they behave in a quarrel.

GEORGE BERNARD SHAW

ART

·······················

Art, like morality, consists in drawing the line somewhere.

G. K. CHESTERTON

Abstract Art: A product of the untalented, sold by the unprincipled to the utterly bewildered.

AL CAPP

A man paints with his brains and not with his hands.
                                      MICHELANGELO

If that's art, I'm a Hottentot!
                                      HARRY S. TRUMAN

*Michelangelo was also a superb applied psychologist. At first, he was
ignored and disdained by his own generation. But he had faith in his
ability and decided to use some psychology on his critics. Knowing
that they were fascinated by excavating in old ruins to dig up
supposedly priceless works of art, he tinted one of his masterpieces
and then had it buried where an excavating party would be sure to
find it. The critics were enraptured. They pronounced it an antique of
rare value. The Cardinal of San Giorgio was so impressed that he
paid a huge sum to add it to his art collection. Then Michelangelo
deftly let the cat out of the bag. The art critics . . . were so far out on a
limb that they had to admit that he was an artistic genius. After
that, Michelangelo was commissioned to do important work.*
                                      GEORGE CRANE

*The function of art is to make that understood which in the form of
argument would be incomprehensible.*
                                      CONSTANTINE BRANCUSI

*When I am finishing a picture I hold some God-made object up to it—
a rock, a flower, the branch of a tree or my hand—as a kind of final
test. If the painting stands up beside a thing man cannot make, the
painting is authentic. If there's a clash between the two, it is bad art.*
                                      MARC CHAGALL

I hope with all my heart there will be painting in heaven.
                                      JEAN-BAPTISTE COROT

He bores me. He ought to have stuck to his flying machine.
                                      AUGUSTE RENOIR, OF LEONARDO DA VINCI

A doctor can bury his mistakes, but an architect can only advise his client to plant vines.

FRANK LLOYD WRIGHT

ARTIST

· ·

What is an artist? He's a man who has antennae, who knows how to hook up to the currents which are in the atmosphere, in the cosmos; he merely has the facility for hooking on, as it were. Who is original? Everything that we are doing, everything that we think, exists already, and we are only intermediaries, that's all, who make use of what is in the air.

HENRY MILLER

ASCENSION

· ·

In the days of His earthly ministry, only those could speak to Him who came where He was. If He was in Galilee, men could not find Him in Jerusalem; if He was in Jerusalem, men could not find Him in Galilee. But His Ascension means that He is perfectly united with God; we are with Him wherever we are present to God; and this is everywhere and always.

WILLIAM TEMPLE

Soar we now where Christ has led; Alleluia!
Following our exalted Head; Alleluia!
Made like Him, like Him we rise; Alleluia!
Ours the cross, the grave, the skies. Alleluia!
CHARLES WESLEY

And He departed from our sight that we might return to our heart, and there find Him. For He departed, and behold, He is here.

SAINT AUGUSTINE

ATHEISM

How to trap an atheist: Serve him a fine meal, then ask him if he believes there is a cook.

ANONYMOUS

Atheism is rather in the lip than in the heart of man.

FRANCIS BACON, *ESSAYS, OF ATHEISM*

It is true, that a little philosophy inclineth man's mind to atheism, but depth in philosophy bringeth men's minds about to religion.

FRANCIS BACON, *ESSAYS, OF ATHEISM*

The atheist who is moved by love is moved by the Spirit of God; an atheist who lives by love is saved by his faith in the God whose existence (under that name) he denies.

WILLIAM TEMPLE

Here Lies an Atheist: All Dressed Up and No Place to Go.

EPITAPH

An atheist is a man who believes himself an accident.

FRANCIS THOMPSON

An atheist is a man who looks through a telescope and tries to explain all that he can't see.

ANONYMOUS

ATONEMENT

This is the mystery of the riches of divine grace for sinners; for by a wonderful exchange our sins are now not ours but Christ's, and Christ's righteousness is not Christ's but ours.

MARTIN LUTHER

Christ took our sins and the sins of the whole world as well as the Father's wrath on His shoulders, and He has drowned them both in Himself so that we are thereby reconciled to God and become completely righteous.

MARTIN LUTHER

The blood of Christ stands not simply for the sting of sin on God but the scourge of God on sin, not simply for God's sorrow over sin but for God's wrath on sin.

P. T. FORSYTH

A great many people are trying to make peace, but that has already been done. God has not left it for us to do; all we have to do—is to enter into it.

D. L. MOODY

I must die or get someone to die for me. If the Bible doesn't teach that, it doesn't teach anything. And that is where the atonement of Jesus Christ comes in.

D. L. MOODY

I would like to examine the three Rs of the atonement—three significant benefits man receives from Christ's work for us on the cross.
    The first is redemption. *Redemption comes from a Greek word that is sometimes translated "ransom." It means "a payment." To a first-century Greek, the term "redemption" suggested a payment to free a slave. If a slave could obtain enough money to buy his freedom, that was called "redemption."*
    Did you know that Jesus' death on the cross was actually a payment of ransom? When He died for us, He paid the price to free us from the slavery of sin. Romans 6:23 says, "The wages of sin is death." Verse 7 of that same chapter says, "For he that is dead is freed from sin."
    The second R of the atonement is reconciliation. *When we think of reconciliation we usually think in terms of two marriage partners who have separated but are getting back together.*

53

"Reconciliation" means "a settling of differences, a bringing together of two conflicting sides."

Man's sin built a wall of separation between him and God. God, a holy and perfectly righteous being, cannot tolerate the presence of sin. Sin is contrary to His nature. Man's decision to sin was a decision to be at enmity with God. Man had declared war.

But that did not change God's love for man. Although God in His perfect righteousness could not tolerate sin, He was not willing to stay at enmity with man. He could not simply overlook sin, so He paid for it Himself in the Person of the Lord Jesus. In that way He was able to declare man righteous without sacrificing His own righteousness.

The third R of the atonement is resurrection. *Without the resurrection there is no meaning to the atonement. Paul wrote in 1 Corinthians 15:17, "If Christ be not raised, your faith is vain; ye are yet in your sins."*

The resurrection is the heart of the gospel. "That he rose again the third day according to the Scriptures" (1 Corinthians 15:4) was central in the apostles' preaching—and with good reason.

It is the resurrection of Christ that gives us the assurance that the atonement was accepted by God. The resurrection was the Holy Spirit's seal of approval on the work of Christ. Paul wrote to the Romans that Christ was "declared to be the Son of God with power, according to the spirit of holiness, by the resurrection of the dead" (Romans 1:4).

G. S.

ATTITUDES

An optimist may see a light where there is none, but why must the pessimist always run to blow it out?

MICHEL DE SAINT-PIERRE

If you wish to travel far and fast, travel light. Take off all your envies, jealousies, unforgiveness, selfishness and fears.

GLENN CLARK

One man gets nothing but discord out of a piano; another gets harmony. No one claims the piano is at fault. Life is about the same. The discord is there, and the harmony is there. Study to play it correctly, and it will give forth the beauty; play it falsely, and it will give forth the ugliness. Life is not at fault.

ANONYMOUS

Forget your past circumstances, whether they be sorrows or joys. The one is not without remedy, the other not perfect. Both are past; why remember them? Why should you carry about parched corn when you dwell among fields white unto harvest? Why carry putrid water in the bottom of a rancid skin, when living in a land of fountains and brooks that run among the hills? Why clasp a handful of poor withered flowers, when the grass is sown with their bright eyes opening to the sunshine.

ALEXANDER MACLAREN

I got a simple rule about everybody. If you don't treat me right— shame on you!

LOUIS ARMSTRONG

He was always leaning forward, pushing something invisible ahead of him.

JAMES THURBER

I would rather be first in a little Iberian village than second in Rome.
JULIUS CAESAR

Any manager who can't get along with a .400 hitter is crazy.
JOE MCCARTHY

In War: Resolution. In Defeat: Defiance. In Victory: Magnanimity. In Peace: Goodwill.

WINSTON CHURCHILL

Growl all day and you'll feel dog tired at night.
ANONYMOUS

We lost because we told ourselves we lost.
LEO TOLSTOY, *WAR AND PEACE*

Don't introduce me to that man! I want to go on hating him, and I can't hate a man whom I know.
CHARLES LAMB (ATTRIBUTED)

An optimist is a driver who thinks that empty space at the curb won't have a hydrant beside it.
CHANGING TIMES

The basis of optimism is sheer terror.
OSCAR WILDE

Two men looked through prison bars—One saw mud, the other stars.
ANONYMOUS

A wise clergyman kept on his desk a special notebook labeled "Complaints of Members." Whenever one of his people began to criticize another's doings, he would say, "I'll just write it out so I can take it up with the board." The sight of the complaint book and the ready pen had its effect. The clergyman kept the book for 40 years, opened it hundreds of times, and never had occasion to write a line in it.
LEEWIN B. WILLIAMS,
THE MASTER BOOK OF HUMOROUS ILLUSTRATIONS

Life would be a perpetual flea hunt if a man were obliged to run down all the innuendoes, inveracities, insinuations and misrepresentations which are uttered against him.
HENRY WARD BEECHER

Irritation in the heart of a believer is always an invitation to the devil to stand by.
ANONYMOUS

Optimism is the cheerful frame of mind that enables a teakettle to sing, though in hot water up to its nose.

ANONYMOUS

We who lived in the concentration camps can remember the men who walked through the huts comforting others, giving away their last piece of bread. They may have been few in number, but they offer sufficient proof that everything can be taken from a man but one thing: the last of his freedoms—to choose one's attitude in any given set of circumstances, to choose one's own way.

VICTOR S. FRANKL

I respect those who resist me, but I cannot tolerate them.

CHARLES DE GUALLE

On the back of an envelope found among his effects after his death in a plane crash, former Atomic Energy Commission Chairman, Gordon Dean, had scrawled:
  1. *Never lose your capacity for enthusiasm.*
  2. *Never lose your capacity for indignation.*
  3. *Never judge people, don't type them too quickly; but in a pinch always assume that a man is good and that at worst he is in the gray area between good and bad.*
  4. *If you can't be generous when it's hard, you won't be when it's easy.*
  5. *The greatest builder of confidence is the ability to do something— almost anything—well.*
  6. *When that confidence comes, then strive for humility; you aren't as good as all that.*
  7. *And the way to become truly useful is to seek the best that other brains have to offer. Use them to supplement your own, and give credit to them when they have helped.*
  8. *The greatest tragedies in world and personal events stem from misunderstanding.*
Gordon Dean lived by that splendid testament.

ROBERT G. LEE

Keep your heart right, even when it is sorely wounded.
J. C. MACAULAY

There is little difference in people, but that little difference makes a big difference. That little difference is attitude. The big difference is whether it is positive or negative.
CLEMENT STONE

Whenever a fellow tells me he is bipartisan, I know he's going to vote against me.
HARRY S. TRUMAN

Let's not be narrow, nasty, and negative.
VERNON GROUNDS

BELIEF

. . . .

Being of Scotch extraction, I always greatly enjoy the Braid Scotch translation of the New Testament. In that you will never find our English word, "believe," but you will find the word "lippen." For instance, John 3:16 reads, "For God sae loved the ward as to give He Son, the only Begotten Ane, that ilka ane wha lippens till Him sudna dee, but hae life for aye." What does that word mean, the word "lippen"? It just means to thrust your whole weight on a thing, trust it implicitly.

A Scotch minister was visiting a poor woman who was in great distress about her soul. She just could not seem to understand. By and by he left her, and on his way back to the manse he was troubled to think he had not been able to help her. He came to a bridge over a burn in front of the house, which he started to cross, going step by step very carefully with his buckthorn cane.

An old Scotch woman called out, "Why, Doctor Man, can ye no lippen the brig?" He laughed and waved his hand and said to himself, "I have the word for my auld lady." So he went back to the cottage. She opened the door and said, "O Doctor, you've come back again?"

He said, "I have the word for you now."

"What is it, Doctor?"

"Can you no lippen to Jesus?"

"Oh, is it just to lippen to Him? Why, surely I can lippen to Him. He will never let me doon, will He?"

They bowed together, and she settled it. That is all God asks you to do. Believe the record He has given concerning Jesus; put your heart's trust in Him. You may be assured that you have life eternal for "he that hath the Son hath life; and he that hath not the Son of God hath not life. These things have I written unto you that believe

*on the name of the Son of God; that ye may know"—not merely
hope, not just have a reasonable assurance, but full assurance—
"that ye have eternal life."*

H. A. IRONSIDE

It is so hard to believe because it is so hard to obey.

SØREN KIERKEGAARD

Belief is a moral act for which the believer is to be held responsible.

H. A. HODGES,
LANGUAGES, STANDPOINTS, AND ATTITUDES,
RIDDEL LECTURES

If God did not exist, it would be necessary to invent Him.

VOLTAIRE

*Belief is a wise wager. Granted that faith cannot be proved, what
harm will come to you if you gamble on its truth and it proves false?
. . . If you gain, you gain all; if you lose, you lose nothing. Wager,
then, without hesitation, that He exists.*

BLAISE PASCAL

*If we let ourselves believe that man began with divine grace, that he
forfeited this by sin, and that he can be redeemed only by divine grace
through the crucified Christ, then we shall find peace of mind never
granted to philosophers. He who cannot believe is cursed, for he
reveals by his unbelief that God has not chosen to give him grace.*

BLAISE PASCAL

*When life becomes all snarled up, offer it to our Lord and let Him
untie the knots.*

A BOOK OF DAYS FOR CHRISTIANS

*Jesus said to him, "Thomas, because you have seen Me, you have
believed. Blessed are those who have not seen and yet have believed."*

JOHN 20:29 NKJV

I asked a man what made his life so radiant and bright. He answered: "Looking, looking toward the Light!"

Even if I knew that tomorrow the world would go to pieces, I would still plant my apple tree.

MARTIN LUTHER

The Gateway to Christianity is not through an intricate labyrinth of dogma, but by a simple belief in the person of Christ.

WILLIAM LYON PHELPS

Belief consists in accepting the affirmations of the soul; unbelief in denying them.

RALPH WALDO EMERSON

If you believe what you like in the gospels, and reject what you don't like, it is not the gospel you believe, but yourself.

SAINT AUGUSTINE

BIBLE

W. C. Fields, a lifetime agnostic, was discovered reading a Bible on his deathbed. "I'm looking for a loop-hole," he explained.

W. C. FIELDS

There's no better book with which to defend the Bible than the Bible itself.

D. L. MOODY

I know the Bible is inspired because it inspires me.

D. L. MOODY

light for every darkness, life in death, the promise of our Lord's return, and the assurance of everlasting glory.

D. L. MOODY

The Bible will keep you from sin, or sin will keep you from the Bible.
D. L. MOODY

The study of God's Word brings peace to the heart. In it, we find a
The impregnable rock of Holy Scriptures.
WILLIAM E. GLADSTONE

In all my perplexities and distresses, the Bible has never failed to give
me light and strength.
ROBERT E. LEE

I must confess to you that the majesty of the Scriptures astonishes me,
the holiness of the evangelists speaks to my heart and has such strik-
ing characters of truth, and is, moreover, so perfectly inimitable, that
if it had been the invention of men, the inventors would be greater
than the greatest heroes.
JEAN-JACQUES ROUSSEAU

Those who spiritualize tell spiritual lies, because they lack spiritual
eyes.
ANONYMOUS

The Bible is God's chart for you to steer by, to keep you from the bot-
tom of the sea, and to show you where the harbor is, and how to
reach it without running on rocks or bars.
HENRY WARD BEECHER

I have read many books, but the Bible reads me.
ANONYMOUS

One man perverts Scripture with his hand, another with his exegesis.
Marcion used the knife, not the pen, massacring Scripture to suit his
own material. Valentinus spared the text, since he did not invent
Scriptures to suit his matter, but matter to suit the Scriptures.
TERTULLIAN

Arguments about Scripture achieve nothing but a stomachache and a headache.

TERTULLIAN

It ain't those parts of the Bible that I can't understand that bother me, it is the parts that I do understand.

MARK TWAIN

Every hour
I read you, kills a sin,
Or lets a virtue in
To fight against it.
IZAAK WALTON

There is no doubt that God has often brought a certain verse to the attention of one of His children in an unusual and almost miraculous manner, for a special need, but the Word was never intended to be consulted in a superstitious manner.

S. MAXWELL CODER,
GOD'S WILL FOR YOUR LIFE

God's Word is pure and sure, in spite of the devil, in spite of your fear, in spite of everything.

R. A. TORREY

On the cover of your Bible and my Bible appear the words "Holy Bible." Do you know why the Bible is called holy? Why should it be called holy when so much lust and hate and greed and war are found in it? I can tell you why. It is because the Bible tells the truth. It tells the truth about God, about man, and about the devil. The Bible teaches that we exchange the truth of God for the devil's lie about sex, for example; and drugs, and alcohol, and religious hypocrisy. Jesus Christ is the ultimate truth. Furthermore, He told the truth. Jesus said that He was the truth, and the truth would make us free.

BILLY GRAHAM

Books of Old Testament—39.
Books of New Testament—27.
Total number of books—66.
Chapters in Old Testament—929.
Chapters in New Testament—260.
Total number of chapters—1,189.
Verses in Old Testament—33,214.
Verses in New Testament—7,959.
Total number of verses—41,173.
Words in Old Testament—593,493.
Words in New Testament—181,253.
Total number of words—774,746.
Letters in Old Testament—2,728,100.
Letters in New Testament—838,380.
Total number of letters—3,566,480.
The shortest chapter is Psalm 117.
Ezra 7:21 contains all the letters of the alphabet except "j."
Esther 8:9 is the longest verse.
John 11:35 is the shortest verse.
There is no word of more than six syllables in the Bible.

ROBERT G. LEE

When you have read the Bible, you will know it is the word of God, because you have found it the key to your own heart, your own happiness and your own duty.

WOODROW WILSON

The Word of God well understood and religiously obeyed is the shortest route to spiritual perfection. And we must not select a few favorite passages to the exclusion of others. Nothing less than a whole Bible can make a whole Christian.

A. W. TOZER, *OF GOD AND MEN*

No one ever graduates from Bible study until he meets its Author face to face.

EVERETT HARRIS

A readiness to believe every promise implicitly, to obey every command unhesitatingly, to stand perfect and complete in all the will of God, is the only true spirit of Bible study.

ANDREW MURRAY

The book which closes the New Testament "shuts up all" "with a seven-fold chorus of hallelujahs and harping symphonies" as Milton says in his stately music, and may well represent for us, in that perpetual cloud of incense rising up fragrant to the Throne of God and of the Lamb, the unceasing love and thanksgiving which should be man's answer to Christ's love and sacrifice.

ALEXANDER MACLAREN

"But the word of God is not bound." That is the inscription on a pillar in the crypt of a church in Rome where Paul is said to have been imprisoned. The heroic apostle, bound with a chain and awaiting death, is not disheartened, discouraged, nor despairing. He has full confidence in the spread of the gospel, and in the conquest of Christ, telling Timothy at Ephesus to be true to Christ and the gospel, for which, he says, "I suffer . . . unto bonds; but the word of God is not bound" (2 Timothy 2:9). How true that statement of the apostle was—and is—is demonstrated by the simple, yet tremendous, fact that nineteen hundred years after Paul wrote from his prison in Rome, "The word of God is not bound," the words are taken as the text for a sermon on the invincible power of the Bible.

CLARENCE E. MACARTNEY

When Thomas Paine showed Benjamin Franklin the manuscript of The Age of Reason, *Franklin advised him not to publish it, saying, "The world is bad enough with the Bible; what would it be without it?"*

ANONYMOUS

When you read God's Word, you must constantly be saying to yourself, "It is talking to me, and about me."

SØREN KIERKEGAARD,
FOR SELF-EXAMINATION

In this one book are the two most interesting personalities in the whole world—God and yourself. The Bible is the story of God and man, a love story in which you and I must write our own ending, our unfinished autobiography of the creature and the Creator.
FULTON OURSLER

England has two books, one which she has made and one which has made her: Shakespeare and the Bible.
VICTOR HUGO

To what greater inspiration and counsel can we turn than to the imperishable truth to be found in this treasure house, the Bible?
QUEEN ELIZABETH II

To me the greatest thing that has happened on this earth of ours is the rise of the human race to the vision of God. That story of the human rise to what I call the vision of God is the story which is told in the Bible.
JAN CHRISTIAN SMUTS

The worth of a book is to be measured by what you can carry away from it.
JAMES BRYCE

Unless we form the habit of going to the Bible in bright moments as well as in trouble, we cannot fully respond to its consolations because we lack equilibrium between light and darkness.
HELEN KELLER

More people are troubled by what is plain in Scripture than by what is obscure.
ROY L. SMITH

The great, God-blessed churches in the world today have one common characteristic: an insistence upon an exposition of God's infallible Word.
O. S. HAWKINS

I am my neighbor's Bible:
  He reads me when we meet,
Today he reads me in my house,
  Tomorrow in the street;
He may be relative or friend,
  Or slight acquaintance be;
He may not even know my name,
  Yet he is reading me.

ANONYMOUS

BIBLE ENDURANCE

Whoever is found reading the Scriptures shall forfeit his life and land.

HENRY V OF ENGLAND

In twenty-five years, the Bible will be a forgotten book.

ROBERT INGERSOLL

I have now gone through the woods with an ax, and felled trees. Here they lie. They will never grow again.

THOMAS PAINE, *THE AGE OF REASON*

Rome also persecuted the Scriptures; but chiefly in this way: that instead of being the custodian of Scripture it became the jailer of Scripture, and for many centuries the Word of God was hidden from the people, and legends and traditions of men became the food of the human mind.

ADOLPH SAPHIR

Knowing this first, that no prophecy of Scripture is of any private interpretation, for prophecy never came by the will of man, but holy men of God spoke as they were moved by the Holy Spirit.

2 PETER 1:20-21 NKJV

Another century and there will not be a Bible on earth.
VOLTAIRE

All Scripture is given by inspiration of God, and is profitable for doctrine, for reproof, for correction, for instruction in righteousness.
2 TIMOTHY 3:16 NKJV

Century follows century—There it stands.
Empires rise and fall and are forgotten—There it stands.
Dynasty succeeds dynasty—There it stands.
Kings are crowned and uncrowned—There it stands.
Emperors decree its extermination—There it stands.
Despised and torn to pieces—There it stands.
Storms of hate swirl about it—There it stands.
Atheists rail against it—There it stands.
Agnostics smile cynically—There it stands.
Profane prayerless punsters caricature it—There it stands.
Unbelief abandons it—There it stands.
Higher critics deny its claim to inspiration—There it stands.
Thunderbolts of wrath smite it—There it stands.
An anvil that has broken a million hammers—There it stands.
The flames are kindled about it—There it stands.
The arrows of hate are discharged against it—There it stands.
Radicalism rants and raves about it—There it stands.
Fogs of sophistry conceal it temporarily—There it stands.
The tooth of time gnaws but dents it not—There it stands.
Infidels predict its abandonment—There it stands.
Modernism tries to explain it away—There it stands.
Devotees of folly denounce it—There it stands.
It is God's highway to Paradise.
It is the light on the pathway in the darkest night.
It leads business men to integrity and uprightness.
It is the great consoler in bereavement.
It awakens men and women opiated by sin.
It answers every great question of the soul.
It solves every great problem of life.

It is a fortress often attacked but never failing.
Its wisdom is commanding and its logic convincing.
Salvation is its watchword. Eternal life its goal.
It punctures all pretense.
It is forward-looking, outward-looking, and upward-looking.
It outlives, outlifts, outloves, outreaches, outranks, outruns all other books.
Trust it, love it, obey it, and Eternal Life is yours.

A. Z. CONRAD

BIBLE STUDY
· ·

Prayer is the "open sesame" of the Bible. Always begin your Bible reading with prayer for divine guidance. All of us in reading some current book have wished the author were present to answer and explain some things, but this is rarely possible. Amazing as it seems, this is possible when reading the Bible.

G. S.

I never saw a useful Christian who was not a student of the Bible.

D. L. MOODY

Bible study is like eating peanuts. The more you eat, the more you want to eat.

PAUL LITTLE

The very same Holy Spirit who led these men to write, longs to lead us today so we can understand. Without the Holy Spirit, the Bible is like an ocean which cannot be sounded, heavens which cannot be surveyed, mines which cannot be explored, and mysteries beyond unraveling. We must—we must—yield to the leadership of the Holy Spirit.

G. S.

First I shake the whole [apple] tree, that the ripest might fall. Then I climb the tree and shake each limb, and then each branch and then each twig, and then I look under each leaf.

MARTIN LUTHER

The Bible is literally God speaking to you. It is God's instrument in salvation (Romans 10:17; 1 Peter 1:25) and God's instrument for growing mature Christians (1 Peter 2:2). It is the blueprint for the Christian.

G. S.

Commentaries are splendid; however, beware of being chained to them. Someone has humorously said, "The Bible throws a lot of light on the commentaries." Any book that takes priority over the Bible becomes a crutch which leads to weakness. To read the words of men and neglect the Word of God is to say the books of men are of greater worth.

G. S.

BOOKS AND READING
· ·

The man who does not read good books has no advantage over the man who can't read them.

MARK TWAIN

Where is human nature so weak as in the bookstore?

HENRY WARD BEECHER

Every man who knows how to read has it in his power to magnify himself, to multiply the ways in which he exists, to make his life full, significant and interesting.

ALDOUS HUXLEY

Reading is to the mind what exercise is to the body.

RICHARD STEELE

The best effect of any book is that it excited the reader to self activity.
THOMAS CARLYLE

The greatest gift is the passion for reading. It is cheap, it consoles, it distracts, it excites, it gives you knowledge of the world and experience of a wide kind. It is a moral illumination.
ELIZABETH HARDWICK

BOREDOM

A bishop was to make his first sermon at the court of Queen Victoria. He asked Disraeli for advice. "How long do you think my first sermon should last, Mr. Prime Minister?" Disraeli replied, "If you preach for forty minutes, Her Majesty will be satisfied; for thirty minutes, she will be delighted. If you preach for only fifteen minutes, Her Majesty will be enthusiastic!"
BENJAMIN DISRAELI

Too many church services start at eleven sharp and end at twelve dull.
VANCE HAVNER

I spent a year in that town, one Sunday.
WARWICK DEEPING

The most terrible thing about materialism, even more terrible than its proneness to violence, is its boredom, from which sex, alcohol, drugs, all devices for putting out the accusing light of reason and suppressing the unrealizable aspirations of love, offer a prospect of deliverance.
MALCOLM MUGGERIDGE

Boredom is the root of all evil—the despairing refusal to be oneself.
SØREN KIERKEGAARD

71

America is said to have the highest per capita boredom of any spot on earth! We know that because we have the greatest number of artificial amusements of any country. People have become so empty that they can't even entertain themselves. They have to pay other people to amuse them, to make them laugh, to try to make them feel warm and happy and comfortable for a few minutes, to try to lose that awful, frightening, hollow feeling—that terrible, dreaded feeling of being lost and alone.

BILLY GRAHAM

BROKENNESS

I have been reflecting on the inestimable value of "broken things." Broken pitchers gave ample light for victory (Judges 7:19–21); broken bread was more than enough for all the hungry (Matthew 14:19–21); broken box gave fragrance to all the world (Mark 14:3, 9); and broken body is salvation to all who believe and receive the Savior (Isaiah 53:5–6, 12; 1 Corinthians 11:24). And what cannot the Broken One do with our broken plans, projects, and hearts?

V. RAYMOND EDMAN

How else but through a broken heart
May Lord Christ enter in?

OSCAR WILDE

BROTHERHOOD

Respect of persons is inconsistent with God's grace. It is inconsistent with God's law. In fact, respect of persons is an act of sin. Racial discrimination and racism are an insult to God.

G. S.

I met a hundred men going to Delhi and everyone is my brother.

INDIAN SAYING

D. L. Moody had a tremendous burden for the downtrodden and neglected. Sunday after Sunday, he would travel up and down the streets of Chicago, gathering the tattered little children into the Sunday school. On one occasion, Moody promised a class of thirteen boys that if they would maintain good conduct and attend Sunday school regularly through the summer and fall, he would give each of them a new suit of clothes for Christmas. Twelve of the boys earned their suits, and Moody had them photographed in their ragged clothes first, captioning it, Will It Pay? then in their new suits, labeling that, It Does Pay! About 1858, Moody opened his own Sunday school in an old saloon building. It soon became so crowded that the mayor of Chicago offered him the North Market Hall for a meeting place. As founder and director, he filled a variety of offices, from janitor to superintendent.

"Sunday was a busy day for me then," Moody wrote. "During the week I would be out of town selling boots and shoes, but I would always manage to be back by Saturday night.

"Often it was late when I got to my room, but I would have to be up by six o'clock to get the hall ready for Sunday school.

"Every Saturday night a German society had a dance there, and I had to roll out the beer kegs, sweep up the sawdust, clean up generally and arrange the chairs. This took most of the morning, and then I had to go out to drum up the scholars.

"By the time two o'clock came we would have the hall full, and then I had to keep order while the speaker of the day led the exercises. . . . When school was over I visited absent scholars and found out why they were not at Sunday school, called on the sick, and invited parents to attend the evening gospel service." Moody was no respecter of persons. He had a love for all men, rich and poor alike.

To this day a plaque appears at the entrance of Moody Church which reads, "Ever welcome to this house of God are the strangers and the poor."

G. S.

To correct the evils, great and small, which spring from want of sympathy and from positive enmity among strangers, as nations or as individuals, is one of the highest functions of civilization.
ABRAHAM LINCOLN

Imagine a large circle and in the center of it rays of light that spread out to the circumference. The light in the center is God; each of us is a ray. The closer the rays are to the center, the closer the rays are to one another. The closer we live to God, the closer we are bound to our neighbor.
ARCHBISHOP FULTON J. SHEEN

We cannot possibly let ourselves get frozen into regarding everyone we do not know as an absolute stranger.
ALBERT SCHWEITZER,
MEMORIES OF CHILDHOOD AND YOUTH

You can't hold a man down without staying down with him.
BOOKER T. WASHINGTON

BURDENS
· ·

I have read in Plato and Cicero sayings that are wise and very beautiful; but I have never read in either of them: "Come unto me all ye that labour and are heavy laden."
SAINT AUGUSTINE

I do not pray for a lighter load, but for a stronger back.
PHILLIPS BROOKS

God gave burdens, also shoulders.
YIDDISH PROVERB

None knows the weight of another's burthen [sic].
GEORGE HERBERT

BUSINESS

The wayside of business is full of brilliant men who started out with a spurt and lacked the stamina to finish. Their places were taken by patient and unshowy plodders who never knew when to quit.

J. R. TODD

Business is like a wheelbarrow—it stands still until someone pushes it.

ANONYMOUS

Some see private enterprise as a predatory target to be shot, others as a cow to be milked, but few are those who see it as a sturdy horse pulling the wagon.

WINSTON CHURCHILL

A man's success in business today turns upon his power of getting people to believe he has something that they want.

GERALD STANLEY LEE

CAPITALISM

The inherent vice of capitalism is the unequal sharing of blessings; the inherent vice of socialism is the equal sharing of miseries.
WINSTON CHURCHILL

Capital as such is not evil; it is its wrong use that is evil.
MOHANDAS GANDHI

Labor is prior to, and independent of, capital. Capital is only the fruit of labor, and could never have existed if labor had not first existed. Labor is the superior of capital, and deserves much the higher consideration. Capital has its rights, which are as worthy of protection as any other rights.
ABRAHAM LINCOLN, MESSAGE TO CONGRESS, 3 DECEMBER 1861

Labor in this country is independent and proud. It has not to ask the patronage of capital, but capital solicits the aid of labor.
DANIEL WEBSTER

CARING, CHARITY, COMPASSION

And now abideth faith, hope, charity, these three; but the greatest of these is charity.
1 CORINTHIANS 13:13

Care is a state in which something does matter; it is the source of human tenderness.
ROLLO MAY

It is our care for the helpless, our practice of lovingkindness that brands us in the eyes of many of our opponents. "Look!" they say, "How they love one another! Look how they are prepared to die for one another."

TERTULLIAN

Lord, make me an instrument of Your peace.
Where there is hatred let me sow love.
Where there is injury, pardon.
Where there is doubt, faith.
Where there is despair, hope.
Where there is darkness, light; and
Where there is sadness, joy.
O Divine Master, grant that I may not so much
Seek to be consoled as to console;
To be understood as to understand;
To be loved as to love;
For it is in giving that we receive;
It is in pardoning that we are pardoned; and
It is in dying that we are born to eternal life.

SAINT FRANCIS OF ASSISI

I feel the capacity to care is the thing which gives life its deepest significance.

PABLO CASALS

Being part of an agenda beyond ourselves liberates us to complement each other rather than compete with each other.

JOSEPH STOWELL

Christianity demands a level of caring that transcends human inclinations.

ERWIN W. LUTZER

Man may dismiss compassion from his heart, but God never will.

WILLIAM COWPER

As we mature spiritually, we exhibit a growing capacity to care for and appreciate one another in the body of Christ, regardless of our differences.

JOSEPH STOWELL

In necessary things, unity; in doubtful things, liberty; in all things, charity.

RICHARD BAXTER

Biblical orthodoxy without compassion is surely the ugliest thing in the world.

FRANCIS SCHAEFFER

> *Perchance that I might learn what pity is,*
> *That I might laugh at erring men no more.*
> MICHELANGELO

> *Taught by that Power that pities me,*
> *I learn to pity them.*
> OLIVER GOLDSMITH

CHANGE

You cannot step twice into the same river, for other waters are continually flowing on.

HERACLITUS

People can cry much easier than they can change.

JAMES BALDWIN

The immutability of God appears in its most perfect beauty when viewed against the mutability of man. In God no change is possible; in men change is impossible to escape. Neither the man is fixed nor his world, and he—and it—are in constant flux.

A. W. TOZER, *THE KNOWLEDGE OF THE HOLY*

Have you ever thought about the collapse of time? From the days of the Lord Jesus Christ until about 1830, man could not travel any faster than a horse. In 1960, a man went into space and traveled at a speed of 18,000 miles an hour. Look how far we have come in so short a time! Sometimes when I read the papers, I think we are trying to run the Space Age with horse-and-buggy moral and spiritual equipment. Technology, you see, has no morals; and with no moral restraints man will destroy himself ecologically, militarily, or in some other way. Only God can give a person moral restraints and spiritual strength. While our world is shaking and crumbling, we need to realize that one thing will never change, and that is God. He is the same today as He was ten million years ago, and He will be the same ten million years from today. We are like grasshoppers; we appear and hop around a bit on the earth and then we are gone.

BILLY GRAHAM

When you're through changing, you're through.

BRUCE BARTON

A truck driver told about the change Christ had made in his life, and I asked him to think of some specific way in which he was different. After a pause he said, "Well, when I find somebody tailgating my truck I no longer drive on the shoulder of the road to kick gravel on him."

BRUCE LARSON

The philosophers have only interpreted the world; the thing, however, is to change it.

KARL MARX

CHARACTER
· ·

Character is the sum and total of a person's choices.
P. B. FITZWATER

During my eighty-seven years, I have witnessed a whole succession of technological revolutions. But none of them has done away with the need for character in the individual or the ability to think.

BERNARD M. BARUCH

Integrity has no need of rules.

ALBERT CAMUS

The happiness of every country depends upon the character of its people, rather than the form of its government.

THOMAS CHANDLER HALIBURTON

When God measures man, He puts the tape around his heart—not his head.

GUIDEPOSTS

The Lord does not look at the things man looks at. Man looks at the outward appearance, but the Lord looks at the heart.

1 SAMUEL 16:7 NIV

Character is like the foundation of a house—it is below the surface.

ANONYMOUS

I am only one, but I am one. I can't do everything, but I can do something. And what I can do, that I ought to do. And what I ought to do, by the grace of God, I shall do.

EDWARD EVERETT HALE

The most important thought I ever had was that of my individual responsibility to God.

DANIEL WEBSTER

God has a program of character development for each one of us. He wants others to look at our lives and say, "He walks with God, for he lives like Christ."

ERWIN W. LUTZER

Those who command themselves, command others.
WILLIAM HAZLITT

Above all else, guard your heart, for it is the wellspring of life.
PROVERBS 4:23 NIV

I have conquered an empire but I have not been able to conquer myself.
PETER THE GREAT

Character in a saint means the disposition of Jesus Christ persistently manifested.
OSWALD CHAMBERS

The chains of habit are too weak to be felt until they are too strong to be broken.
SAMUEL JOHNSON

There never will exist anything permanently noble and excellent in the character which is a stranger to resolute self-denial.
SIR WALTER SCOTT

A dear old Quaker lady, distinguished for her youthful look, was asked what she used to preserve her appearance. She replied sweetly, "I use for the lips, truth; for the voice, prayer; for the eyes, pity; for the hand, charity; for the figure, uprightness; and for the heart, love.
JERRY FLEISHMAN,
LADIES HOME JOURNAL

The integrity of the upright guides them, but the unfaithful are destroyed by their duplicity.
PROVERBS 11:3 NIV

Character is not made in a crisis—it is only exhibited.
ROBERT FREEMAN

Few persons are made of such strong fiber that they will make a costly outlay when surface work will pass as well in the market.

E. M. BOUNDS

Resolutions Concerning Myself

I will be joyful, that life may give me wings.
I will be courageous, that there shall be no binding fears.
I will be balanced, that neither work, nor play, nor rest, nor worship shall lose its proper share.
I will be self-reliant, that thoughts of failure shall not hold me back.
I will be self-controlled, that emotions shall not be dominant.
I will be intelligent, that straight thinking and knowledge shall direct all actions.
I will be healthy, that my body shall not fail to respond.
I will be clean in spirit, mind and action, that there shall be no shame.
I will be good-tempered, that annoyance shall not irritate.
I will be patient, that discouragement shall not seem final.
I will be persistent, that the will may carry through to completion.
I will be prepared, that emergency shall not find me in confusion.
      Paul, the great apostle, who left a trail of gospel glory across the Gentile world wrote:
      "With the mind I myself serve the law of God" (Romans 7:25).
      "I could wish that myself were accursed from Christ for my brethren, my kinsmen according to the flesh" (Romans 9:3).
      "I have made myself servant unto all" (I Corinthians 9:19).
      "But I determined this with myself" (2 Corinthians 2:1).
      "In all things I have kept myself from being burdensome unto you, and so will I keep myself" (2 Corinthians 11:9).

ROBERT G. LEE

Character is always lost when a high ideal is sacrificed on the altar of conformity and popularity.

ANONYMOUS

Mr. Jefferson came into Congress in June, 1775, and brought with him a reputation for literature, science, and a happy talent of composition. Writings of his were handed about, remarkable for the peculiar felicity of expression. Though a silent member in Congress, he was so prompt, frank, explicit, and decisive upon committees and in conversation—not even Samuel Adams was more so—that he soon seized upon my heart.

JOHN ADAMS

Prolific writer Oscar Wilde confessed, "I let myself be lured into long spells of senseless and sensual ease. . . . Tired of being on the heights, I deliberately went to the depths in search of new sensations. . . . I grew careless of the lives of others. I forgot that every little action of the common day makes or unmakes character, and that therefore what one has done in the secret chamber, one has some day to cry aloud from the house-top. I ceased to be lord over myself. I was no longer the captain of my soul, and did not know it. I allowed pleasure to dominate me. I ended in horrible disgrace.

OSCAR WILDE

Character is what you are in the dark.

D. L. MOODY

Learn to say no; it will be of more use to you than to be able to read Latin.

CHARLES HADDON SPURGEON

CHEERFULNESS
· ·

Happiness is essentially a state of going somewhere wholeheartedly.

W. H. SHELDON

It is not fitting, when one is in God's service, to have a gloomy face or a chilling look.

SAINT FRANCIS OF ASSISI

Mirth is God's medicine. Everybody ought to bathe in it. Grim care, moroseness, anxiety—all this rust of life ought to be scoured off by the oil of mirth. It is better than emery. Every man ought to rub himself with it. A man without mirth is like a wagon without springs, in which everyone is caused disagreeably to jolt by every pebble over which it runs.

HENRY WARD BEECHER

O Holy Spirit, descend plentifully into my heart. Enlighten the dark corners of this neglected dwelling and scatter there Thy cheerful beams.

SAINT AUGUSTINE

Those who bring sunshine into the lives of others, cannot keep it from themselves.

JAMES M. BARRIE

Happiness adds and multiplies, as we divide it with others.

A. NIELEN

Delicate humor is the crowning virtue of the saints.

EVELYN UNDERHILL

A happy family is but an earlier heaven.

JOHN BOWRING

People are always good company when they are doing what they really enjoy.

SAMUEL BUTLER

There is no danger of developing eyestrain from looking on the bright side of things.

ANONYMOUS

Cheerfulness and contentment are great beautifiers and are famous preservers of good looks.

CHARLES DICKENS

To watch the corn grow, or the blossoms set; to draw hard breath over the ploughshare or spade; to read, to think, to love, to pray, are the things that make men happy.

JOHN RUSKIN

The truest greatness lies in being kind,
The truest wisdom in a happy mind.

ELLA WHEELER WILCOX

The Happiest Man

Happy is he who by love's sweet song
Is cheered today as he goes along.
Happier is he who believes that tomorrow
Will ease all pain and take away all sorrow.
Happiest he who on earthly sod
Has faith in himself, his friends, and God.

Happiness depends, as Nature shows,
Less on exterior things than most suppose.

WILLIAM COWPER

We have no right to consume happiness without producing it than to consume wealth without producing it.

GEORGE BERNARD SHAW

CHILDREN
· ·

Children are not casual guests in our home. They have been loaned to us temporarily for the purpose of loving them and instilling a foundation of values on which their future lives will be built.

JAMES C. DOBSON

Men are generally more careful of the breed of their horses and dogs than of their children.

WILLIAM PENN

Too many parents are not on spanking terms with their children.
ANONYMOUS

It is easiest to lead a child from five to ten years to a definite acceptance of Christ.

I rejoice in the work done by rescue missions, where we see the wrecks of manhood and womanhood changed into noble men and women. But this is not the work that produces the most satisfactory Christians. The younger we get a child to accept Christ and begin Christian training, the more beautiful the product.

The overwhelming majority in our churches today were converted before twenty-one years of age.

Whatever your church does, let it do its full duty by the children.
R. A. TORREY

Little girl's definition of conscience: "Something that makes you tell your mother before your brother or sister does."
ANONYMOUS

I saw tomorrow marching
On little children's feet;
Within their forms and faces read
Her prophecy complete.

I saw tomorrow look at me
From little children's eyes;
And thought how carefully we'd teach
If we were really wise.
ANONYMOUS

If we had paid no more attention to our plants than we have to our children, we would now be living in a jungle of weeds.
LUTHER BURBANK

Give me the children until they are seven and anyone may have them afterwards.
FRANCIS XAVIER

Birds in their little nests agree;
And 'tis a shameful sight,
When children of one family
Fall out, and chide, and fight.
ISAAC WATTS

Young people should be helped, sheltered, ignored, and clubbed if necessary.

AL CAPP

It needs courage to let our children go, but we are trustees and stewards and have to hand them back to life—to God. As the old saying puts it: "What I gave I have." We have to love them and lose them.
ALFRED TORRIE

CHRIST
· ·

I love to hear my Lord spoken of, and wherever I have seen the print of His shoe in the earth, there have I coveted to put mine also.
JOHN BUNYAN

The Christian is not one who has gone all the way with Christ. None of us has. The Christian is one who has found the right road.
CHARLES L. ALLEN

When Jesus comes, the shadows depart.
INSCRIPTION

Christianity takes for granted the absence of any self-help and offers a power which is nothing less than the power of God.
A. W. TOZER, THE DIVINE CONQUEST

He is no fool, who gives what he cannot keep, to gain what he cannot lose.

JIM ELLIOT

God speaks to me not through the thunder and the earthquake, nor through the ocean and the stars, but through the Son of Man, and speaks in a language adapted to my imperfect sight and hearing.

WILLIAM LYON PHELPS

The men who followed Him were unique in their generation. They turned the world upside down because their hearts had been turned right side up. The world has never been the same.

BILLY GRAHAM

The Lord has turned all our sunsets into sunrise.

CLEMENT OF ALEXANDRIA

Jesus promised His disciples three things: that they would be entirely fearless, absurdly happy, and that they would get into trouble.

W. RUSSELL MALTBY

Above all the grace and the gifts that Christ gives to his beloved is that of overcoming self.

SAINT FRANCIS OF ASSISI

The greatest thing about any civilization is the human person, and the greatest thing about this person is the possibility of his encounter with the person of Jesus Christ.

CHARLES MALIK

*Association with the Lord can bring
To any life a dignity and grace,
And ever looking up to Him will give
The high, white look of Christ to any face.*

GRACE NOLL CROWELL

I thank God for the honesty and virility of Jesus' religion which makes us face the facts and calls us to take a man's part in the real battle of life.

HENRY VAN DYKE

No one else holds or has held the place in the heart of the world which Jesus holds. Other gods have been as devoutly worshiped; no other man has been so devoutly loved.

JOHN KNOX

Here is the Truth in a little creed,
Enough for all the roads we go:
In Love is all the law we need,
In Christ is all the God we know.

EDWIN MARKHAM

Jesus Christ, the condescension of divinity, and the exaltation of humanity.

PHILLIPS BROOKS

We believe that the history of the world is but the history of His influence and that the center of the whole universe is the cross of Calvary.

ALEXANDER MACLAREN

In every pang that rends the heart
The Man of Sorrows has a part.

MICHAEL BRUCE

To become Christlike is the only thing in the whole world worth caring for, the thing before which every ambition of man is folly and all lower achievement vain.

HENRY DRUMMOND

By a Carpenter mankind was made, and only by that Carpenter can mankind be remade.

DESIDERIUS ERASMUS

I am pretty sure that we err in treating these sayings as paradoxes. It would be nearer the truth to say that it is life itself which is paradoxical and that the sayings of Jesus are simply a recognition of that fact.

THOMAS TAYLOR

Two thousand years ago there was One here on this earth who lived the grandest life that ever has been lived yet—a life that every thinking man, with deeper or shallower meaning, has agreed to call divine.

FREDERICK W. ROBERTSON

There is but one God, the Father, of whom are all things, and we in him; and one Lord Jesus Christ, by whom are all things, and we by him.

1 CORINTHIANS 8:6

Jesus never gained disciples under false pretenses. He never hid His scars, but rather declared, "Behold my hands and feet."

G. S.

Charles Lamb was once discussing the greatest literary characters of all time when the names of both William Shakespeare and Jesus Christ were mentioned. "The major difference between these two," said Charles Lamb, "is that if Shakespeare came into this room we would all stand in honor and respect. But if Jesus Christ were here, we would all humbly bow and worship Him."

G. S.

In his famous painting of Christ knocking at the door, artist Holman Hunt has purposely omitted from the door a knob or handle. Why? Because that is on the inside, and you, and you alone, can open the door to Jesus.

G. S.

Jesus whom I know as my Redeemer cannot be less than God!
SAINT ATHANASIUS

Christ is the Bible's fullness, the Bible's center, the Bible's fascination. It is all about Jesus—in the Old Testament. The Old Testament conceals, infolds, promises, pictures, prophesies, localizes, symbolizes Christ. The New Testament reveals, unfolds, presents, produces, pro-

claims, universalizes and sacrifices Christ. Yes, the Old Testament and New Testament alike tell of Jesus, the great Fact of history, the great Force of history, the great Future of history. Of this book it can truly be said: "The Glory of God doth lighten it, and the Lamb is the Light thereof!" The name of Jesus, the Supreme Personality, the center of a world's desire, is on every page—in expression, or symbol, or prophecy, or psalm, or proverb. Take Jesus out of the Bible—and it is like taking calcium out of lime, carbon out of diamonds, truth out of history, matter out of physics, mind out of metaphysics, numbers out of mathematics, cause and effect out of philosophy. Through this book the name of Jesus, the Revealed, the Redeeming, the Risen, the Reigning, the Returning Lord, runs like a line of glimmering light. The thought of Jesus, the Desire of all nations, threads this great book like a crystal river winds its way through a continent.

ROBERT G. LEE

Alexander, Caesar, Charlemagne, and myself founded empires; but on what foundation did we rest the creations of our genius? Upon force. Jesus Christ founded an empire upon love; and at this hour millions of men would die for Him.

NAPOLEON BONAPARTE

Each eye can have its vision separately; but when we are looking at anything . . . our vision, which in itself is divided, joins up and unites in order to give itself as a whole to the object that is put before it.

JOHN CALVIN, ON CHRIST'S TWO NATURES

The most pressing question on the problem of faith is whether a man, as a civilized being . . . can believe in the divinity of the Son of God, Jesus Christ, for therein rests the whole of our faith.

FYODOR DOSTOYEVSKY

Jesus is the God whom we can approach without pride and before whom we can humble ourselves without despair.

BLAISE PASCAL

You should point to the whole man Jesus and say, "That is God."
                                                    MARTIN LUTHER

CHRISTIANITY
· ·

[Christianity] provides a unified answer for the whole of life.
                                    FRANCIS SCHAEFFER, *ESCAPE FROM REASON*

Whatever makes men good Christians, makes them good citizens.
                                                    DANIEL WEBSTER

*I have now disposed of all my property to my family. There is one
thing more I wish I could give them, and that is the Christian religion.*
                                                    PATRICK HENRY

*Christianity, above all, has given a clear-cut answer to the demands
of the human soul.*
                                                    ANONYMOUS

*The test of Christian character should be that a man is a joy-bearing
agent to the world.*
                                                    HENRY WARD BEECHER

*Most of us spend the first six days of each week sowing wild oats; then
we go to church on Sunday and pray for a crop failure.*
                                                    FRED ALLEN

*The difference between heart belief and head belief is the difference
between salvation and damnation.*
                                                    G. S.

A Christian is a combination of Christ and you.
                                                    G. S.

Salvation is an offer, not a demand.
                                                                    G. S.

God doesn't have any grandchildren.
                                                E. STANLEY JONES

Is your Christianity ancient history—or current events?
                                                SAMUEL M. SHOEMAKER

*If we take the first three words of John 1:13 and the last two words,
we have the phrase, "which were born . . . of God." That's a good
definition. A Christian is one who is born of God.*
                                                                    G. S.

*From history's pages we learn of a cowardly young soldier in the
army of Alexander the Great. Whenever the battle grew fierce, the
young soldier would yield. The general's pride was cut because this
timid soldier also bore the name Alexander. One day Alexander the
Great sternly addressed him and said, "Stop being a coward or drop
that good name."*

*The call to all Christians is the same today. May we faithfully live
up to all the name Christian implies. "Lord, what will You have me
to do?"*
                                                                    G. S.

*It is only when all our Christian ancestors are allowed to become our
contemporaries that the real splendor of the Christian faith and the
Christian life begins to dawn upon us.*
                                                LYNN HAROLD HOUGH

*Real Christianity is lovely. There is a quality about a Spirit-filled,
radiant Christian that draws and attracts others and causes them to
"enjoy favor with all the people." The truth is that the gospel is not
nearly as offensive as some of its proponents!*
                                                O. S. HAWKINS

The Christianity which is shared is the Christianity which is convincing.

LYNN HAROLD HOUGH

If Jesus Christ be God and died for me, then no sacrifice can be too great for me to make for Him.

C. T. STUDD

CHRISTIAN LIVING

The great difference between present-day Christianity and that of which we read in these letters is that to us it is primarily a performance, to them it was a real experience . . . To these men it is quite plainly the invasion of their lives by a new quality of life altogether. They do not hesitate to describe this as Christ "living in" them.

J. B. PHILLIPS, *LETTERS TO YOUNG CHURCHES*

If you make a great deal of Christ, He will make a great deal of you; But if you make but little of Christ, He will make but little of you.

R. A. TORREY

It is a bad world, Donatus, an incredibly bad world. But I have discovered in the midst of it a quiet and good people who have learned the great secret of life. They have found a joy and wisdom which is a thousand times better than any of the pleasures of our sinful life. They are despised and persecuted, but they care not. They are masters of their souls. They have overcome the world. These people, Donatus, are Christians . . . and I am one of them.

SAINT CYPRIAN

A good example is far better than a good precept.

D. L. MOODY

No book will make you grow like the Bible.

G. S.

The question is not "How much may I indulge in and still be saved?" God forbid! I must rather ask, "What about Christ's will and the example I set for my fellow Christians?"

ROBERT A. COOK

We are set apart unto God, in one sense of the term, the moment we receive Christ, for we are bought with the price of His blood. Some day we shall be set apart from sin forever, by being taken to glory with Christ. But I Thessalonians 4:3 speaks of our present responsibility. God wants us to take our stand against every form of known sin, and to maintain that stand consistently.

S. MAXWELL CODER,
GOD'S WILL FOR YOUR LIFE

A rule I have had for years is: to treat the Lord Jesus Christ as a personal friend. His is not a creed, a mere doctrine, but it is He Himself we have.

D. L. MOODY

Never think that Jesus commanded a trifle, nor dare to trifle with anything He has commanded.

D. L. MOODY

There are many of us that are willing to do great things for the Lord, but few of us are willing to do little things.

D. L. MOODY

Dead things cannot grow. Before there can be spiritual growth, there must be spiritual life.

G. S.

Where one man reads the Bible, a hundred read you and me.

D. L. MOODY

I have had more trouble with myself than with any other man.

D. L. MOODY

A young girl was asked: "Whose preaching brought you to Christ?"
"It wasn't anybody's preaching; it was Aunt Mary's practicing,"
she replied. The beginning of anxiety is the end of faith, and the
beginning of true faith is the end of anxiety.

GEORGE MUELLER

Periods of staleness in the life are not inevitable but they are common.
He is a rare Christian who has not experienced times of spiritual
dullness. Sometimes our trouble is not moral but physical. The
Christian who gets tired in the work of the Lord and stays tired with-
out relief beyond a reasonable time will go stale.

We can keep from going stale by getting proper rest, by practicing
complete candor in prayer, by introducing variety into our lives, by
heeding God's call to move onward and by exercising quiet faith
always.

A. W. TOZER, *THE INCREDIBLE CHRISTIAN*

Seven Indispensable Things

1. *Without shedding of blood is no remission (Hebrews 9:22).*
2. *Without faith it is impossible to please God (Hebrews 11:6).*
3. *Without works faith is dead (James 2:26).*
4. *Without holiness no man shall see the Lord (Hebrews 12:14).*
5. *Without love I am nothing (I Corinthians 13:2).*
6. *Without chastisement ye are not sons (Hebrews 12:8).*
7. *Without me ye can do nothing (John 15:5).*

ROBERT G. LEE

Regardless of the day or the hour; whether in seeming good times or
bad, the Christian lives in the world for the good of the world and for
the sake of the world.

HAROLD LINDSELL,
A CHRISTIAN PHILOSOPHY OF MISSIONS

What the world requires of the Christians is that they should contin-
ue to be Christians.

ALBERT CAMUS

Much of our drive to build separate but equal facilities (for use by evangelicals) is the desire to forget the war we are in. We can't forget it very well with drunks stumbling over our feet, so we go to "Christian" hotels. Non-Christians upset us, not so much because they curse and carouse (we have worse sins of our own), but because they remind us of evaded responsibility. From time to time this guilt gets intolerable (down deep we do love Christ), so we mount our chrome-trimmed chargers, and like knights of old, we gallop out of our castles in search of the dragon. We usually find him in jail, or a skid-row mission or other captive audience (even a fraternity) where we can dump our gospel load and get out again with a minimum of personal involvement or time wasted. Then back to the castle we tear, mission completed. With the draw-bridge slammed shut behind us, we sing "Safe Am I" and settle down again. Often our castle is psychological, but none the less real.

JOHN GOODWIN

The touch of God makes the difference between success and failure. God touched Isaiah's lips to give him purity (Isaiah 6:1–7) and Jeremiah's lips to give him power (Jeremiah 1:9–10; Luke 21:15). He touched Jacob's hip and gave him a limp (Genesis 32:25), thus helping him to become a "prince with God." God touched Daniel and set him on his feet (Daniel 8:18), gave him strength (Daniel 10:18), and opened his mouth for ministry (Daniel 10:15–16). The call of God and the touch of God must go together or we fail.

WARREN WIERSBE

The gradual disappearance of the idea and feeling of majesty from the Christ is a sign and a portent. Our God has now become our servant to wait on our will. "The Lord is my shepherd," *we say, instead of "*The Lord *is my shepherd," and the difference is as wide as the world.*

A. W. TOZER, *THE DIVINE CONQUEST*

The Christian is a person who makes it easy for others to believe in God.
ROBERT M. MCCHEYNE

The Two Natures

An American Indian was giving his testimony in a gathering of Christian members of his tribe. He told of his conversion and of how in the beginning he felt as though he would never sin again; he was so happy in knowing His Saviour. But, he explained, as time went on he became conscious of an inward conflict, which he described somewhat as follows:

"It seems, my brothers, that I have two dogs fighting in my heart: one is a very good dog, a beautiful white dog, and he is always watching out for my best interests. The other is a very bad dog, a black dog, who is always trying to destroy the things that I want to see built up. These dogs give me a lot of trouble because they are always quarreling and fighting each other."

One of his hearers looked up and asked laconically, "Which one wins?" The other instantly replied, "Whichever one I say 'Sic 'im' to."

Surely there could not be a more apt illustration of the two natures in the believer. "If we walk in the Spirit we shall not fulfill the lusts of the flesh." But if we pander to the flesh, we will be certain to go down in defeat.

H. A. IRONSIDE

Christianity is either relevant all the time or useless anytime. It is not just a phase of life; it is life itself.

RICHARD HALVERSON

We need to grow because growth is God's plan. We must bend or be broken.

G. S.

Faith makes a Christian.
Life proves a Christian.
Trial confirms a Christian.
Death crowns a Christian.
ANONYMOUS

Salvation is just the beginning of what God wants to do for you.
G. S.

*Father Abraham, whom have you in heaven? Any Episcopalians?
No! Any Presbyterians? No! Any Independents or Methodists? No,
no, no! Whom have you there? We don't know those names here. All
who are here are Christians. . . . Oh, is this the case? Then God help
us to forget party names and to become Christians in deed and truth.*
GEORGE WHITEFIELD

*Ivan Albright painted a picture now hanging in the Chicago Art
Institute of an eight-foot door shaped like the lid of an old casket. The
door is scarred and bruised, supposedly by the difficult experiences of
life. A funeral wreath of wilted flowers hangs on the closed door. The
colors are dull and somber. The painting is entitled, "That Which I
Should Have Done I Did Not Do." What a sad thought!*
G. S.

CHRISTMAS

*Christmas is not a myth, not a tradition, not a dream. It is a glorious
reality. It is a time of joy. Bethlehem's manger crib became the link
that bound a lost world to a loving God. From that manger came a
Man who not only taught us a new way of life, but brought us into a
new relationship with our Creator. Christmas means that God is
interested in the affairs of people; that God loves us so much that He
was willing to give His Son.*
BILLY GRAHAM

*O Father, may that Holy star
Grow every year more bright,
And send its glorious beams afar
To fill the world with light.*
WILLIAM CULLEN BRYANT

Cold on His cradle the dew drops are shining,
Low lies His head with the beasts of the stall.
REGINALD HEBER

For to us a child is born, to us a son is given. . . . And He will be
called Wonderful Counselor, Mighty God, Everlasting Father, Prince
of Peace.
ISAIAH 9:6 NIV

Merson's painting entitled "No Room" depicts a scene of deep shad-
ows, cold stars, a lonely street, and howling dogs, as a hard-hearted
innkeeper closes the door and turns Mary away, saying, "No room
here."

Yes, in the lowliest place in the world—a barn—the sinless King
was born. For the Son of God, the Prince of Peace, there was no
room!
G. S.

In his book entitled When Iron Gates Yield, *author Geoffrey Bull*
tells of spending Christmas Eve in a Tibetan inn, en route to a com-
munist prison camp. As he walked into the stable to feed the horses
and mules, he says, "My boots squashed in the manure and straw.
The horrible smell of the animals was nauseating, and I thought, 'to
think Christ came all the way from heaven to some wretched, eastern
stable, and what is more, He came for me.'"
G. S.

No fact in history is so well attested as is the birth, life, and death of
Jesus Christ. Encyclopædia Britannica *devotes more words to Jesus*
than to Aristotle, Cicero, Julius Caesar, or the great Napoleon. No life
has been so carefully examined, so carefully noted. No life has
reached down so many centuries with so great an impact on so many
millions of people.
G. S.

I imagine the wise men were asked, "Well, why do you want to take this foolish and dangerous trip? Why are you going to all this trouble?" "Why?" the wise men must have replied. "Because we have heard a story from Scripture; we have seen the star in the sky; and we have felt a stirring in our souls."

Like Abraham of old, the wise men went out, not knowing whither they went. And wise men of every generation have done the same. William Carey, an English shoemaker, read our Lord's Great Commission. He realized the responsibility of taking the Gospel to every creature. In the face of severe opposition and ridicule, he traveled to that far-off land of India and labored seven years before he saw even one soul come to Christ. He worked relentlessly and translated the Bible into several languages. And he became known as the "father of modern missions."

David Livingstone demonstrated the same venture of faith as he pioneered with the Gospel message throughout the continent of Africa. C. T. Studd, an all-star cricketer from Cambridge, England, forsook fame and fortune and poured out his life in missionary work. He, too, traveled by faith. When Jim Elliot and four other men were murdered by the Auca Indians, some were critical of their attempts to penetrate that savage people with the Gospel. "What a waste," some people cried. "How foolish to throw your life away for nothing." But when the book of God is finally opened, all of these will be listed as wise men, men who ventured forth in faith.

G. S.

God walked down the stairs of heaven with a Baby in his arms.
PAUL SCHERER

Christ was born in the first century, yet He belongs to all centuries. He was born a Jew, yet He belongs to all races. He was born in Bethlehem, yet He belongs to all countries.
GEORGE W. TRUETT

He who has not Christmas in his heart will never find it under a tree.
ROY L. SMITH

In the pure soul, although it sing or pray,
The Christ is born anew from day to day;
The life that knoweth Him shall bide apart
And keep eternal Christmas in the heart.

ELIZABETH STUART PHELPS

The purpose and cause of the incarnation was that He might illuminate the world by His wisdom and excite it to the love of Himself.

PETER ABELARD

Whatever else be lost among the years,
Let us keep Christmas still a shining thing:
Whatever doubts assail us, or what fears,
Let us hold close one day, remembering
Its poignant meaning for the hearts of men.
Let us get back our childlike faith again.

GRACE NOLL CROWELL,
FROM *LET US KEEP CHRISTMAS*

Christmas waves a magic wand over this world, and behold, everything is softer and more beautiful.

NORMAN VINCENT PEALE

CHURCH
· ·

It's about time we quit playing church in these services that start at eleven o'clock sharp and end at twelve o'clock dull.

VANCE HAVNER

One of the problems of the Church is that it is made up of people like you and me. The Church is a divine institution, founded by Jesus, but it is also a human institution. It is not a hothouse operating under ideal conditions.

G. S.

A little boy was taken by his parents to a new church which had long services, both morning and evening. On his third Sunday the boy noticed on the annex wall a list of the names of those who had lost their lives in World War II. The father explained, "They are the names of the men and women who died in the service."

The boy asked, "Which one, morning or evening?"

VANCE HAVNER

Many people are in a rut and a rut is nothing but a grave—with both ends kicked out.

VANCE HAVNER

I heard of a man who said to the preacher, "I want to sing in your choir."

The preacher replied, "But you don't belong here. Where do you have your membership?"

He said, "I don't belong to any local church. I belong to the invisible church."

The pastor said, "Then I suggest that you join the invisible choir."

VANCE HAVNER

It is one of the ironies of the ministry that the very man who works in God's name is often hardest put to find time for God. The parents of Jesus lost Him at church, and they were not the last ones to lose Him there.

VANCE HAVNER

The Church is not a gallery for the exhibition of eminent Christians, but a school for the education of imperfect ones.

HENRY WARD BEECHER

One hundred religious persons knit into a unity by careful organization do not constitute a church any more than eleven dead men make a football team. The first requisite is life, always.

A. W. TOZER, MAN, THE DWELLING PLACE OF GOD

Though the church has many critics, it has no rivals.
ANONYMOUS

The Bible knows nothing of solitary religion.
JOHN WESLEY

Churchgoers are like coals in a fire. When they cling together, they keep the flame aglow; when they separate, they die out.
BILLY GRAHAM

Church attendance is as vital to a disciple as a transfusion of rich, healthy blood to a sick man.
D. L. MOODY

[The local church is] the outcrop of the church universal.
P. T. FORSYTH

One day the telephone rang in the Rector's office of the Washington church which President Franklin Roosevelt attended. An eager voice inquired, "Tell me, do you expect the President to be in church this Sunday?"

"That," the Rector explained patiently, "I cannot promise. But we expect God to be there, and we fancy that will be incentive enough for a reasonably large attendance."
JOHN T. WATSON

The Church cannot be content to live in its stained-glass house and throw stones through the picture window of modern culture.
ROBERT MCAFEE BROWN

You can have the largest church auditorium, the biggest Sunday School, and run up a steeple on the church so high that it interferes with astronauts circling the earth, but the angels in heaven won't give a holy grunt until some old sinner comes down the aisle and gets right with Jesus.

BOB HARRINGTON

People with problems need the Church just like sick people need a hospital.

G. S.

A group touring Westminster Abbey in London heard the guide list the famous people buried within its walls. During a momentary silence a little old lady's voice blurted out loud and clear, "Anybody been saved here lately?"

ANONYMOUS

The greatest hindrances to the evangelization of the world are those within the church.

JOHN R. MOTT

A languid church breeds unbelief as surely as a decaying oak fungus. In a condition of depressed vitality, the seeds of disease, which a full vigor would shake off, are fatal. Raise the temperature, and you kill the insect germs.

ALEXANDER MACLAREN

Wherever we find the Word of God surely preached and heard, and the sacraments administered according to the institution of Christ, there, it is not to be doubted, is a church of God.

JOHN CALVIN, *THE INSTITUTES*

A church is a hospital for sinners, not a museum for saints.

L. L. NASH

Sign in lot: Church parking only. We will not forgive those who trespass against us.

ANONYMOUS

What makes a church great in the eyes of God? Participation, proclamation, preservation, and propagation. Every church ought to exhibit all four.

O. S. HAWKINS

*The [Early] Church was not an organization merely, not a move-
ment, but a walking incarnation of spiritual energy. The Church
began in power, moved in power and moved just as long as she had
power. When she no longer had power, she dug in for safety and
sought to conserve her gains. But her blessings were like the manna:
when they tried to keep it overnight it bred worms and stank. So we
have had monasticism, scholasticism, institutionalism; and they have
all been indicative of the same thing: absence of spiritual power. In
Church history, every return to New Testament power has marked a
new advance somewhere, and every diminution of power has seen the
rise of some new mechanism for conservation and defense. If this
analysis is reasonably correct, then we are today in a state of very low
spiritual energy.*

A. W. TOZER

*The difference between listening to a radio sermon and going to
church . . . is almost like the difference between calling your girl on
the phone and spending an evening with her.*

D. L. MOODY

*The church is so subnormal that if it ever got back to the New
Testament normal it would seem to people to be abnormal.*

VANCE HAVNER

*In the 1880s the nation's best-known infidel, Robert Ingersoll,
announced that "the churches are dying out all over the land."
Charles McCabe of the Methodist Church Extension Society replied by
telegram:*

*Dear Robert: All hail the power of Jesus' name—we are building
more than one Methodist church for every day in the year, and pro-
pose to make it two a day!*

G. S.

*An instinctive taste teaches men to build their churches with spire
steeples which point as with a silent finger to the sky and stars.*

SAMUEL T. COLERIDGE

The church exists to train its members through the practice of the presence of God to be servants of others, to the end that Christlikeness may become common property.

WILLIAM ADAMS BROWN

The Christian church is a society of sinners. It is the only society in the world, membership in which is based upon the single qualification that the candidate shall be unworthy of membership.

CHARLES C. MORRISON

All is holy where devotion kneels.

OLIVER WENDELL HOLMES, SR.

No church will ever be a great church in the eyes of God without its membership being all together and all filled. Unity and unction are essential elements to the making of a great church in the eyes of God.

O. S. HAWKINS

CITIES
· ·

In his work The Meaning of the City *(Wm. B. Eerdmans, 1970), the French social critic and commentator, Jacques Ellul, points out that the first biblically recorded cities were founded by men who rejected God. They were the products of self-will and self-ambition.*

But Ellul goes on to acknowledge, "Our task is therefore to represent Him [God] in the heart of the city."

G. S.

We will neglect our cities to our peril, for in neglecting them we neglect the nation.

JOHN F. KENNEDY,
MESSAGE TO CONGRESS, 30 JANUARY 1962

It is significant that when our Lord, in His earthly ministry, sent out the twelve and later the seventy, He sent them to cities. And in a prophetic footnote, looking down to the end of the age, He added, "You will not have gone through the cities of Israel before the Son of Man comes" (Matthew 10:23 NKJV).

G. S.

As we follow the expansion of the first-century church, we see how it follows the contours of the urbanized Roman empire. This church faced mountainous problems. But its members put their complete confidence in God. "God is able!" was their password into the very strongholds of paganism.

G. S.

Either these [unsaved] people are to be evangelized, or the leaven of communism and infidelity will assume such enormous proportions that it will break out in a reign of terror such as this country has never known.

D. L. MOODY

I have never felt salvation in nature. I love cities above all.
MICHELANGELO

Man's course begins in a garden, but it ends in a city.
ALEXANDER MACLAREN

Protestantism has somehow inherited a false perspective which says, "God made the country; man made the city." Even the names of many churches bear this out: Pleasantdale Community Church, Brookside Baptist, Shady Rest Presbyterian, Mountainside Methodist. Sometimes we get so restful we give the impression of a cemetery! We smile and nod and avoid the closeness within our fellowship that discloses flaws and problems and conflicts. The appearance from the outside may very well be one of living in a trance, a dream world where life is unreal.

G. S.

There was never an hour when the opportunities of the church were what they are at this moment. There never was a moment since Calvary when the city cried for the help of Christians as it is crying now. The heart of the modern metropolis has been largely abandoned by the modern churches and the new theologians; and these great centers—threatening to become the black holes of our cities—have been flung at our feet as our special charges. Evangelical ministers and evangelistic churches will either shine there or darkness will reign; we will either be the salt to the city, or corruption and decay are its destiny. If we put Christ upon the throne of our affections, if we make His church the medium of our endeavors, if we tithe our time and tithe our income, we will conquer. Thousands will yet throng the courts of the Lord, the walls of His church will be compelled to widen by their incoming, and into every dark spot of the city we will send our young men and maidens, carrying the torchlight of life, and our mission stations will become the lighthouses for the storm-tossed of every region, and hospitals for those suffering from moral hurts, yea, homes into which Christ shall walk, and with His voice raise the dead.

WILLIAM B. RILEY

Scripture makes it clear that God's compassion reaches out to the great centers of population.

Remember how God set Lot and the angels to warn the people of Sodom? Then, God's concern was reflected in the burden of Abraham as he interceded with God for Sodom.

Again we see God's compassion for another great city when He sent Jonah to Nineveh, and in the end spared the city after its repentance. We sense something of God's great pity when He asked Jonah, "Should not I have compassion on Nineveh, the great city in which there are more than 120,000 people who do not know the difference between their right and left hand . . . ?" (Jonah 4:11 NASB).

G. S.

The city may have started with Cain, but it will climax with Christ. We need to keep in mind that the destiny of the redeemed is a city.

G. S.

I like the cadence of the jackhammer. I like the sight of a huge crane hoisting steel beams into place. I like the flow of concrete, the clicking of a million heels on finished pavement. I like the feel of sweat, of tears, and flesh. Here is action; here is life. In the crush of multitudes, the power of the living Jesus can still be sensed. Let us not limit our spiritual experience to the Grand Canyon.

G. S.

Why should we minister in the city centers? The churches of the New Testament set the example.

The apostles concentrated their efforts in the throbbing cities of their day. The ministries in those metropolitan areas were life-and-death struggles. The environment was not easy or compatible with the revolutionary new values introduced by the disciples of Christ.

Ephesus, located at the mouth of the Cayster River, was notorious for its luxury and moral looseness. Diana was the chief object of worship, and opposition to the gospel was fierce.

Corinth, with a population of 600,000, was the largest city in Greece. It was an important seaport, a garrison town, and a strategic highway junction. The Corinthians were particularly prone to sexual promiscuity and enjoyed dragging each other off to court over any little difference of opinion. The city seethed with a mass of merchants, philosophers, ex-soldiers, and peddlers of vice.

Rome, metropolitan center of the Roman empire, was riddled with perversions, court plots, and murders. Its prosperity and immorality eventually brought about its downfall.

In these centers of life, Christianity took root and flowered throughout the known world. The disciples went neither to the fringes of the towns nor to the tents of the migrants. They saw no future for the gospel in isolation.

G. S.

CIVIL DISOBEDIENCE
· ·

Guidelines for Civil Disobedience

1. *Disobedience, if necessary, must be without violence. To be violent and to hurt someone is contrary to the teaching of the Word of God.*
2. *The law being disobeyed must be clearly contrary to the Word of God. This was Peter and John's situation. They were commanded by their Lord to bear witness to the things they had seen and heard. The command of the authorities to be silent was clearly in conflict with God's word to them.*
3. *In general, disobedience must not be against civil rulers, because these rulers (both good ones and bad ones) fall within God's permissive and directive will.*

   Peter and Paul lived and served while wicked Nero held sway, yet both commanded believers to be submissive to the government. The direct teaching of Scripture requires civil obedience (Romans 13:1–7; 1 Peter 2:13–17).

   Henry David Thoreau is often referred to by present-day dissenters. Thoreau stated, "It is not desirable to cultivate a respect for the law, so much as for the right." But, we must ask, who decides what is right? The government may make a mistake, but so may the people. If seven people disobey, that is one thing. But if seven million disobey, that is anarchy.
4. *Christians must be willing to bear the consequences that disobedience to civil authority involves. Peter and John, and Paul, too, were so committed to Jesus Christ that they were willing to suffer ridicule, jail, and death to get out the gospel. The Scriptures imply that ordinarily the commandments of God and the commandments of men should not be in conflict. But it also establishes that God is the Lord of the Christian's conscience. However, for the most part, obedience is in and disobedience is out. If we are forbidden to bear witness to salvation in Christ, we must disobey that command. If we are ordered by authorities to do evil in the sight of God, we must disobey.*

   But there is so much which can be done without disobeying!

We must ask, what is the church willing to do today to get out the gospel? Can we be complacent when the world is in such great need?

G. S.

The workers have nothing to lose but their chains. They have a world to win. Workers of the world, unite!

KARL MARX

Have respect for authority. Jesus Christ was under the authority of His Father in heaven. . . . He lived for one thing: to fulfill the will of the Father. Everyone is subject to some kind of authority. There is one chain of command and the ultimate authority is God at the top. What is the authority in your life? Is it your selfishness? Your lust? Your greed? Or have you turned it all over to God and said, "Lord, You are going to be my authority"? . . . When you are under authority, you are then able to assume authority.

BILLY GRAHAM

CIVILIZATION

Civilization today reminds me of an ape with a blowtorch playing in a room full of dynamite. It looks like the monkeys are about to operate the zoo, and the inmates are taking over the asylum.

VANCE HAVNER

Civilization is a stream with banks. The stream is sometimes filled with blood from people killing, stealing, shouting and doing things historians usually record, while on the banks, unnoticed, people build homes, make love, raise children, sing songs, write poetry and even whittle statues. The story of civilization is the story of what happened on the banks. Historians are pessimists because they ignore the banks for the river.

WILL AND ARIEL DURANT

Civilization is a movement and not a condition, a voyage and not a harbor.

ARNOLD TOYNBEE

To be able to fill leisure intelligently is the last product of civilization.
ARNOLD TOYNBEE

COMFORT

God does not comfort us to make us comfortable but to make us comforters.

J. HENRY JOWETT

> *So, amid the conflict, whether great or small,*
> *Do not be discouraged, God is over all;*
> *Count your many blessings, angels will attend,*
> *Help and comfort give you to your journey's end.*
> JOHNSON OATMAN, JR.

God often comforts us, not by changing the circumstances of our lives, but by changing our attitude toward them.

S. H. B. MASTERMAN

> *And He that doth the ravens feed,*
> *Yea, providently caters for the sparrow,*
> *Be comfort to my age!*
> WILLIAM SHAKESPEARE, *AS YOU LIKE IT*

COMMITMENT

> *Take my life, and let it be*
> *Consecrated, Lord, to thee.*
> FRANCES RIDLEY HAVERGAL

God calls us to be 100 percent committed. His resources can make us willing to take a stand with our friends and neighbors. Ours need not be the day of the placid pulpit and the comfortable pew. Dante said, "The hottest places in hell are reserved for those who in times of great moral crisis maintain their neutrality."

G. S.

What an opportunity to realize that our generation, which lauds the excellence of its scientific accomplishments, perceives God—and the validity of His existence—by our actions! One basis of our judgment before God is the quality of life we live: "The fire will test each one's work, of what sort it is" (1 Corinthians 3:13).

G. S.

Men must have goals which, in their eyes, merit effort and commitment; and they must believe that their efforts will win them self-respect and the respect of others.

JOHN W. GARDNER

COMMITTEES

One of the reasons why the Ten Commandments are so short and to the point is the fact they were given direct and did not come out of committees.

H. G. HUTCHESON

Committee—a group of men who keep minutes and waste hours.

MILTON BERLE

A committee is a thing which takes a week to do what one good man can do in an hour.

ELBERT HUBBARD

A camel looks like a horse that was planned by a committee.

ANONYMOUS

COMMUNICATION

If you cry "Forward" you must be sure to make clear the direction in which to go. Don't you see that if you fail to do that and simply call out the word to a monk and a revolutionary, they will go in precisely opposite directions?

ANTON CHEKHOV

It must be that evil communications corrupt good dispositions.
MENANDER

Good, the more communicated, more abundant grows.
JOHN MILTON

Genuine poetry can communicate before it is understood.
T. S. ELIOT

Communication is depositing a part of yourself in another person.
ANONYMOUS

Pure truth cannot be assimilated by the crowd; it must be communicated by contagion.

HENRI FRÉDÉRIC AMIEL

Communication is a two-way street. And while we revel in the reality that we can always get through to heaven, our concern should be whether our Lord can always get through to us.
JOSEPH STOWELL

COMPROMISE

The swift wind of compromise is a lot more devastating than the sudden jolt of misfortune.

CHARLES SWINDOLL

A new Decalogue has been adopted by some of our day, the first words of which reads, "Thou shalt not disagree," and a new set of Beatitudes too, which begins, "Blessed are they that tolerate every-thing, for they shall not be made accountable for anything." It is now the accepted thing to talk over religious differences in public with the understanding that no one will try to convert another or point out errors in his belief. Imagine Moses agreeing to take part in a panel discussion with Israel over the golden calf; or Elijah engaging in a gentlemanly dialogue with the prophets of Baal. Or try to picture Jesus seeking a meeting of minds with the Pharisees to iron out differ-ences.

The blessing of God is promised to the peacemaker, but the reli-gious negotiator had better watch his step. Darkness and light can never be brought together by talk. Some things are not negotiable.

A. W. TOZER, *MAN, THE DWELLING PLACE OF GOD*

Some Christians who once championed sound doctrine beat a retreat once in a while and from stratospheric heights announce that they will not "stoop to controversy." When a man contends for the faith in New Testament style, he does not stoop! . . . Contending for the faith is not easy. It is not pleasant business. It has many perils. It is a thank-less job, and it is highly unpopular in this age of moral fogs and spir-itual twilights. This is a day of diplomats, not prophets. It is nicer to be an appeaser than an opposer. It is the day of Erasmus, not Luther; of Gamaliel, not Paul.

VANCE HAVNER

The instances are exceedingly rare of man immediately passing over a clear marked line from virtue into declared vice and corruption. There are middle tints and shades between the two extremes; there is some-thing uncertain on the confines of the two empires which they must pass through, and which renders the change easy and imperceptible.

EDMUND BURKE

Please all, and you will please none!

AESOP

In the year 1939, the Spanish Civil War was almost over. Just outside Madrid, the rebel General Mola prepared to attack. Someone asked which of his four columns would be the first to enter the besieged city. To the inquirer's surprise, he replied, "The fifth." General Mola was simply saying that his most important forces were the band of rebel sympathizers already in the city, already fighting for him behind the loyalist lines.

General Mola's remark coined the term "fifth column," a synonym for traitorous forces. During World War II, it was a fifth column in Norway that brought about that country's collapse. Norway's leader, Vidkun Quisling, became a puppet premier of Adolf Hitler's German Nazis, and when, at the end of the war, Norway was freed, Quisling was put to death for treason.

Betrayal is an ugly business and yet very common in history. Down through the centuries, even the church has had its Quislings.

G. S.

The greatness of Christianity did not arise from attempts to make compromises with those philosophical opinions of the ancient world which had some resemblance to its own doctrine, but from the unrelenting and fanatical proclamation and defense of its own teaching.

ADOLF HITLER, *MEIN KAMPF*

CONFESSION
· ·

"Blessed art thou, Simon Barjonas." Yes, He blessed him right there because he confessed Him to be the Son of God. He was hungry to get someone to confess Him. Then let everyone take his stand on the side of the Lord; confess Him here on earth, and He will confess you when you get to heaven. He will look around upon you with pride, because you stood up for Him here. If you want the blessing of heaven, and the peace that passeth all understanding, you must be ready and willing to confess Him. Do you know how Peter fell? He fell as a thousand people fall, because they don't confess the Son of God.

D. L. MOODY

Forgiveness is always free. But that doesn't mean that confession is always easy. Sometimes it is hard. Incredibly hard. It is painful (sometimes literally) to admit our sins and entrust ourselves to God's care.

ERWIN W. LUTZER

There is no refuge from confession but suicide; and suicide is confession.

DANIEL WEBSTER

We confess to little faults only to persuade ourselves that we have no great ones.

FRANÇOIS DUC DE LA ROCHEFOUCAULD

In confession . . . we open our lives to healing, reconciling, restoring, uplifting grace of Him who loves us in spite of what we are.

LOUIS CASSELS

CONFIDENCE
· ·

Supreme confidence in one's ability to "deliver" in times of crisis or need is a quality much to be desired. It is possessed by all too few of us. Our tendency is to yield, to retreat, or to crack up when the going gets tough. Each of us has his or her "breaking point," dependent upon the degree of courage and faith and resolution . . . built into our lives. Where one person gives up, another person may be just beginning. If you are not going forward, you are going backward. Nothing stands still in life. You must keep on putting forth the best efforts of which you are capable to maintain the position you have gained.

HAROLD SHERMAN

It's fine to believe in ourselves, but we mustn't be too easily convinced.

BETTER HOMES AND GARDENS

Self-confidence is the first requisite to great undertakings.

SAMUEL JOHNSON

God knows best; he hasn't arranged your anatomy so as to make it easy for you to pat yourself on the back.

ANONYMOUS

CONFLICT
· ·

I believe in getting into hot water. I think it keeps you clean.

G. K. CHESTERTON

The best armor is to keep out of range.

ITALIAN PROVERB

A quarrel is quickly settled when deserted by one party; there is no battle unless there be two.

SENECA

The key to solving conflict is found in affirming God's will. When we do this, our desires become God's desires, and then His power becomes our power.

G. S.

> *Let dogs delight to bark and bite,*
> *For God hath made them so;*
> *Let bears and lions growl and fight,*
> *For 'tis their nature too. . . .*
> *But children you should never let*
> *Such angry passions rise,*
> *Your little hands were never made*
> *To tear each other's eyes.*

ISAAC WATTS

CONSCIENCE
· ·

Two things fill me with constantly increasing admiration and awe, the longer and more earnestly I reflect on them: the starry heavens without and the moral law within.

IMMANUEL KANT

A seared conscience is one whose warning voice has been suppressed and perverted habitually, so that eventually instead of serving as a guide, it only confirms the person in his premeditatedly evil course.

ROBERT J. LITTLE

Though the dungeon, the scourge, and the executioner be absent, the guilty mind can apply the goad and scorch with blows.

LUCRETIUS

What is conscience? God put within each one of us something that cries aloud against us, whenever we do that which we know to be wrong. Conscience is the detective that watches the direction of our steps and decries every conscious transgression. Conscience is a vigilant eye before which each imagination, thought, and act is held up for either censure or approval. I believe there is no greater argument for the existence of God in the world today than conscience. There is no greater proof of the existence of a moral law and lawgiver in the universe than this little light of the soul. It is God's voice to the inner man. Conscience is our wisest counselor and teacher, our most faithful and most patient friend.

BILLY GRAHAM

A man's conscience, like a warning line on the highway, tells him what he shouldn't do—but it does not keep him from doing it.

FRANK A. CLARK

CONSECRATION

God is not so much concerned with your ability as with your availability.

THE BIBLE FRIEND

The mark of a saint is not perfection, but consecration. A saint is not a man without faults, but a man who has given himself without reserve to God.

BROOKE FOSS WESTCOTT

The greatness of a man's power is the measure of his surrender.

GENERAL WILLIAM BOOTH

I go out to preach with two propositions in mind. First, everyone ought to give his life to Christ. Second, whether or not anyone gives Him his life, I will give Him mine.

JONATHAN EDWARDS

CONTENTMENT

Being "contented" ought to mean in English, as it does in French, being pleased. Being content with an attic ought not to mean being unable to move from it and resigned to living in it: it ought to mean appreciating all there is in such a position.

G. K. CHESTERTON

True contentment is the power of getting out of any situation all that there is in it.

G. K. CHESTERTON

If we have not quiet in our minds, outward comfort will do no more for us than a golden slipper on a gouty foot.

JOHN BUNYAN

I don't want to own anything that won't fit into my coffin.
FRED ALLEN

To have what we want is riches; but to be able to do without is power.
GEORGE MACDONALD

All the misfortunes of men spring from their not knowing how to live quietly at home in their own rooms.
BLAISE PASCAL

Is your place a small place?
Tend it with care!
He set you there.

Is your place a large place?
Guard it with care!
He set you there.

Whatever your place, it is
Not yours alone, but His,
Who set you there.

JOHN OXENHAM

"I have learned in whatsoever state I am, therewith to be content" *(Philippians 4:11).*
Christ is enough to satisfy the hearts of all who confide in Him and who leave everything in His hands. Such need never be cast down by seeming misfortunes.
A Christian asked another how he was getting along. Dolefully his friend replied, "Oh, fairly well, under the circumstances."
"I am sorry," exclaimed the other, "that you are under the circumstances. The Lord would have us living above all circumstances, where He Himself can satisfy our hearts and meet our every need for time and eternity."
H. A. IRONSIDE

Be happy with what you have and are,
be generous with both,
and you won't have to hunt for happiness.
WILLIAM E. GLADSTONE

If we noticed little pleasures,
As we notice little pains—
If we quite forgot our losses
And remembered all our gains.

If we looked for people's virtues
And their faults refused to see.
What a comfortable, happy, cheerful place
This world would be!
FORBES MAGAZINE OF BUSINESS

CONTRITION
· ·

During a long life I have had to eat my own words many times, and I
have found it a very nourishing diet.
WINSTON CHURCHILL

Four things which are not in thy treasury,
I lay before thee, Lord, with this petition:—
My nothingness, my wants,
My sins, and my contrition.
ROBERT SOUTHEY

If you bethink yourself of any crime
Unreconcil'd as yet to heaven and grace,
Solicit for it straight.
WILLIAM SHAKESPEARE, OTHELLO

Man, wretched man, whene'er he stoops to sin,
Feels, with the act, a strong remorse within.
JUVENAL

To err is human; but contrition felt for the crime distinguishes the virtuous from the wicked.

VITTORIO ALFIERI

COUNTENANCE

A solemn, unsmiling, sanctimonious old iceberg that looked like he was waiting for a vacancy in the Trinity.

MARK TWAIN

One of Abraham Lincoln's advisers urgently recommended a certain man for a post in the President's cabinet. When Lincoln declined to follow the suggestion, he was asked to give his reasons.

"I don't like the man's face," the President explained.

"But the poor man isn't responsible for his face," his advocate insisted.

"Every man over 40 is responsible for his face," Lincoln replied.

FRANCES PARKINSON KEYES

He had a face like a benediction.

MIGUEL DE CERVANTES

One ABC of Christianity: "Always Be Cheerful" (1 Thessalonians 5:16 Berkeley).

ANONYMOUS

COURAGE

Here I stand; I can do no other. God help me. Amen!

MARTIN LUTHER,
SPEECH AT THE DIET OF WORMS, 18 APRIL 1521

Theodore Roosevelt is attributed to have said about his predecessor to the presidency, William McKinley, "As much backbone as a chocolate eclair."

G. S.

Courage is the first of human qualities because it is the quality which guarantees all others.

WINSTON CHURCHILL

I am only one, but I am one.
I can't do everything, but
I can do something.
And what I can do, I ought to do.
And what I ought to do, by the
Grace of God, I shall do.

EDWARD EVERETT HALE

The Courage That My Mother Had

The courage that my mother had
Went with her, and is with her still:
Rock from New England quarried;
Now granite in a granite hill.

The golden brooch my mother wore
She left behind for me to wear;
I have no thing I treasure more:
Yet, it is something I could spare.

Oh, if instead she'd left to me
The thing she took into the grave!—
That courage like a rock, which she
Has no more need of, and I have.

EDNA ST. VINCENT MILLAY,
COLLECTED POEMS

The signing of the Declaration of Independence took courage. When Charles Carroll signed his name, someone asked, "How will anyone know which Charles Carroll is meant among all those with that name?"

"Well, let there be no mistake," said the courageous patriot, and he signed in bold letters, "Charles Carroll of Carrollton."

G. S.

Noah was a brave man to sail in a wooden boat with two termites.
ANONYMOUS

Today many people are living in the bondage of fear. In a recent study, a psychiatrist said that the greatest problem facing his patients was fear. Afraid of going insane, committing suicide, being alone, or afraid of heart disease, cancer, disaster, or death. We are becoming a nation of fearful people. Down through the centuries in times of trouble, temptation, trial, bereavement, and crisis, God has brought courage to the hearts of those who love Him. The Bible is crowded with assurances of God's help and comfort in every kind of trouble which might cause fears to arise in the human heart. Today the Christian can come to the Scriptures with full assurance that God is going to deliver the person who puts his trust and confidence in God. Christians can look into the future with promise, hope, and joy, and without fear, discouragement, or despondency.
BILLY GRAHAM

Here is the answer which I will give to President Roosevelt. . . . Give us the tools, and we will finish the job.
WINSTON CHURCHILL,
BROADCAST 9 FEBRUARY 1941

Without belittling the courage with which men have died, we should not forget those acts of courage with which men . . . have lived. The courage of life is often a less dramatic spectacle than the courage of a final moment; but it is no less a magnificent mixture of triumph and tragedy. A man does what he must . . . in spite of personal consequences, in spite of obstacles and damages and pressures—and that is the basis of all human morality.
JOHN F. KENNEDY, *PROFILES IN COURAGE*

When John Huss was about to be burned to death, they asked him to give up his teachings. Huss answered, "What I have taught with my lips, I now seal with my blood."
*   That is courage.*
G. S.

127

COURTESY

The test of good manners is to be able to put up pleasantly with bad ones.
WENDELL WILLKIE

There is no such thing as being a gentleman at important moments; it is at unimportant moments that a man is a gentleman. . . . If once his mind is possessed in any strong degree with the knowledge that he is a gentleman he will soon cease to be one.
G. K. CHESTERTON

Life is short, but there is always time for courtesy.
RALPH WALDO EMERSON

Love does not behave in a discourteous manner. Greed does; selfishness does; fear does—but not love.
G. S.

It is almost a definition of a gentleman to say that he is one who never inflicts pain.
JOHN HENRY NEWMAN

If you would win the world, melt it, do not hammer it.
ALEXANDER MACLAREN

"One of the most tactful men I ever knew," says a California manufacturer, "was the man who fired me from my first job. He called me in and said, 'Son, I don't know how we're ever going to get along without you, but starting Monday we're going to try.'"
JAMES M. BRAUDE

COVETOUSNESS

The man who covets is always poor.
CLAUDIAN

Envy is thin because it bites but never eats.
SPANISH PROVERB

Abraham Lincoln once walked down the street with his two sons, both of whom were crying. "What's the matter with your boys?" asked a passerby. "Exactly what is wrong with the whole world," said Lincoln. "I have three walnuts, and each boy wants two."

Lust in one form or another is the common sin that plagues all of mankind.
G. S.

Those that much covet are with gain so fond,
For what they have not, that which they possess,
They scatter and unloose it from their bond,
And so, by hoping more, they have but less.
WILLIAM SHAKESPEARE,
THE RAPE OF LUCRECE

CREATION

What can be more foolish than to think that all this rare fabric of heaven and earth could come by chance, when all the skill of science is not able to make an oyster.
JEREMY TAYLOR

I asked the whole frame of the world about my God; and he answered, "I am not He, but He made me."
SAINT AUGUSTINE, *CONFESSIONS*

My heart is awed within me when I think
Of the great miracle that still goes on,
In silence, round me—the perpetual work
Of thy creation, finished, yet renewed forever.
Written on thy works I read
The lesson of thy own eternity
WILLIAM CULLEN BRYANT

All created things are living in the Hand of God. The senses see only the action of the creatures; but faith sees in everything the action of God.

J. P. DE CAUSSADE,
ABANDONMENT TO DIVINE PROVIDENCE

Either God is in the whole of nature, with no gaps, or He's not there at all.

L. A. COULSON, *SCIENCE AND CHRISTIAN BELIEF*

CRITICISM
· ·

Here we write well when we expose frauds and hypocrites. We are great at counting warts and blemishes and weighing feet of clay. In expressing love, we belong among the undeveloped countries.

SAUL BELLOW

People ask you for criticism, but they only want praise.

W. SOMERSET MAUGHAM

He who throws dirt always loses ground.

ANONYMOUS

If what they are saying about you is true, mend your ways.
If it isn't true, forget it, and go on and serve the Lord.

H. A. IRONSIDE

A thick skin is a gift from God.

KONRAD ADENAUER

Draw deep from the well of Biblical criticism, but do not give your congregation too much of the rope to chew.

W. RUSSELL MALTBY

CROSS
. . . .

> *May I be willing, Lord, to bear*
> *Daily my cross for thee;*
> *Even thy cup of grief to share,*
> *Thou hast borne all for me.*
>   JENNIE EVELYN HUSSEY

And he who does not take his cross and follow after Me is not worthy of Me.

MATTHEW 10:38 NKJV

But God forbid that I should glory except in the cross of our Lord Jesus Christ, by whom the world has been crucified to me, and I to the world.

GALATIANS 6:14 NKJV

If I see aright, the cross of popular evangelicalism is not the cross of the New Testament. It is, rather, a new bright ornament upon the bosom of a self-assured and carnal Christianity. The old cross slew men, the new cross entertains them. The old cross condemned; the new cross amuses. The old cross destroyed confidence in the flesh; the new cross encourages it.

A. W. TOZER, *THE DIVINE CONQUEST*

God is generous. The cross is the sign of addition.

G. S.

Once when Lord Tennyson was on vacation in a country village he asked an old Methodist woman, "Is there any news?"

"Well," she replied, "there is only one piece of news that I know, and that is that Christ died for my sins."

Tennyson responded, "That is old news, and good news, and new news."

G. S.

We are not saved by theories, but by fact, and what is the fact? For whom did Christ die? Christ died for sinners. Well, then, He died for me.

ARTHUR STANTON

Christ, who, being the holiest among the mighty, and mightiest among the holy, lifted with His pierced hands empires off their hinges and turned the stream of centuries out of its channel, and still governs the ages.

JEAN PAUL RICHTER

The most crucial event of all history, the one crisis that forms a watershed by which we number our years, write all our history, and reckon our relationship with God—the crucifixion of Christ—was one of those events that passed without much notice. Yet it is the cross of Christ to which all previous history looked forward and to which all history since looks back. It is the crucifixion that gives meaning to the flow of human history. It is Christ's death that makes sense of the pattern of events from the beginning of history.

Yes, the cross is the hinge of history. The great events that were compressed into the four days surrounding Christ's death touch the lives and hopes of everyone.

G. S.

Do you see the Person of the cross? He is the sinless one, the only man ever of whom it could accurately be said, "[He] did no sin, neither was guile found in His mouth" (1 Peter 2:22). He was "in all points tempted like as we are, yet without sin" (Hebrew 4:15). He was "holy, harmless, undefiled, separate from sinners" (Hebrews 7:26).

He was perfectly righteous, perfectly holy, and sinless; yet He died willingly for our sin. First Peter 2:23–24 tells us, "When he was reviled, [he] reviled not again; when he suffered, he threatened not; but committed himself to him that judgeth righteously: Who his own self bare our sins in his own body on the tree, that we, being dead to sins, should live unto righteousness."

G. S.

God made a show of the powers of evil and darkness and at Calvary He put them to rout.
JAMES S. STEWART

C. I. Scofield once wrote, "God was not changed, for He had always loved the world; nor was the world changed, for it continued in sinful rebellion against God. But by the death of Christ the relationship between God and the world was changed." God took away the wall between Himself and man the day Christ died.
G. S.

The Cross of Christ must be either the darkest spot of all in the mystery of existence or a searchlight by the aid of which we may penetrate the surrounding gloom.
BURNETT H. STREETER

In the cross is health, in the cross is life, in the cross is protection from enemies, in the cross is heavenly sweetness, in the cross strength of mind, in the cross joy of the Spirit, in the cross the height of virtue, in the cross perfection of holiness. There is no health of the soul, no hope of eternal life, save in the cross.
THOMAS À KEMPIS

The man with a cross no longer controls his destiny; he lost control when he picked up his cross. That cross immediately became to him an all-absorbing interest, an overwhelming interference. No matter what he may desire to do, there is but one thing he can do; that is, move on toward the place of crucifixion.
A. W. TOZER, OF GOD AND MEN

I am crucified with Christ: nevertheless I live; yet not I, but Christ liveth in me: and the life which I now live in the flesh I live by the faith of the Son of God, who loved me, and gave Himself for me.
GALATIANS 2:20

But God forbid that I should glory, save in the cross of our Lord Jesus Christ, by whom the world is crucified unto me, and I unto the world.
GALATIANS 6:14

There are no crown-wearers in heaven who were not cross-bearers here below.
CHARLES HADDON SPURGEON

> *Upon a life I have not lived,*
> *Upon a death I have not died—*
> *Another's life, Another's death,*
> *I stake my whole eternity.*
> ANONYMOUS

Then Jesus beholding him loved him, and said unto him, "One thing thou lackest: go thy way, sell whatsoever thou hast, and give to the poor, and thou shalt have treasure in heaven: and come, take up the cross, and follow me."
MARK 10:21

Until a person sees that there is no hope within himself to satisfy the righteous demands of the law, the cross is simply a farce to him.
O. S. HAWKINS

The cross is the center of the world's history. The incarnation of Christ and the crucifixion of our Lord are the pivot round which all the events of the ages revolve. The testimony of Christ was the spirit of prophecy, and the growing power of Jesus is the spirit of history.
ALEXANDER MACLAREN

Then said Jesus unto His disciples, "If any man will come after me, let him deny himself, and take up his cross, and follow me."
MATTHEW 16:24

How soon would faith freeze without a cross!
SAMUEL RUTHERFORD

The Cross is not only the symbol for the life of man; it is equally the symbol for the life of God, and it may indeed be said that the Cross is in the heart of God.

JOHN T. WATSON

DEATH

At death we cross from one territory to another, but we'll have no trouble with visas. Our representative is already there, preparing for our arrival. As citizens of heaven, our entrance is incontestable.
ERWIN W. LUTZER

"My sword I give to him that shall succeed me in my pilgrimage, and my courage and skill to him that can get it. My marks and scars I carry with me, to be a witness for me that I have fought his battles who now will be my rewarder." When the day that he must go hence was come, many accompanied him to the riverside, into which as he went he said: "Death, where is thy sting?" And as he went down deeper, he said: "Grave, where is thy victory?" So he passed over, and all the trumpets sounded for him on the other side.
JOHN BUNYAN, *THE PILGRIM'S PROGRESS*

"Speculations!" said the dying man in astonishment. "I know nothing about speculations; I'm resting on certainties. 'I know whom I have believed, and am persuaded that he is able to keep that which I have committed unto him against that day'" (2 Timothy 1:12).
SIR MICHAEL FARADAY

Death may be the King of terrors . . . but Jesus is the King of kings!
D. L. MOODY

Christ taught an astonishing thing about physical death: not merely that it is an experience robbed of its terror but that as an experience it does not exist at all. To "sleep in Christ," like one that wraps the drapery of his couch about him, and lies down to pleasant dreams.
WILLIAM CULLEN BRYANT

Death is but a passage. It is not a house, it is only a vestibule. The grave has a door on its inner side.

ALEXANDER MACLAREN

Death is the most democratic experience in life for we all participate in it. We think of its happening only to other people. We don't like to grow old and we don't like to die. The Bible teaches that death is an enemy of man and God. But it also teaches that this enemy, death, will ultimately be destroyed forever; that in fact it has already been defeated at the Cross and resurrection of Jesus Christ. Death, for a Christian, brings permanent freedom from evil. It also means the believer will be like Jesus. We shall be like Christ in love. So much of self is involved in what we do here; but one day, in Christ, we will have perfect love. What a glorious time it will be when we get to heaven!

BILLY GRAHAM

When Michelangelo, already well along in years, was discussing life with an old friend, the latter commented, "Yes, after such a good life, it's hard to look death in the eye."

"Not at all!" contradicted Michelangelo. "Since life was such a pleasure, death coming from the same great Source cannot displease us."

TEMMLER WERKE

Truth sits upon the lips of dying men.

MATTHEW ARNOLD

I am ready to meet God face to face tonight and look into those eyes of infinite holiness, for all my sins are covered by the atoning blood.

R. A. TORREY

Death is not the end; it is only a new beginning. Death is not the master of the house; he is only the porter at the King's lodge, appointed to open the gate and let the King's guests into the realm of eternal day.

JOHN HENRY JOWETT

I Have a Rendezvous with Death

I have a rendezvous with Death
At some disputed barricade,
When Spring comes back with rustling shade
And apple blossoms fill the air—
I have a rendezvous with Death
When Spring brings back blue days and fair.

It may be he shall take my hand,
And lead me into his dark land,
And close my eyes and quench my breath—
It may be I shall pass him still.
I have a rendezvous with Death
On some scarred slope of battered hill,
When Spring comes round again this year
And the first meadow flowers appear.

God knows 'twere better to be deep
Pillowed in silk and scented down,
Where Love throbs out in blissful sleep,
Pulse nigh to pulse, and breath to breath,
Where hushed awakenings are dear . . .
But I've a rendezvous with Death
At midnight in some flaming town,
When Spring trips north again this year;
And I to my pledged word am true,
I shall not fail that rendezvous.

ALAN SEEGER, AMERICAN VOLUNTEER
(KILLED IN FRANCE WHILE SERVING WITH THE
FRENCH FOREIGN LEGION, 1916, AGE 28)

And thou, most kind and gentle death,
Waiting to hush our latest breath;
O Praise Him—Alleluia!
Thou leadest home the child of God
And Christ our Lord the way hath trod.

SAINT FRANCIS OF ASSISI

As a well-spent day brings happy sleep, so life well used brings happy death.

LEONARDO DA VINCI

Death is the great adventure beside which moon landings and space trips pale into insignificance.

JOSEPH BAYLY

Death always waits. The door of the hearse is never closed.

JOSEPH BAYLY, *THE VIEW FROM A HEARSE*

The conquest of death is the final achievement of religion. No religion is worth its name unless it can prove itself more than a match for death.

L. P. JACKS, *THE INNER SENTINEL*

When I am dead, my dearest,
Sing no sad songs for me.
CHRISTINA ROSSETTI

To die is landing on some distant shore.

JOHN DRYDEN

Old man, exhausted by ordeal, detached from human deeds, feeling the approach of the eternal cold, but always watching in the shadows for the gleam of hope.

CHARLES DE GAULLE

Good-bye world . . . Good-bye to clocks ticking . . . and Mama's sunflowers. And food and coffee. And new-ironed dresses and hot baths . . and sleeping and waking up. Oh, earth, you're too wonderful for anybody to realize you.

THORNTON WILDER, *OUR TOWN*

Precious in the sight of the Lord is the death of his saints.

PSALM 116:15

You haven't lost anything when you know where it is. Death can hide but not divide.

VANCE HAVNER

I'd like to get home before dark because although you're saved, you're never safe as far as your testimony's concerned until you get home. They will all remember the big blunder you made on the last mile of the way and forget all the good things you did all the way back up the road.

VANCE HAVNER

Yea, though I walk through the valley of the shadow of death, I will fear no evil: for thou art with me; thy rod and thy staff they comfort me.

PSALM 23:4

Every man must do two things alone; he must do his own believing and his own dying.

MARTIN LUTHER

God buries His workmen but carries on His work.

CHARLES WESLEY

The wicked is driven away in his wickedness: but the righteous hath hope in his death.

PROVERBS 14:32

And fear not them which kill the body, but are not able to kill the soul: but rather fear him which is able to destroy both soul and body in hell.

MATTHEW 10:28

His maker kissed his soul away,
And laid his flesh to rest.

ISAAC WATTS

How strange this fear of death is! We are never frightened at a sunset.
GEORGE MACDONALD

For we brought nothing into this world, and it is certain we can carry nothing out.
1 TIMOTHY 6:7

And as it is appointed unto men once to die, but after this the judgment.
HEBREWS 9:27

He that hath the Son hath life; and he that hath not the Son of God hath not life.
1 JOHN 5:12

And God shall wipe away all tears from their eyes; and there shall be no more death, neither sorrow, nor crying, neither shall there be any more pain: for the former things are passed away.
REVELATION 21:4

If we really think that home is elsewhere and that this life is a "wandering to find home," why should we not look forward to the arrival?
C. S. LEWIS

DECAY AND DECLINE
· ·

History teaches us that when a barbarian race confronts a sleeping culture, the barbarian always wins.
ARNOLD TOYNBEE

Within the Roman empire, law and order prevailed, and never [before] did almost everybody "have it so good" . . . no foreign power could challenge Rome. . . . Why did this . . . civilization decline at all? and why did it decline so rapidly that, within another 100 years, the Roman Empire was plunged irreversibly into anarchy and penury, ravaged by foreign aggressors and doomed to extinction?
ROBERT STRAUSS-HUPE

According to Edward Gibbon, in his classic work, The Decline and Fall of the Roman Empire, *there were five major causes for the decline and fall of the Roman empire.*

1. *The breakdown of the family and the increase of divorce.*
2. *The spiraling rise of taxes and extravagant spending.*
3. *The mounting desire for pleasure and the brutalization of sports.*
4. *The continual production of armaments to face ever increasing threats of enemy attacks.*
5. *The decay of religion into many confusing forms, leaving the people without a uniform faith.*

It is very significant that these factors exist today.

G. S.

DECISIONS

There is no more miserable human being than one in whom nothing is habitual but indecision.

WILLIAM JAMES

The great thing in the world is not so much where we stand, as in what direction we are moving.

OLIVER WENDELL HOLMES, SR.

[They are] decided only to be undecided, resolved to be irresolute, adamant for drift, solid for fluidity, all-powerful to be impotent.

WINSTON CHURCHILL, *WHILE ENGLAND SLEPT*

I determined never to stop until I had come to the end and achieved my purpose.

DAVID LIVINGSTONE

Destiny is not a matter of chance, it is a matter of choice; it is not a thing to be waited for, it is a thing to be achieved.

WILLIAM JENNINGS BRYAN

A man with a half volition goes backwards and forwards, and makes no way on the smoothest road; a man with a whole volition advances on the roughest, and will reach his purpose, if there be even a little worthiness in it. The man without a purpose is like a ship without a rudder—a waif, a nothing, a no man. Have a purpose in life and having it, throw such strength of mind and muscle into your work as God has given you.

THOMAS CARLYLE

Formula for Achievement

Plan more work than you can do;
        Then do it.
Bite off more than you can chew;
        Then chew it.
Hitch your wagon to a star;
        Keep your seat;
And there you are!

ANONYMOUS

. . . the refusal to choose is a form of choice; disbelief is a form of belief.

FRANK BARRON

No answer is also an answer.

GERMAN PROVERB

In making our decisions, we must use the brains that God has given us. But we must also use our hearts which He also gave us.

FULTON OURSLER

A man who has not learned to say, "No"—who is not resolved that he will take God's way, in spite of every dog that can bay or bark at him, in spite of every silvery voice that woos him aside—will be a weak and a wretched man till he dies.

ALEXANDER MACLAREN

How few of us could honestly crystallize the aims that guide our life into any single sentence? We try the impossible feat of riding on two horses at once. We resolve and retract, and hesitate and compromise. The ship heads now one way and now another, and that not because we are wisely tacking—that is to say, seeking to reach one point by widely varying courses—but because our hand is so weak on the helm that we drift wherever the wash of the waves and the buffets of the wind carry us.

ALEXANDER MACLAREN

A man so various, that he seems to be
Not one, but all Mankind's Epitome:
Still in Opinions, always in the wrong;
Was everything by starts, and Nothing long:
But, in the course of one revolving moon,
Was Chymist, Fidler, Statesman, and Buffoon.
JOHN DRYDEN

I'm glad for the Bible. It gives me a chance to see how other men chose—and the results. There's the contrast between Abraham's choice and Lot's choice before Sodom. There's Moses' choice of his fellows rather than the riches of Egypt. There's Joseph's choice in the prison house of Potiphar, and Daniel's choice of the king's vegetables rather than his meats. Paul paid a glorious price when he chose his lot with the early Christians. Christ made marvelous choices when he set his face toward Jerusalem, at the Garden of Gethsemane, and the Judgment Hall.

Adam's choice cost him Eden; Esau's, his birthright; Achan's, his life; Lot's, his home and herds; Absalom's, his father's throne; Saul's, his kingdom; the rich young ruler's, the companionship of Christ. Judas lost his apostleship; Demas, his discipleship. Pilate, Agrippa, and Felix chose wrong and missed immortality. Ananias' choice fooled no one but himself. Caleb and Joshua chose well, while Jonah's first choice nearly shipwrecked himself and the crew.

Ye older ones, what would your answer be as a father, as a mother, as a Christian leader, if, concerning our young people, God would

145

say to you today, "Ask what I shall make of these young people"?
Would your answer prove you know how to choose the things that
matter most? Would your answer prove you are a wise leader—for
them?

ROBERT G. LEE

DEDICATION
· ·

You will not be carried to Heaven lying at ease upon a feather bed.

SAMUEL RUTHERFORD

The condition of an enlightened mind is a surrendered heart.

ALAN REDPATH

> *What can I give Him,*
> *Poor as I am?*
> *If I were a shepherd*
> *I would bring a lamb.*
> *If I were a wise man*
> *I would do my part—*
> *Yet what can I give Him,*
> *Give Him my heart.*

CHRISTINA ROSSETTI

Obedience is the fruit of faith.

CHRISTINA ROSSETTI

It is a great deal easier to do that which God gives us to do, no matter
how hard it is, than to face the responsibilities of not doing it.

J. R. MILLER

The Christian life is a positive allegiance to Jesus Christ. It is becom-
ing so occupied with Him that the values and standards of the world
around us have little influence.

G. S.

The world has yet to see what God will do with a man who is fully and wholly consecrated to the Holy Spirit.

HENRY VARLEY

By the grace of God, I'll be that man.

D. L. MOODY

If Jesus Christ died and died for me, then no sacrifice can be too great for me to make for Him.

C. T. STUDD

I wish to preach, not the doctrine of ignoble ease, but the doctrine of the strenuous life.

THEODORE ROOSEVELT

Nothing earthly will make me give up my work in despair.

DAVID LIVINGSTONE

The fall of man has created a perpetual crisis. It will last until sin has been put down and Christ reigns over a redeemed and restored world. Until that time the earth remains a disaster area and its inhabitants live in a state of extraordinary emergency.

To me it has always been difficult to understand those evangelical Christians who insist upon living in the crisis as if no crisis existed. They say they serve the Lord, but they divide their days so as to leave plenty of time to play and loaf and enjoy the pleasures of the world as well. They are at ease while the world burns.

A. W. TOZER, BORN AFTER MIDNIGHT

I will place no value on anything I have or may possess except in relation to the kingdom of Christ.

DAVID LIVINGSTONE

God doesn't seek for golden vessels, and does not ask for silver ones, but He must have clean ones.

D. L. MOODY

Men join the church. They take that Holy Name upon themselves. They enter into covenant with each other in the name of the Father and of the Son and of the Holy Spirit, inviting the Holy Trinity to witness and support their purpose of faithfulness, purity, love, cooperation, liberality, of personal effort to win a lost world to Christ. Yet American churches are filled with men and women who flagrantly and frivolously and constantly ignore the obligations of the voluntary covenants. Thousands of church members have changed residence without changing church membership. They stand aloof from the local church. They take no local responsibility for Christ. They settle into becoming church drifters and sermon drifters and sermon tasters. God will not hold such guiltless. He has declared it in His Word.

J. C. MASSEE

Some people object to taking vows, but in the Bible you will find many great men of God directed by covenants, promises, vows and pledges. A carnal man refuses the discipline of such commitments. He says, "I want to be free. It is legalism." There are many religious tramps in the world who will not be bound by anything.

Now there are five vows I have in mind which we do well to make and keep.

1. Deal thoroughly with sin.

2. Never own anything—get rid of the sense of possessing.

3. Never defend yourself.

4. Never pass anything on about anybody else that will hurt him.

5. Never accept any glory.

Remember that these five vows are not something you write in the back of your Bible and forget. They have got to be written in your own blood.

A. W. TOZER,
"FIVE VOWS FOR SPIRITUAL POWER"

Your powers are dead or dedicated. If they are dedicated, they are alive with God and tingle with surprising power. If they are saved up, taken care of for their own ends, they are dead.

E. STANLEY JONES

Resolved: Very much to exercise myself in this, all my life long, namely, with the greatest openness of which I am capable, to declare my ways to God, and lay open my soul to Him, all my sins, temptations, difficulties, sorrows, fears, hopes, desires, and everything, and every circumstance.

JONATHAN EDWARDS

Each believer stands on one side or the other of dedication. Either we have made this lifelong commitment or we have not. Either we have faced the issue of who is to be the master of our lives or we have been plucking up one sin at a time.

CHARLES CALDWELL RYRIE,
BALANCING THE CHRISTIAN LIFE

There are two kinds of people: those who say to God, "Thy will be done," and those to whom God says, "All right, then, have it your way."

C. S. LEWIS, *THE GREAT DIVORCE*

DEEDS
· ·

Every man feels instinctively that all the beautiful sentiments in the world weigh less than a single lovely action.

JAMES RUSSELL LOWELL

I expect to pass through this world but once. Any good therefore that I can do, or any kindness that I can show to any fellow creature, let me do it now. Let me not defer or neglect it, for I shall not pass this way again.

ANONYMOUS

O Lord, how many read the Word, and yet from vice are not deterred.

ANONYMOUS

People forget how fast you did a job—but they remember how well you did it.

HOWARD W. NEWTON

We are told that the palmyra is the most useful plant in the world. Upward of eight hundred uses are recorded for its various parts.

Are we palmyra Christians—good for many things? Are we possessed of the spirit that will make us good for many things—or good for nothing?

It was D. L. Moody who quoted from a tombstone these words:

> *Do all the good you can,*
> *To all the people you can,*
> *In all the ways you can,*
> *As long as ever you can.*

If that were engraved on our hearts and were to find expression in our lives, we would be palmyra-palm servants of Christ.

ROBERT G. LEE

Nothing can be made of nothing; he who has laid up no material can produce no combination.

SIR JOSHUA REYNOLDS

The man who has accomplished all that he thinks worthwhile has begun to die.

E. T. TRIGG

Chop your own wood, and it will warm you twice.

HENRY FORD'S FIREPLACE MOTTO

A good deed is never lost. He who sows courtesy, reaps friendship; he who plants kindness, gathers love; pleasure bestowed on a grateful mind was never sterile, but generally gratitude begets reward.

BASIL

> *Sitting still and wishing*
> *Makes no person great.*
> *The good Lord sends the fishing*
> *But you must dig the bait.*

ANONYMOUS

DEFEAT
· ·

When the frustration of my helplessness seemed greatest, I discovered God's grace was more than sufficient. And after my imprisonment, I could look back and see how God used my powerlessness for His purpose. What He has chosen for my most significant witness was not my triumphs or victories, but my defeat.

CHARLES COLSON

Defeat is a school in which truth always grows strong.

HENRY WARD BEECHER

If you think you are beaten, you are,
If you think that you dare not, you don't,
If you'd like to win, but you think you can't,
It's almost certain you won't.

If you think you'll lose, you've lost,
For out in the world you'll find
Success begins with a fellow's will—
It's all in the state of mind.

If you think you are out-classed, you are;
You've got to think high to rise;
You've got to be sure of yourself before
You can ever win a prize.

Life's battles don't always go
To the stronger or faster man;
But soon or late the man who wins
Is the man who thinks he can.

ANONYMOUS

Most human organizations that fall short of their goals do so not because of stupidity or faulty doctrines, but because of internal decay and rigidification. They grow stiff in the joints. They get in a rut. They go to seed.

JAMES GARDNER

When the Confederate army retreated after Gettysburg, General Lee wrote to Jefferson Davis a remarkable letter in which he said: "We must expect reverses, even defeats. They are sent to teach us wisdom and prudence, to call forth greater energies, and to prevent our falling into greater disasters." True of a nation's life, this is also profoundly true of the life of the individual. And what shall we say of sickness, sorrow, and affliction? Shall these things overwhelm us, or shall we be able to say with that great spirit who kept both his soul and his body under the dominion of a great and holy purpose, "Nay, in all these things we are more than conquerors through him that loved us" (Romans 8:37)?

CLARENCE E. MACARTNEY

A man is not defeated by his opponents but by himself.

JAN CHRISTIAN SMUTS

My lowest days as a Christian (and there were low ones—seven months' worth of them in prison, to be exact) have been more fulfilling and rewarding than all the days of glory in the White House.

CHARLES COLSON

DELAY
· ·

Procrastination is my sin.
It brings me naught but sorrow.
I know that I should stop it.
In fact, I will—tomorrow!

GLORIA PITZER

Throughout history, it has been the inaction of those who could have acted, the indifference of those who should have known better, the silence of the voice of justice when it mattered most, that has made it possible for evil to triumph.

HAILE SELASSIE

He was going to be all that a mortal should be—
  Tomorrow
No one would be better than he—
  Tomorrow
Each morning he stacked up the letters he'd write—
  Tomorrow
It was too bad indeed he was too busy to see Bill,
but he promised to do it—
  Tomorrow
The greatest of workers this man would have been—
  Tomorrow
The world would have known him had he ever seen—
  Tomorrow
But the fact is he died and faded from view,
and all that was left when living was through
Was a mountain of things he intended to do—
  Tomorrow

ANONYMOUS

Defer no time, delays have dangerous ends.

WILLIAM SHAKESPEARE, *1 HENRY VI*

DEPRESSION, DESPAIR

The Christian's chief occupational hazards are depression and discouragement.

JOHN R. STOTT

Despair of ever being saved, "except thou be born again," or of seeing God "without holiness," or of having part in Christ except thou "love Him above father, mother, or thy own life." This kind of despair is one of the first steps to heaven.

RICHARD BAXTER

> *Now, God be prais'd, that to believing souls*
> *Gives light in darkness, comfort in despair!*
>   WILLIAM SHAKESPEARE, *2 HENRY VI*

DETERMINATION

I will go anywhere, provided it be forward.
                    DAVID LIVINGSTONE

One cold February day a snail started climbing an apple tree. As he inched slowly upward, a worm stuck its head from a crevice in the bark to offer some advice. "You're wasting your energy. There isn't a single apple up there."
    There will be when I get there," he said.
                    ANONYMOUS

A thick skin is a gift from God.
                    KONRAD ADENAUER

I put a piece of paper under my pillow, and when I could not sleep I wrote in the dark.
                    HENRY DAVID THOREAU

Earnestness is not by any means everything; it is very often a subtle form of pious pride because it is obsessed with the method and not with the Master.
                    OSWALD CHAMBERS

Millions of people in our culture make decisions for Christ, but there is a dreadful attrition rate. . . . In our kind of culture anything, even news about God, can be sold if it is packaged freshly; but when it loses its novelty, it goes on the garbage heap. There is a great market for religious experience in our world; there is little enthusiasm for the patient acquisition of virtue, little inclination to sign up for a long apprenticeship.
                    EUGENE PETERSON

Once while St. Francis of Assisi was hoeing his garden, he was asked, "What would you do if you were suddenly to learn that you were to die at sunset today?" He replied, "I would finish hoeing my garden."
ANONYMOUS

When things go wrong as they sometimes will,
When the road you're trudging seems all uphill,
When the funds are low and the debts are high,
And you want to smile, but you have to sigh.

When care is pressing you down a bit,
Rest if you must, but don't you quit.
Life is queer with its twists and turns,
As every one of us sometimes learns,
And many a failure turns about
When he might have won had he stuck it out.
Don't give up though the pace seems slow—
You may succeed with another blow!

Success is failure turned inside out—
The silver tint of the clouds of doubt,
And you never can tell just how close you are,
It may be near when it seems so far.

So stick to the fight when you're hardest hit—
It's when things seem worst that you must not quit.
ANONYMOUS

DEVIL
· ·

The devil is a better theologian than any of us and is a devil still.
A. W. TOZER, *MAN, THE DWELLING PLACE OF GOD*

Satan is neither omnipotent nor free to do everything he pleases. Prince of the world he may be, but the Prince of Peace has come and dealt him a death blow.
HAROLD LINDSELL,
THE WORLD, THE FLESH, AND THE DEVIL

"Christ in you, the hope of glory." I'm not afraid of the devil. The devil can handle me—he's got judo I never heard of. But he can't handle the One to whom I'm joined; he can't handle the One to whom I'm united; he can't handle the One whose nature dwells in my nature.

A. W. TOZER

The devil doesn't know how to sing, only how to howl.
FRANCIS THOMPSON

If the devil could be persuaded to write a bible, he would title it, "You Only Live Once."

SYDNEY HARRIS

I would like to suggest three evil devices that make up most of Satan's repertoire.

The first is opposition. The very name Satan means opposer, and he has opposed the work of God from the day he fell. To the Christian he is the chief adversary. First Peter 5:8 says, "Be sober, be vigilant; because your adversary the devil, as a roaring lion, walketh about, seeking whom he may devour."

Another of Satan's devices is imitation. Often he is more successful at imitation than he could be with blatant opposition. Satan has always imitated God. It was his desire to be like God that led to his fall in the first place.

Whatever God does, Satan is sure to substitute his own imitation. When Moses demonstrated the power of God to Pharaoh with miracles, Satan enabled Pharaoh's magicians to imitate those miracles. Throughout the Old Testament when God raised up His prophets, Satan countered by raising up false prophets.

A third device of Satan is accusation. He is called the "accuser of our brethren" in Revelation 12:10. That same verse says that Satan accuses believers before God day and night. It is the picture of one pointing his finger at others, accusing of wrongdoing, shortcoming, false motives, and sin.

G. S.

The devil can cite Scripture for his purpose.

WILLIAM SHAKESPEARE,
THE MERCHANT OF VENICE

The devil hath power to assume a pleasing shape.

WILLIAM SHAKESPEARE, HAMLET

The devil does not stay where music is.

MARTIN LUTHER

*The devil will let a preacher prepare a sermon if it will keep him
from preparing himself.*

VANCE HAVNER

*As I see it, there are two possible mistakes to be made. One is to over-
estimate the power of Satan, and the other is to underestimate it.*

*A believer who overestimates Satan's power can live an entire
lifetime in fear, always terrified of what Satan might do. Satan likes
nothing better than to stir up that kind of fear in a believer, because it
destroys his effectiveness for the Lord.*

*On the other hand, a person who underestimates the power and
cunning of Satan may become unconcerned with Satan's activity and
be lulled into complacency. That is where Satan can do his most dam-
aging work.*

G. S.

*Our songs and psalms sorely vex and grieve the devil, whereas our
passions and impatiences, our complainings and cryings, our, "Alas"
and "Woe is me" please him well, so that he laughs in his fist. He
takes delight in tormenting us, especially when we confess, praise,
preach and laud Christ.*

MARTIN LUTHER

DEVOTIONS

· ·

We are to be shut out from men, and shut in with God.

ANDREW MURRAY

I came to see that my relationship to my Lord Jesus Christ, with the passing years, had eroded away something like a marriage gone humdrum. What did I do when I found a little pocket of spare time, on a Sunday, or a holiday? I couldn't wait to get together with other people—people I liked, people with whom I had something in common—so we could share ideas and experiences. Or I read a stimulating book. Or I went out to enjoy nature. I even plunged further into my work, doing things that I normally didn't have time for. But to go to Jesus—to give Him first claim on even my spare time—that I did not do.

M. BASILEA SCHLINK

An essential condition of listening to God is that the mind should not be distracted by thoughts of resentment, ill-temper, hatred or vengeance, all of which are comprised in the general term, the wrath of man.

R. V. G. TASKER

Whatever is your best time in the day, give that to communion with God.

HUDSON TAYLOR

I have only missed my morning watch once or twice this term. . . . I can easily believe that it is next in importance to accepting Christ. For I know that when I don't wait upon God in prayer and Bible study, things go wrong.

WILLIAM BORDEN

How rare it is to find a soul quiet enough to hear God speak.

FRANÇOIS FÈNELON

Cut your morning devotions into your personal grooming. You would not go out to work with a dirty face. Why start the day with the face of your soul unwashed?

ROBERT A. COOK

Andrew Bonar, a great man of God, had three rules that he lived by. Rule 1—Not to speak to any person before speaking to Jesus Christ. Rule 2—Not to do anything with his hands until he had been on his knees. Rule 3—Not to read the papers until he had read his Bible.

G. S.

To be a Christian without prayer is no more possible than to be alive without breathing.

MARTIN LUTHER

If we don't maintain a quiet time each day, it's not really because we are too busy; it's because we do not feel it is important enough. . . .

There's an old navy rule: when ships readjust their compass, they drop anchor in a quiet spot. . . .

Late nights kill the quiet time. . . . Quiet time is not just a helpful idea, it's necessary to spiritual growth.

G. S.

DIFFICULTIES

Bumps are the things we climb on.

WARREN WIERSBE

Nothing will ever be attempted if all possible objections must first be removed.

SAMUEL JOHNSON

When it is dark enough, men see the stars.

RALPH WALDO EMERSON

A Christian is like a tea bag—he's not worth much until he's been through some hot water.

ANONYMOUS

> *Out of the presses of pain*
> *Cometh the soul's best wine;*
> *The eyes that have shed no rain*
> *Can shed but little shine.*

A. B. SIMPSON

Storms make oaks take deeper root.

GEORGE HERBERT

Stand still . . . and refuse to retreat. Look at it as God looks at it and draw upon His power to hold up under the blast.

CHARLES SWINDOLL

The lowest ebb is the turn of the tide.

HENRY WADSWORTH LONGFELLOW

Many men owe the grandeur of their lives to their tremendous difficulties.

CHARLES HADDON SPURGEON

The eternal stars shine out as soon as it is dark enough.

THOMAS CARLYLE

Troubles are often the tools by which God fashions us for better things.

HENRY WARD BEECHER

Difficulties are stepping stones to success.

ANONYMOUS

Into each life some rain must fall, some days be dark and dreary.

HENRY WADSWORTH LONGFELLOW

Our greatest glory is not in never falling, but in rising each time we fall.
OLIVER GOLDSMITH

Be assured that, if God waits longer than you could wish, it is only to make the blessing doubly precious! God waited four thousand years, till the fullness of time, ere He sent His Son. Our times are in His hands; He will avenge His elect speedily; He will make haste for our help, and not delay one hour too long.
ANDREW MURRAY

If we could see beyond today, as God can see,
If all the clouds should roll away, the shadows flee;
O'er present griefs we would not fret,
Each sorrow we would soon forget;
For many joys are waiting yet for you and me.
"If we could see, if we could know," we often say.
But God in love a veil doth throw across our way.
We cannot see what lies before
And so we cling to Him the more,
He leads us till this life is o'er;
Trust and obey.
ANONYMOUS

As in nature, as in art, so in grace; it is rough treatment that gives souls, as well as stones, their lustre. The more the diamond is cut the brighter it sparkles; and in what seems hard dealing, there God has no end in view but to perfect His people.
THOMAS GUTHRIE

When the storms of life come down upon you, keep your eyes fixed on Jesus.
G. S.

People have a natural tendency to flee to the mountains when things get tough.
STUART BRISCOE, *WHAT WORKS*

What is difficulty? Only a word indicating the degree of strength requisite for accomplishing particular objects; a mere notice of the necessity for exertion; a bugbear to children and fools; only a mere stimulus to men.

SAMUEL WARREN

God drives a deep snare through many a wayside heart, and the coulter of affliction breaks up many a spirit that it may afterwards yield "the peaceable fruit of righteousness."

ALEXANDER MACLAREN

Jesus Christ is no security against storms, but He is perfect security in storms. He has never promised you an easy passage, only a safe landing.

ANONYMOUS

Every life has dark tracts and long stretches of sombre tint, and no representation is true to fact which dips its pencil only in light, and flings no shadows on the canvas.

ALEXANDER MACLAREN

*Job feels the Rod
Yet blesses GOD.*
NEW ENGLAND PRIMER

*If you have God for your "enduring substance," you can face all varieties of condition, and be calm, saying—
"Give what Thou canst, without Thee I am poor,
And with Thee rich, take what Thou wilt away."*

ALEXANDER MACLAREN

DIPLOMACY
· ·
Diplomacy is the art of saying "Nice doggie!" till you can find a rock.
WYNN CATLIN

A diplomat is a man who always remembers a woman's birthday but never remembers her age.

ROBERT FROST

[Advice to a young diplomat]: Tell the truth, and so puzzle and confound your adversaries.

HENRY WOTTON

DISCIPLINE

Look upon your chastening as God's chariots sent to carry your soul into the high places of spiritual achievement.

HANNAH WHITALL SMITH

The diamond cannot be polished without friction, nor the man perfected without trials.

CHINESE PROVERB

I bear my willing witness that I owe more to the fire, and the hammer, and the file, than to anything else in the Lord's workshop. I sometimes question whether I have ever learned anything except through the rod. When my schoolroom is darkened, I see most.

CHARLES HADDON SPURGEON

Discipline is the soul of an army. It makes small numbers formidable; procures success to the weak, and esteem to all.

GEORGE WASHINGTON,
LETTER OF INSTRUCTION TO THE VIRGINIA
REGIMENTS, 29 JULY 1759

You can judge the quality of their faith from the way they behave. Discipline is an index to doctrine.

TERTULLIAN

Better to be pruned to grow than cut up to burn.

JOHN TRAPP

DOUBT
· ·

Doubt is the hammer that breaks the window clouded with human fancies and lets in the pure light.

GEORGE MACDONALD

All of us at times have passed through the sea of doubt. Bunyan speaks of being "much tumbled up and down in his thoughts." However, without question we may know now that we have eternal life. Jesus said, "He that believeth on me hath everlasting life" (John 6:47). Anything that contradicts the words of Jesus is a lie. "Let God be true, but every man a liar" (Romans 3:4).

G. S.

At the conclusion of a mass meeting, I was greeting people when a distinguished-looking man approached me and asked, "May I talk with you about my salvation? I'm desperately confused." He went on to state that he had acknowledged the Lord as Saviour but had little peace and Christian confidence. "As I listened to your message, I decided I must settle it."

I replied. "First, look into your life to discover if all is right between yourself and the Lord. Carnal believers are usually full of doubts. If the Holy Spirit is grieved through self-will of sin, He cannot witness effectively to your salvation because there is contradiction. For this reason the witness of the Holy Spirit is often dimmed. Second, after discovering the wrong, openly confess it to the Lord. Third, deal with it and do works to prove your repentance."

"That's it," he interrupted. "I've grown careless; there's sin in my life, and I must make it right."

We bowed our heads in a holy hush as he sought God's gracious forgiveness. It was evident that the Lord was in the room, for when we arose from our knees the doctor was changed. His expression, his voice, his whole attitude radiated blessed assurance. Careless living will always create doubt, then the opposite is also true. Doubt leads to careless living.

G. S.

Don't doubt in the dark what God has revealed in the light.
V. RAYMOND EDMAN

It's shocking to realize how many people are made miserable by the disease called doubt. Uncertainty has robbed thousands of people of the joy of salvation.

People who even read their Bibles, earnestly pray, faithfully attend church, and live uprightly in all their dealings with others, may yet have no assurance of forgiveness and be living defeated lives.

Is the assurance of salvation possible? What does the Bible say? In 2 Corinthians 13:5, Paul writes, "Examine yourselves, whether ye be in the faith." In 2 Peter 1:10 we are told, "Give diligence to make your calling and election sure." The assurance of salvation is one of God's beautiful gifts. Every believer ought to know that he possesses salvation.

G. S.

DREAMS
· ·

We grow great by dreams. All big men are dreamers. They see things in the soft haze of a spring day or in the red fire of a long winter's evening. Some of us let these great dreams die, but others nourish and protect them; nurse them through bad days till they bring them to the sunshine and light which comes always to those who sincerely hope that their dreams will come true.

WOODROW WILSON

One of the most tragic things I know about human nature is that all of us tend to put off living. We are all dreaming of some magical rose garden over the horizon—instead of enjoying the roses that are blooming outside our windows today.

DALE CARNEGIE

I like the dreams of the future better than the history of the past.

THOMAS JEFFERSON

Our heart oft times wakes when we sleep, and God can speak to that, either by words, by proverbs, by signs and similitudes, as well as if one was awake.

JOHN BUNYAN

DUTY
· ·

Let men laugh when you sacrifice desire to duty, if they will. You have time and eternity to rejoice in.

THEODORE PARKER

> *The things which must be, must be for the best,*
> *God helps us do our duty and not shrink*
> *And trust His mercy humbly for the rest.*

OWEN MEREDITH

He who is false to present duty breaks a thread in the loom, and will find the flaw when he may have forgotten its cause.

HENRY WARD BEECHER

In doing what we ought we deserve no praise, because it is our duty.

SAINT AUGUSTINE

EASTER

The simplest meaning of Easter is that we are living in a world in which God has the last word.

An Easter Carol

Tomb, thou shalt not hold Him longer;
Death is strong, but Life is stronger;
Stronger than the dark, the light;
Stronger than the wrong, the right;
Faith and Hope triumphant say,
Christ will rise on Easter Day.
PHILLIPS BROOKS

Because He lives I can face tomorrow,
Because He lives all fear is gone.
Because I know He holds the future,
And life is worth the living,
Just because He lives.
WILLIAM GAITHER

And He departed from our sight that we might return to our heart,
and there find Him. For He departed, and behold, He is here.
SAINT AUGUSTINE

Look at the sequence: risen from the dead, therefore alive for ever;
therefore our contemporary; therefore able to confront us face to face.
JAMES S. STEWART

He takes men out of time and makes them feel eternity.
RALPH WALDO EMERSON

And the graves were opened; and many bodies of the saints which slept arose, and came out of the graves after his resurrection, and appeared unto many.

MATTHEW 27:52–53

EDUCATION
· ·

A new graduate rushed out of his college on graduation day and shouted, "Here am I, world. I have my A.B.!" The world answered: "Sit down, young man, and I'll teach you the rest of the alphabet."

On being congratulated on what he had done for Harvard University as its president, Charles W. Eliot said, "It is true, as you say, that Harvard has become a store-house of knowledge. But I scarcely deserve credit for that. It is simply that the freshmen bring so much and the seniors take away so little."

CHARLES W. ELIOT

America's greatness has been the greatness of a free people who shared certain moral commitments. Freedom without moral commitment is aimless and promptly self-destructive.

JOHN W. GARDNER

I have no startling panacea for the spirit or the blueprint for attainment. But being asked for personal philosophy I perforce have to make the reply intensely personal. It is an alien act for me. That being understood, and personal reference condoned, I want to repeat all that I basically know, which turns out to be exactly what almost all of us know: Love God, be loyal to country, be true to self.

CONRAD HILTON

Educate men without religion and you make of them but clever Devils.

ARTHUR WELLESLEY

Education is the knowledge of how to use the whole of oneself. Many men use but one or two faculties out of the score with which they are endowed. A man is educated who knows how to make a tool of every faculty—how to open it, how to keep it sharp, and how to apply it to all practical purposes.

HENRY WARD BEECHER

Talk to a man about himself and he will listen for hours.

BENJAMIN DISRAELI

Every man who knows how to read has it in his power to magnify himself, to multiply the ways in which he exists, to make his life full, significant and interesting.

ALDOUS HUXLEY

America's founding fathers did not intend to take religion out of education. Many of the nation's greatest universities were founded by evangelists and religious leaders; but many of these have lost the founders' concept and become secular institutions. Because of this attitude, secular education is stumbling and floundering.

BILLY GRAHAM

EGOTISM
· ·

Don't talk about yourself; it will be done when you leave.

WILSON MIZNER

We reproach people for talking about themselves; but it is the subject they treat best.

ANATOLE FRANCE

He who falls in love with himself will have no rivals.

BENJAMIN FRANKLIN

Be yourself is about the worst advice you can give some people.

ANONYMOUS

He who does not think much of himself is much more esteemed than he imagines.

JOHANN WOLFGANG VON GOETHE

EMPATHY

Sometimes I'm asked by kids why I condemn marijuana when I haven't tried it. The greatest obstetricians in the world have never been pregnant.

ART LINKLETTER

When James Burrill Angell, for thirty-eight years president of the University of Michigan, was asked the secret of his success, he answered: "Grow antennae, not horns."

G. S.

When a good man is hurt all who would be called good must suffer with him.

EURIPIDES

> *World-wide apart, and yet akin,*
> *As showing that the human heart,*
> *Beats on forever as of old.*

HENRY WADSWORTH LONGFELLOW

Yet, taught by time, my heart has learned to glow
For other's good, and melt at other's woe.

HOMER

ENCOURAGEMENT

Correction does much, but encouragement does more. Encouragement after censure is as the sun after a shower.

JOHANN WOLFGANG VON GOETHE

It takes so little to make us sad,
Just a slighting word or a doubting sneer,
Just a scornful smile on some lips held dear;
And our footsteps lag, though the goal seemed near,
And we lose courage and hope we had—
So little it takes to make us sad.

It takes so little to make us glad,
Just a cheering clasp of a friendly hand,
Just a word from one who can understand;
And we finish the task we long had planned,
And we lose the doubt and the fear we had—
So little it takes to make us glad.

IDA GOLDSMITH MORRIS

The deepest principle in human nature is the craving to be appreciated.

WILLIAM JAMES

ENDURANCE

Something that irritates you and won't let you go. That's the anguish of it. Do this book, or die. You have to go through that. Talent is insignificant. I know a lot of talented ruins. Beyond talent lie all the usual words: discipline, love, luck, but, most of all, endurance.

ANONYMOUS

Endurance is not just the ability to bear a hard thing, but to turn it into glory.

WILLIAM BARCLAY

ENEMIES

The best way to destroy your enemy is to make him your friend.

ABRAHAM LINCOLN

171

*I have had a lot of adversaries in my political life, but no ememies
that I can remember.*

GERALD FORD

One enemy can do more hurt than ten friends can do good.
JONATHAN SWIFT

One enemy is too much.

GEORGE HERBERT

*Give us grace and strength to forbear and to persevere. Give us
courage and gaiety and the quiet mind, spare to us our friends, soften
to us our enemies.*

ROBERT LOUIS STEVENSON

*Man's chief enemy is his own unruly nature and the dark forces pent
up within him.*

ERNEST JONES

A man cannot be too careful in the choice of his enemies.
OSCAR WILDE

You shall judge a man by his foes as well as by his friends.
JOSEPH CONRAD

*We look upon the enemy of our souls as a conquered foe, so he is, but
only to God, not to us.*

OSWALD CHAMBERS

ENTHUSIASM
· ·

*How poor a guide enthusiasm is when it is not informed with the
mind and spirit of Christ.*

JAMES STALKER,
THE TRIAL AND DEATH OF JESUS CHRIST

Nothing great was ever achieved without enthusiasm.
RALPH WALDO EMERSON

Enthusiasm makes ordinary people extraordinary.
ANONYMOUS

When I hear a man preach, I like to see him act as if he were fighting bees.
ABRAHAM LINCOLN

Fires can't be made with dead embers, nor can enthusiasm be stirred by spiritless men. Enthusiasm in our daily work lightens effort and turns even labor into pleasant tasks.
JAMES MARK BALDWIN

Enthusiasm is a telescope that yanks the misty, distant future into the radiant, tangible present.
ANONYMOUS

The word enthusiasm *really means to be filled or inspired by God. If any people ought to radiate enthusiasm and joy, we should.*

We read that the apostolic church was "Praising God, and having favour with all the people" (Acts 2:47). Their unanimous acceptance was related to their spirit of praise. There is a charisma in praise. "Praise is comely for the upright" (Psalm 33:1).

A sad, half-hearted, reluctant Christian is an enigma. But when the joy of the Lord is our strength, we must say with Peter, "We cannot but speak" what we know and believe. Ask the Lord to make you a winsome witness, and I guarantee you that you will win some. Enthusiasm isn't everything but it is important.
G. S.

EPITAPHS
· ·

Here lies one whose name was writ in water.
JOHN KEATS

Rev. Adoniram Judson,
Born August 9th, 1788,
Died April 12th, 1850.
Malden his birthplace,
The ocean his sepulchre,
Converted Burmans and
The Burman Bible
His Monument
His record is on high.

OF THE LINGUIST AND
MISSIONARY TO BURMA

I for happiness beyond the grave.

THOMAS PAINE

He that doeth the will of God abideth forevereth.

OF D. L. MOODY

Statesman, yet friend of truth,
A soul sincere,
In action faithful and in honor clear.

OF WILLIAM JENNINGS BRYAN

In heart a Lydia, and in tongue a Hanna,
In zeal a Ruth, in wedlock a Susanna,
Prudently simple, providentially wary.
To the world a Martha, and to heaven a Mary.

OF DAME DOROTHY SELBY

This is the grave of Mike O'Day
Who died maintaining his right of way.
His right was clear, his will was strong,
But he's just as dead as if he'd been wrong.

EQUALITY

One day, the South will know that when these disinherited children of God sat down at lunch counters, they were in reality standing up for the best in the American dream and the most sacred values in our Judeo-Christian heritage.

MARTIN LUTHER KING, JR.

If liberty and equality, as is thought by some, are chiefly to be found in democracy, they will be best attained when all persons alike share in the government to the utmost.

ARISTOTLE

It is the mark of the cultured man that he is aware of the fact that equality is an ethical and not a biological principle.

ASHLEY MONTAGU

For the colonel's lady an' Judy O'Grady,
Are sisters under their skins.

RUDYARD KIPLING

Equality is the life of conversation; and he is as much out who assumes to himself any part above another, as he who considers himself below the rest of society.

SIR RICHARD STEELE

We hold these truths to be sacred and undeniable; that all men are created equal and independent, that from that equal creation they derive rights inherent and inalienable, among which are the preservation of life, and liberty, and the pursuit of happiness.

THOMAS JEFFERSON,
ORIGINAL DRAFT OF THE DECLARATION OF
INDEPENDENCE, JUNE 1776

ETERNITY
· ·

I know what Eternity is, though I cannot define the word to satisfy a metaphysician. The little child taught by some grandmother Lois, in a cottage, knows what she means when she tells him "you will live forever," though both scholar and teacher would be puzzled to put it into other words.

ALEXANDER MACLAREN

Forever is a long bargain.

GERMAN PROVERB

All that is not eternal is eternally out of date.
C. S. LEWIS

> *Life is real! Life is earnest!*
> *And the grave is not its goal;*
> *Dust thou art, to dust returnest,*
> *Was not spoken by the soul.*
HENRY WADSWORTH LONGFELLOW

Puritan writer Thomas Watson said, "Eternity to the godly is a day that has no sunset; eternity to the wicked is a night that has no sunrise." Eternity is the grand climax of all history. It is the age to come when every person will acknowledge Jesus as Lord. Eternity will bring to this world all God intended for us. Sin will have been judged and banished. Rewards will have been presented. Life will continue with new vitality, meaning, and perfection. What an age that will be!
G. S.

We have all eternity to celebrate our victories, but only one short hour before sunset in which to win them.

ROBERT MOFFAT

ETHICS
· ·

Evangelical faith without Christian ethics is a travesty on the gospel.
V. RAYMOND EDMAN

Actually, there is only one "first question" of government, and it is "How should we live?" or (this is the same question) "What kind of people do we want our citizens to be?"
GEORGE WILL

I say statecraft is soulcraft. Just as all education is moral education because learning conditions conduct, most legislation is moral legislations because it conditions the action and the thought of the nation in broad and important spheres in life.
GEORGE WILL

Ethics and equity and the principles of justice do not change with the calendar.
DAVID LAWRENCE

Nothing that is morally wrong can be politically right.
WILLIAM E. GLADSTONE

Let us raise a standard to which the wise and honest can repair; the rest is in the hands of God.
GEORGE WASHINGTON

EVANGELISM
· ·

The salvation of a single soul is more important than the production or preservation of all the epics and tragedies in the world.
C. S. LEWIS

Being an extrovert isn't essential to evangelism—obedience and love are.
REBECCA M. PIPPERT

Evangelism is just one beggar telling another beggar where to find bread.

D. T. NILES

The Holy Spirit can't save saints or seats. If we don't know any non-Christians, how can we introduce them to the Savior?

PAUL LITTLE, *HOW TO GIVE AWAY YOUR FAITH*

The world has more winnable people than ever before . . . but it is possible to come out of a ripe field empty-handed.

DONALD MCGAVRAN

Evangelism as the New Testament describes it is not child's play. Evangelism is work, often hard work. Yet it is not drudgery. It puts a person in good humor, and makes him truly human.

OSWALD C. J. HOFFMAN

Evangelism is the spontaneous overflow of a glad and free heart in Jesus Christ.

ROBERT MUNGER

Our business is to present the Christian faith clothed in modern terms, not to propagate modern thought clothed in Christian terms. . . . Confusion here is fatal.

J. I. PACKER

To call a man evangelical who is not evangelistic is an utter contradiction.

G. CAMPBELL MORGAN

While women weep, as they do now, I'll fight; while little children go hungry, I'll fight; while men go to prison, in and out, in and out, as they do now, I'll fight; while there is a drunkard left, while there is a poor lost girl upon the streets, where there remains one dark soul without the light of God—I'll fight! I'll fight to the very end!

GENERAL WILLIAM BOOTH,
THE END OF HIS VERY LAST SPEECH

EVOLUTION
· ·

After listening to a lecture on evolution by a science professor, a student wrote a poem and titled it "The Amazing Professor." The poem read:

> *Once I was a tadpole when I began to begin.*
> *Then I was a frog with my tail tucked in.*
> *Next I was a monkey on a coconut tree.*
> *Now I am a doctor with a Ph.D.*

ANONYMOUS

One of the stupidest theories of Western life.

MALCOLM MUGGERIDGE,
FROM THE *SUNDAY TIMES*,
LONDON TIMES (NEWSPAPER), 17 FEBRUARY 1980

EXAMPLE
· ·

He that gives good advice builds with one hand; he that gives good counsel and example builds with both; but he that gives good admonition and bad example builds with one hand and pulls down with the other.

FRANCIS BACON

Every life is a profession of faith, and exercises an inevitable and silent propaganda. As far as lies in its power, it tends to transform the universe and humanity into its own image. Thus we have all a cure of souls. Every man is a centre of perpetual radiation like a luminous body; he is, as it were, a beacon which entices a ship upon the rocks if it does not guide it into port. Every man is a priest, even involuntarily; his conduct is an unspoken sermon, which is forever preaching to others—but there are priests of Baal, of Moloch, and of all the false gods. Such is the high importance of example.

HENRI FRÉDÉRIC AMIEL

Well done, is better than well said.

BENJAMIN FRANKLIN

It is easier to exemplify values than teach them.
THEODORE HESBURGH

A man who lives right, and is right, has more power in his silence than another has by his words.
PHILLIPS BROOKS

The first great gift we can bestow on others is a good example.
THOMAS MORELL

EXCELLENCE
· ·

There never will exist anything permanently noble and excellent in the character which is a stranger to resolute self-denial.
SIR WALTER SCOTT

Lord, grant that I may always desire more than I can accomplish.
MICHELANGELO

Whoever I am, or whatever I am doing, some kind of excellence is within my reach.
JOHN W. GARDNER

Some people have greatness thrust upon them. Very few have excellence thrust upon them. . . . They achieve it. They do not achieve it unwittingly by doing what comes naturally and they don't stumble into it in the course of amusing themselves. All excellence involves discipline and tenacity of purpose.
JOHN W. GARDNER

Only a mediocre person is always at his best.
W. SOMERSET MAUGHAM

Great spirits have always found violent opposition from mediocrities.
ALBERT EINSTEIN

*Excellence is never cheap. It is costly. Constant care, serious prepara-
tion, and continual application are required. Excellence involves
desire plus discipline plus determination.*

G. S.

*Over my desk at home hangs a poster of an Olympic runner, and
its caption reads, "Run in such a way that you may WIN"
(1 Corinthians 9:24 NASB).*

G. S.

*There is a canyon of difference between doing your best to glorify God
and doing whatever it takes to glorify yourself. The quest for excellence is a mark of maturity. The quest for power is childish.*

MAX L. LUCADO

*If a society holds conflicting views about excellence—or cannot rouse
itself to the pursuit of excellence—the consequences will be felt in everything that it undertakes. The disease may not attack every organ, but
the resulting debility will be felt in all parts of the system. Everything
that it does and everything that it strives for will be affected.*

JOHN W. GARDNER

*Quality is never an accident. It is always the result of intelligent
effort. There must be the will to produce a superior thing.*

JOHN RUSKIN

EXCUSES
· ·

To regard or judge with indulgence; pardon or forgive.
RANDOM HOUSE DICTIONARY

We have forty million reasons for failure, but not a single excuse.
RUDYARD KIPLING

The person who is good for excuses, is good for little else.
BENJAMIN FRANKLIN

In the cartoon strip "Peanuts," Lucy blames missing the fly ball on the sun, the moon, the wind, the stars, and even the toxic substance in her baseball glove.

Someone had painted on a tenement building wall, "Humpty Dumpty was pushed."

He who excuses himself, accuses himself.
GABRIEL MEURIER

Excuses only satisfy the people who make them.
G. S.

Then said I: "Ah, Lord God! Behold, I cannot speak, for I am a youth."
JEREMIAH, JEREMIAH 1:6 NKJV

Reasons are usually sincere, whereas an excuse is a rationalization, or at best a weak reason.
G. S.

The woman you put here with me—she gave me some fruit from the tree, and I ate it.
ADAM, GENESIS 3:12 NIV

So he said to Him, "O my Lord, how can I save Israel? Indeed my clan is the weakest in Manasseh, and I am the least in my father's house."
GIDEON, JUDGES 6:15 NKJV

Then Moses said to the Lord, "O my Lord, I am not eloquent, neither before nor since You have spoken to Your servant; but I am slow of speech and slow of tongue."
MOSES, EXODUS 4:10-11 NKJV

The slothful man says, "There is a lion outside! I shall be slain in the streets!"
PROVERBS 22:13 NKJV

An excuse is worse than a lie, for an excuse is a lie, guarded.
ALEXANDER POPE

But they all with one accord began to make excuses. The first said to him, "I have bought a piece of ground, and I must go and see it. I ask you to have me excused." And another said, "I have bought five yoke of oxen, and I am going to test them. I ask you to have me excused." Still another said, "I have married a wife, and therefore I cannot come." So that servant came and reported these things to his master. Then the master of the house, being angry, said to his servant, "Go out quickly into the streets and lanes of the city, and bring in here the poor and the maimed and the lame and the blind."
LUKE 14:18-21 NKJV

Excuses I have heard:

—*I can't come because the baby wet and I have to change her, wash her off, and calm her down.*
—*I'm afraid I'm going to have a nervous breakdown and if I have a breakdown, I want to have it at home.*
—*Billie locked himself in the bathroom, and we can't remember how to open the door.*
—*Richie ate our paycheck.*
—*Peter mistook Ex-lax for chocolate kisses.*
—*Jimmie was playing filling station and put eight gallons of water in our gas tank.*

Rationalization: It's what we do when we substitute false explanations for true reasons . . . . when we cloud our motives with a smoke screen of nice-sounding excuses.
CHARLES SWINDOLL

The serpent deceived me, and I ate.
EVE, GENESIS 3:13 NIV

No Excuse Sunday

Cots will be placed in the foyer for those who say, "Sunday is my only day to sleep in."

We have steel helmets for those who say, "The roof would cave in if I ever came to church."

Blankets will be furnished for those who think the church is too cold, and fans for those who say it is too hot.

We have hearing aids for those who say, "The preacher speaks too softly," and cotton balls for those who say, "He preaches too loudly."

Score cards will be available for those who wish to list the hypocrites present.

Some relatives will be in attendance for those who like to go visiting on Sundays.

There will be TV dinners for those who can't go to church and cook dinner also.

One section will be devoted to trees and grass for those who like to worship God in nature.

Finally, the sanctuary will be decorated with Christmas poinsettias and Easter lilies for those who have never seen the church without them.

FROM A CHURCH BULLETIN

If our philandering, gambling, shopping, or even our criminal conduct is the result of "illness" rather than the result of poor character, or immoral decisions, we are off the hook, we have abolished sin by medicalizing it.

CHARLES J. SYKES, *A NATION OF VICTIMS*

A boss said to his new young accountant, "Do you believe in life after death?"

When the puzzled accountant said that he did, the boss seemed relieved. "You see—about a half-hour after you left to attend your grandfather's funeral yesterday afternoon, he came in here to see you!"

The new preacher looked sternly at Deacon Smith. "I heard you went to a ball game instead of church last Sunday."

"That's a lie," said the deacon indignantly. "And I've got the fish to prove it!"

An excuse is the skin of a reason stuffed with a lie.

FAILURE

Not failure, but low aim, is a crime.

ERNEST HOLMES

Thomas Edison was taunted by some wag before he had successfully invented the incandescent light bulb, "Ten thousand experiments and you haven't learned a thing."

"You're wrong," responded Edison, "I've learned ten thousand ways not to invent the incandescent electric light."

G. S.

In God's world, for those who are in earnest, there is no failure. No work truly done, no word earnestly spoken, no sacrifice freely made, was ever made in vain.

FREDERICK W. ROBERTSON

The glory is not in never failing, but in rising every time you fall.

ANONYMOUS

Those who have failed miserably are often the first to see God's formula for success.

ERWIN W. LUTZER

FAITH

It is a masterpiece of the devil to make us believe that children cannot understand religion. Would Christ have made a child the standard of faith if He had known that it was not capable of understanding His words?

D. L. MOODY

I'm tired of hootenanny religion, the new brand of Christianity that pagans do not feel embarrassed to join. I'm tired of Batman, the Beatniks, the Beatles, the "God is dead" movement, the new morality, situation ethics, existentialism, and the latest theological aberration out of Germany. If my faith were so weak that a professor down in Georgia could shake it, I'd get another kind.

I'm tired of hearing in our church bodies that we must get away from our humble beginnings, shake the hayseed out of our hair, and come of age. I hear a lot today about grandstand seats in glory, but I don't hear much about the baptism of Christ's suffering. We're wearing a lot of medals these days, and not many scars.

VANCE HAVNER

Faith makes all things possible . . . love makes all things easy.

D. L. MOODY

> *Lord, give me faith!—to live from day to day,*
> *With tranquil heart to do my simple part,*
> *And, with my hand in Thine, just go Thy way.*
>
> *Lord, give me faith!—to trust, if not to know;*
> *With quiet mind in all things Thee to find,*
> *And, child-like, to go where Thou wouldst have me go.*
>
> *Lord, give me faith!—to leave it all to Thee,*
> *The future is Thy gift, I would not lift*
> *The veil Thy love has hung 'twixt it and me.*

JOHN OXENHAM

Faith, as Paul saw it, was a living, flaming thing leading to surrender and obedience to the commandments of Christ.

A. W. TOZER

You should not believe your conscience and your feelings more than the word which the Lord who receives sinners preaches to you.

MARTIN LUTHER

The apostolic church faced mountainous problems with complete confidence in God. "God is able" was their password into pagan territory. Only a fool would have attempted in human strength what they did. Ancient Israel met defeat at Kadesh-Barnea because the people doubted God's ability to see them through. They forgot too soon. The miracle of the Red Sea, the provision of the manna, all faded from their minds, as they considered their own weakness. Problems? Yes, they had problems. Each of us faces his own little custom-designed set of temptations and problems. Every one of us—at our own point of greatest weakness—has a magnificent chance to display God's power. "If God be for us, who can be against us?" (Romans 8:31).

G. S.

The great evangelist George Whitefield once asked a coal miner in Cornwall, England, what he believed.

"Oh," said he, "I believe what my church believes."

Whitefield then inquired, "And what does your church believe?"

"Well," he answered, "the church believes what I believe."

Seeing that he was getting nowhere, Whitefield then asked, "What do you both believe?"

The coal worker answered, "We both believe the same thing."

This sort of unintelligent faith is pathetic and only perpetuates error.

G. S.

Sight is not faith, and hearing is not faith, neither is feeling faith; but believing when we neither see, hear, nor feel is faith; and everywhere the Bible tells us our salvation is to be by faith. Therefore we must believe before we feel, and often against our feelings, if we would honor God by our faith.

HANNAH WHITALL SMITH

Faith and obedience are bound up in the same bundle; he that obeys God trusts God; and he that trusts God obeys God. He that is without faith is without works, and he that is without works is without faith.

CHARLES HADDON SPURGEON

189

We walk by faith, not by sight.

2 CORINTHIANS 5:7

The beginning of anxiety is the end of faith, and the beginning of true faith is the end of anxiety.

GEORGE MUELLER

Faith is: dead to doubts, dumb to discouragements, blind to impossibilities.

ANONYMOUS

Faith is a reasoning trust, a trust which reckons thoughtfully and confidently upon the trustworthiness of God.

JOHN R. STOTT

Attempt something so impossible that unless God is in it, it's doomed to failure.

JOHN HAGGAI

Faith is a living, daring confidence in God's grace, so sure and certain that a man could stake his life on it a thousand times.

MARTIN LUTHER

A faith that hasn't been tested can't be trusted.

ADRIAN ROGERS

Faith is deliberate confidence in the character of God whose ways you may not understand at the time.

OSWALD CHAMBERS

We must never cease to earnestly contend for the faith which was once for all delivered to the saints. And how? By loving the faith. By learning the faith. By living the faith. And by loosing the faith. That charge was delivered to the church, and no one else will be responsible . . . if the foundations be destroyed!

O. S. HAWKINS

Faith . . . is a steady and certain knowledge of the Divine benevolence towards us, which being founded on the truth of the gratuitous promise in Christ, is both revealed to our minds, and confirmed to our hearts, by the Holy Spirit.

JOHN CALVIN

No Christian has ever been known to recant on his death bed.

C. M. WARD

I believe though I do not comprehend, and I hold by faith what I cannot grasp with the mind.

SAINT BERNARD OF CLAIRVAUX

Justifying faith implies, not only a divine evidence or conviction that "God was in Christ, reconciling the world unto Himself," but a sure trust and confidence that Christ died for my sins, that He loved me and gave Himself for me.

JOHN WESLEY

Faith makes: The uplook good, the outlook bright, the future glorious.

ANONYMOUS

There is no great future for any people whose faith has burned out.

RUFUS M. JONES

My faith has no bed to sleep upon but omnipotence.

SAMUEL RUTHERFORD

Faith is the refusal to panic.

D. MARTYN LLOYD-JONES

Faith, mighty faith, the promise sees,
And looks to God alone;
Laughs at impossibilities,
And cries, it shall be done.

CHARLES WESLEY

191

FAMILY
· ·

The family is the most basic unit of government. As the first commu-
nity to which a person is attached and the first authority under
which a person learns to live, the family establishes society's most
basic values.

CHARLES COLSON

In a broken nest there are few whole eggs.

CHINESE PROVERB

A man ought to live so that everybody knows he is a Christian . . .
and most of all, his family ought to know.

D. L. MOODY

Divorces had multiplied, and the family seemed about to be dissolved.
Augustus strove to arrest this downward tendency by edicts and laws
in encouragement of marriage and in the restraint of divorces. But
the trouble was too deep-seated in the failing moral and religious life
of the times to be reached and remedied by any measure of the state.

PHILIP VAN NESS MYERS

The fine edge of character had been blunted in the Rome of the second
century A.D. The stern face of the traditional father of the family had
faded out; instead we see on every hand the flabby face of the son of
the house, the eternal spoiled child of society, who has grown accus-
tomed to luxury and lost all sense of discipline. . . .
    Some evaded the duty of maternity for fear of losing their looks.
Some were not content to live their lives by their husband's side.

JEROME CARCOPINO,
DAILY LIFE IN ANCIENT ROME

What are your answers to the three questions the prophet asked the
Shunammite woman? "Is it well with you? Is it well with your hus-
band [or wife]? Is it well with the child?" (II Kings 4:26)

WARREN WIERSBE

Let France have good mothers and she will have good sons.
NAPOLEON BONAPARTE

What if God should place a diamond in your hand and tell you to inscribe on it a sentence which should be read at the Last Day and shown there as an index of your thoughts and feelings! What care, what caution would you exercise in the selection! (The diamond is your child.)
RUSSELL PAYSON

The family is the school of duties . . . founded on love.
FELIX ADLER

Apart from religious influence, the family is the most important unit of society. It would be well if every home were Christian, but we know that it is not so. The family and the home can never exert their proper influence while ignoring the Biblical standards. The Bible calls for discipline and a recognition of authority. If children do not learn this at home, they will go out into society without the proper attitude toward authority and law. There is always the exceptional child, but the average tells us that the child is largely what the home has made him. The only way to provide the right home for your children is to put the Lord above them, and fully instruct them in the ways of the Lord. You are responsible before God for the home you provide for them.
BILLY GRAHAM

The babe at first feeds upon the mother's bosom, but it is always on her heart.
HENRY WARD BEECHER

God could not be everywhere, and therefore He made mothers.
OLD JEWISH SAYING

All I am, or can be, I owe to my angel mother.
ABRAHAM LINCOLN

A man never sees all that his mother has been to him until it is too late.
W. D. HOWELLS

If there is something one cannot do without, it is Mother. Father loves her, daughter imitates her, son ignores her, salesmen thrive on her, motorists hurry around her, teacher phones her, and the woman next door confides in her.

She can be sweeter than sugar, more sour than a lemon, all smiles, and crying her heart out within any given two-minute period.

She likes sewing, detective stories, having her birthday remembered, church, a new dress, the cleaning woman, Father's praise, a little lipstick, flowers and plants, canasta, dinner out on Sunday, policemen, one whole day in bed, crossword puzzles, sunny days, tea, and the newspaper boy.

She dislikes doing the dishes, Father's boss, having her birthday forgotten, the motorist behind her, spring cleaning, Junior's report card, rainy days, the neighbor's dog, stairs, and the man who was supposed to cut the grass.

She can be found standing by, bending over, reaching for, kneeling under, and stretching around, but rarely sitting on.

She has the beauty of a spring day, the patience of a saint, the appetite of a small bird, and the memory of a large elephant.

She knows the lowest prices, everybody's birthday, what you should be doing, and all your secret thoughts.

She is always straightening up after, reminding you to, and taking care of, but never asking for.

Yes, a Mother is one thing that nobody can do without. And when you have harassed her, buffeted her about, tried her patience, and worn her out, and it seems that the end of the world is about to descend upon you, then you can win her back with four little words, "Mom, I love you!"

WILLIAM A. GREENBAUM II

Parents wonder why the streams are bitter when they themselves have poisoned the fountain.

JOHN LOCKE

'Mid pleasures and palaces though we may roam,
Be it ever so humble, there's no place like home.
                                    JOHN HOWARD PAYNE

Parents: persons who spend half their time worrying how a child will
turn out, and the rest of the time wondering when a child will turn in.
                                    TED COOK

At the bottom as it were of Roman society and forming its ultimate
unit, was the family. . . . The typical Roman family consisted of the
father . . . and mother, the sons, together with their wives and sons,
and the unmarried daughters. . . . The most important feature or ele-
ment of this family group was the authority of the father. It would be
difficult to overestimate the influence of this group upon the history
and destiny of Rome. It was the cradle of at least some of those splen-
did virtues of the early Romans that contributed so much to the
strength and greatness of Rome, and that helped to give her the
dominion of the world.
                                    PHILIP VAN NESS MYERS

There is an old proverb: "The shoemaker's wife is always the worst
shod." The families of many very busy Christian teachers suffer woe-
fully for want of remembering "He first findeth his own brother."
                                    ALEXANDER MACLAREN

            Who ran to help me when I fell,
            And would some pretty story tell,
            Or kiss the place to make it well? My mother.
                                    JANE TAYLOR

When I was a boy of fourteen, my father was so ignorant I could
hardly stand to have the old man around. But when I got to be twen-
ty-one, I was astonished at how much the old man had learned.
                                    MARK TWAIN

A family is a place where principles are hammered and honed on the anvil of everyday living.

CHARLES SWINDOLL

FEAR
· ·

God incarnate is the end of fear; and the heart that realizes that He is in the midst . . . will be quiet in the middle of alarm.

F. B. MEYER

To hate and to fear is to be psychologically ill . . . it is, in fact, the consuming illness of our time.

H. A. OVERSTREET

The Lord is my light and my salvation; whom shall I fear? the Lord is the strength of my life; of whom shall I be afraid?

PSALM 27:1

Shame arises from the fear of men, conscience from the fear of God.

SAMUEL JOHNSON

Less base the fear of death than fear of life.

EDWARD YOUNG

On March 4, 1933 during the dark days of the depression, President Franklin D. Roosevelt said in a radio speech, "The only thing we have to fear is fear itself."

On September 7, 1851, the naturalist Henry David Thoreau wrote in his journal, "Nothing is so much to be feared as fear."

Three centuries before that, the French essayist Montaigne wrote, "The thing of which I have most fear is fear."

People in all ages of history have fought their fears in one way or another, but the only thing that really conquers fear is faith in the Lord: "I will trust, and not be afraid" (Isaiah 12:2).

Only he who can say, "The Lord is my strength," can say, "Of whom shall I be afraid?"

ALEXANDER MACLAREN

FELLOWSHIP

A gentleman is one who puts more into the world than he takes out.

GEORGE BERNARD SHAW

Who practices hospitality entertains God Himself.

ANONYMOUS

Fellowship with God means warfare with the world.

CHARLES E. FULLER

No man is an island.

JOHN DONNE

A habit of devout fellowship with God is the spring of all our life, and the strength of it.

H. E. MANNING

FORGIVENESS

He who cannot forgive others breaks the bridge over which he must pass himself.

GEORGE HERBERT

God pardons like a mother, who kisses the offense into everlasting forgiveness.

HENRY WARD BEECHER

God has a big eraser.

BILLY ZEOLI

This is certain, that a man that studieth revenge keeps his wounds green, which otherwise would heal and do well.

FRANCIS BACON

The best thing to give to your enemy is forgiveness; to an opponent, tolerance; to a friend, your heart; to your child, a good example; to a father, deference; to your mother, conduct that will make her proud of you; to yourself, respect; to all men, charity.

ARTHUR J. BALFOUR

"I can forgive, but I cannot forget," is only another way of saying, "I cannot forgive."

HENRY WARD BEECHER

I will not permit any man to narrow and degrade my soul by making me hate him.

BOOKER T. WASHINGTON

When Andrew Jackson was being interviewed for church member-ship, the pastor said, "General, there is one more question which I must ask you. Can you forgive all your enemies?"

Andrew Jackson was silent as he recalled his stormy life of bitter fighting. Then he responded, "My political enemies I can freely for-give; but as for those who attacked me for serving my country and those who slandered my wife—Doctor, I cannot forgive them!"

The pastor made it clear to Jackson that before he could become a member of the church and partake of the broken bread and the cup, his hatred and bitterness must be confessed and dealt with before God.

Again there was an awkward silence. Then Jackson affirmed that if God would help him, he would forgive his enemies.

G. S.

The discretion of a man deferreth his anger; and it is his glory to pass over a transgression.

PROVERBS 19:11

Rejoice not when thine enemy falleth, and let not thine heart be glad when he stumbleth.
                                        PROVERBS 24:17

And forgive us our debts, as we forgive our debtors. . . . For if ye forgive men their trespasses, your heavenly Father will also forgive you: but if ye forgive not men their trespasses, neither will your Father forgive your trespasses.
                                        MATTHEW 6:12, 14-15

Forgiveness is not an occasional act, it is a permanent attitude.
                                        MARTIN LUTHER KING, JR.

And when ye stand praying, forgive, if ye have ought against any: that your Father also which is in heaven may forgive you your trespasses.
                                        MARK 11:25

And be ye kind one to another, tenderhearted, forgiving one another, even as God for Christ's sake hath forgiven you.
                                        EPHESIANS 4:32

It is in pardoning that we are pardoned.
                                        SAINT FRANCIS OF ASSISI

FORTUNE
. . . .

Fortune does not so much change men, as it unmasks them.
                                        ANONYMOUS

Fortune favors the prepared mind.
                                        LOUIS PASTEUR

He that waits upon fortune is never sure of a dinner.
                                        BENJAMIN FRANKLIN

Therefore if a man look sharply and attentively, he shall see Fortune: for though she be blind, yet she is not invisible.

FRANCIS BACON

Fortune truly helps those who are of good judgment.

EURIPIDES

If a man's fortune does not fit him, it is like the shoe in the story; if too large it trips him up, if too small it pinches him.

HORACE

FRANKNESS
· ·

During World War II, the Civil Defense authorities had posters printed which read: "Illumination must be extinguished when premises are vacated." When he saw these signs, President Roosevelt exclaimed, "Why can't they just say 'Put out the lights when you leave'?"

FRANKLIN DELANO ROOSEVELT

A trouble-making woman once told John Wesley, "God has given me the talent of speaking my mind."

Mr. Wesley snapped back, "God wouldn't mind if you buried that talent."

G. S.

We are franker towards others than towards ourselves.

FRIEDERICH NIETZSCHE

People who talk much say nothing.

ANONYMOUS

FREEDOM

· ·

Any nation that thinks more of its ease and comfort than its freedom will soon lose its freedom; and the ironical thing about it is that it will lose its ease and comfort too.

W. SOMERSET MAUGHAM

All theory is against freedom of the will; all experience for it.

SAMUEL JOHNSON

Liberty is the only thing you cannot have unless you are willing to give it to others.

WILLIAM ALLEN WHITE

I disapprove of what you say, but I will defend to the death your right to say it.

VOLTAIRE *(ATTRIBUTED)*

Yesterday the greatest question was decided which ever was debated in America; and a greater perhaps never was, nor will be, decided among men. A resolution was passed without one dissenting colony, "that these United Colonies are, and of right ought to be, free and independent States."

JOHN ADAMS,
LETTER TO ABIGAIL ADAMS, 3 JULY 1776

FRIENDSHIP

· ·

Some men still have their first dollar. The man who is really rich is the one who still has his first friend.

Keep a fair-sized cemetery in your back yard, in which to bury the faults of your friends.

HENRY WARD BEECHER

To gather with God's people in united adoration of the Father is as necessary to the Christian life as prayer.

MARTIN LUTHER

We will win the world when we realize that fellowship, not evangelism, must be our primary emphasis. When we demonstrate the Big Miracle of Love, it won't be necessary for us to go out - they will come in.

JESS MOODY

You may poke a man's fire after you've known him for seven years.

ENGLISH PROVERB

Associate with men of good quality, if you esteem your own reputation; for it is better to be alone than in bad company.

GEORGE WASHINGTON

Old friends are best. King James used to call for his old shoes; they were easiest for his feet.

JOHN SELDEN

Friendship is one of the sweetest joys of life. Many might have failed beneath the bitterness of their trial had they not found a friend.

CHARLES HADDON SPURGEON

You can't eat your friends and have them too.

BUDD SCHULBERG

There is a destiny that makes us brothers,
No one goes his way alone;
All that we send into the lives of others,
Comes back into our own.

EDWIN MARKHAM

He whose hand is clasped in friendship cannot throw mud.

ANONYMOUS

Ten Commandments of Human Relations

1. *Speak to people. There is nothing as nice as a cheerful word of greeting.*
2. *Smile at people. It takes seventy-two muscles to frown, only fourteen to smile.*
3. *Call people by name. The sweetest music to anyone's ears is the sound of his own name.*
4. *Be friendly and helpful. If you would have friends, be friendly.*
5. *Be cordial. Speak and act as if everything you do is a genuine pleasure.*
6. *Be genuinely interested in people. You can like almost anybody if you try.*
7. *Be generous with praise—cautious with criticism.*
8. *Be considerate with the feelings of others. There are usually three sides to a controversy; yours, the other fellow's and the right one.*
9. *Be alert to give service. What counts most in life is what we do for others.*
10. *Add to this a good sense of humor, a big dose of patience and a dash of humility, and you will be rewarded many-fold.*

ROBERT G. LEE

A friend should bear a friend's infirmities,
But Brutus makes mine greater than they are.

WILLIAM SHAKESPEARE,
CASSIUS IN *JULIUS CAESAR*

You can make more friends in two months by becoming interested in other people than you can in two years by trying to get other people interested in you.

DALE CARNEGIE

We cannot tell the precise moment when friendship is formed. As in filling a vessel drop by drop, there is at last a drop which makes it run over, so in a series of kindnesses there is at last one that makes the heart run over.

SAMUEL JOHNSON

A friend attributed the secret of his popularity to one particular word. "Years ago," he said, "upon hearing a statement with which I disagreed, I used to say, 'Baloney,' and people began to avoid me like the plague. Now I substitute 'Amazing' for 'Baloney,' and my phone keeps ringing and my list of friends continues to grow."

CAPPER'S WEEKLY

A friend is a present you give yourself.

ROBERT LOUIS STEVENSON

In the progress of personality, first comes a declaration of independence, then a recognition of interdependence.

HENRY VAN DYKE

A friend is one to whom one may pour out all the contents of one's heart, chaff and grain together, knowing that the gentlest of hands will take and sift it, keep what is worth keeping, and with a breath of kindness, blow the rest away.

ANONYMOUS

It brings comfort to have companions in whatever happens.

SAINT JOHN CHRYSOSTOM

Three men are my friends: he that loves me, he that hates me, and he that is indifferent to me. Who loves me teaches me tenderness. Who hates me teaches me caution. Who is indifferent to me teaches me self-reliance.

THESE TIMES

Those who best knew Sir Walter Scott used to say of him, "He spoke to every man he met as if he were a blood relative."

G. S.

The dearest friend on earth is a mere shadow compared to Jesus Christ.

OSWALD CHAMBERS

FUTURE
· ·

I've read the last page of the Bible. It's all going to turn out all right.
BILLY GRAHAM

Ignorance of God's prophetic outline, failure to know God's program for the Church, the nations, and Israel, is the cause of the overwhelming amount of error and misunderstanding of the events of the future.
M. R. DEHAAN

We should all be concerned about the future because we will have to spend the rest of our lives there.
CHARLES F. KETTERING

We Break New Seas Today

We break new seas today—
Our eager keels quest unaccustomed waters,
And, from the vast uncharged waste in front,
The mystic circles leap
To greet our prows with mightiest possibilities,
Bringing us—What?
Dread shoals and shifting banks?
And calms and storms?
And clouds and biting gales?
And wreck and loss?
And valiant fighting times?
And, maybe, death!—and so, the Larger Life!

For, should the Pilot deem it best
To cut the voyage short,
He sees beyond the sky-line, and
He'll bring us into Port!
JOHN OXENHAM

The future is as bright as the promises of God.
WILLIAM CAREY

The nineteenth-century American preacher William Jackson once said, "Here on earth our greatest joys are empty and imperfect. But in the presence of God, we shall have fullness of joy. Our cup of joy will be full. There will be no room for sorrow. Here our sweetest pleasures are but momentary. They fly away, and are replaced by bitter disappointment. But at God's right hand, there are 'pleasures forevermore.'"

G. S.

In eternity all the promises of God for His children will be fulfilled. There will be no strife between nations, for all men will want God's will. All of creation and redeemed mankind will continue as God meant them to be, perfect in unity and working together for the glory of God.

G. S.

Never be afraid to trust an unknown future to a known God.
CORRIE TEN BOOM

> *One short life for watching with the Saviour,*
> *Eternal years to walk with Him in white,*
> *One short life to bravely meet disaster,*
> *Eternal years to reign with Him in light,*
> *One brief life for weary toils and trials,*
> *Eternal years for calm and peaceful rest,*
> *One brief life for patient self-denials,*
> *Eternal years for life, where life is best.*
> ANONYMOUS

Some men see things as they are and say why. I dream things that never were and say why not.
ROBERT F. KENNEDY

GIVING

. . . .

Do your giving while you're living, then you're knowing where it's going.

The nine-tenths prove man's love, but the one-tenth tests man's legal obedience.

HERSCHEL HOBBS

There never was a person who did anything worth doing, who did not receive more than he gave.

HENRY WARD BEECHER

I have somewhere met with the epitaph on a charitable man which has pleased me very much. I cannot recollect the words, but here is the sense of it: "What I spent I lost; what I possessed is left to others; what I gave away remains with me."

JOSEPH ADDISON

Not what we give, but what we share—
For the gift without the giver is bare;
Who gives himself with his alms feeds three—
Himself, his hungering neighbor, and me.

JAMES RUSSELL LOWELL,
THE VISION OF SIR LAUNFAL

For the Macedonian Christians, giving was not a chore but a challenge, not a burden but a blessing. Giving was not something to be avoided, but a privilege to be desired.

G. S.

He who bestows his goods upon the poor,
Shall have as much again, and ten times more.

JOHN BUNYAN, *PILGRIM'S PROGRESS*

Said a good man to me when I asked him, "How do you manage to
give so much?"—"The Lord is all the time shoveling it on me, and I
would be overwhelmed if I did not give." God shovels wealth upon
us, and if we do not shovel it back, we will be buried beneath it as by
an avalanche of ruin.

DASHIELL

I do not believe one can settle how much we ought to give. I am afraid
the only safe rule is to give more than we can spare.

C. S. LEWIS, *MERE CHRISTIANITY*

When we come to the end of life, the question will be, "How much
have you given?" not "How much have you gotten?"

G. S.

Jesus Christ is the supreme Example of giving.

G. S.

The Dead Sea is the dead sea, because it continually receives and
never gives.

ANONYMOUS

Seldom repress a generous impulse.

G. S.

If your OUTGO is greater than your INCOME,
then your UPKEEP is headed for a DOWNFALL.

UNKNOWN

A bit of fragrance always clings to the hand that gives you roses.

PROVERB

GOD
· ·

What I believe about God is the most important thing about me.
                                    A. W. TOZER

Seek to cultivate a buoyant, joyous sense of the crowded kindnesses of God in your daily life.
                            ALEXANDER MACLAREN

The most important thought that ever occupied my mind is that of my individual responsibility to God.
                                DANIEL WEBSTER

God has marvelous ways of taking our worst tragedies and turning them into His most glorious triumphs.
                                JOSEPH STOWELL

The intrinsic drive to please the significant people in our lives reflects the fact that we were built to bring pleasure to someone outside of ourselves—God. The highest satisfaction of life is knowing in our spirits that He indeed is pleased with us.
                                JOSEPH STOWELL

I find that doing of the will of God leaves me no time for disputing about His plans.
                            GEORGE MACDONALD

It is difficult to make a man miserable while he feels he is worthy of himself and claims kindred to the great God who made him.
                                ABRAHAM LINCOLN

The only way God could impose peace on the world would be to robotize our wills and rob every human being of the power of choice. He has not chosen to do that. He has given every person a free will.
                                JOHN HAGGAI

God is concerned with nations, but nations also need to be concerned with God. No nation can have a monopoly on God, but God will bless any nation whose people seek and honor His will as revealed by Christ and declared through the Holy Spirit.

JOHN HAGGAI

GOD'S CHARACTER
· ·

Having given us the package, do you think God will deny us the ribbon?

OSWALD C. J. HOFFMAN

If God is dead, then the great capitulation of the force standing over against man has been made, and man is free to move forward and to occupy the God-like positions.

Henceforth, man is free to make of himself what he will. . . . If God is dead everything is permitted, even the resort to the animality of an amoral natural force. The decision that the ward is over, and man has won, and God is dead is the inspiration and despair of contemporary movements such as nihilism and existentialism.

LESLIE PAUL

It is not a difficult matter to learn what it means to delight ourselves in the Lord. It is to live so as to please Him, to honor everything we find in His Word, to do everything the way He would like to have it done, and for Him.

S. MAXWELL CODER

What do you conceive God to be like? Some would say that to believe at all in a personal God requires a giant leap of faith—but I am convinced that belief in God is a far more reasonable position than atheism. Nature, the personal experience of literally billions of people, and something innate in the heart of man all testify to the existence of God.

G. S.

Down through the years God's love has shined through misery, tears, and sin like a shaft of sunlight on a dark day. We see God's love in His revelation, in His mercy, in His patience, and in His redemption. We see the love of God as the infinite One becomes an infant in Bethlehem's manger. We see it in His life and ministry. And most of all we see it as He hangs on the cross, dying for our sins.

G. S.

I know not, but God knows;
Oh, blessed rest from fear!
All my unfolding days
To Him are plain and clear
Each anxious, puzzled "Why?"
From doubt or dread that grows,
Finds answer in this thought:
I know not, but He knows.

I cannot, but God can;
Oh, balm for all my care!
The burden that I drop
His hand will lift and bear,
Though eagle pinions tire—
I walk where once I ran,
This is my strength to know:
I cannot, but God can.

ANNIE JOHNSON FLINT

An infinite God can give all of Himself to each of His children. He does not distribute Himself that each may have a part, but to each one He gives all of Himself as fully as if there were no others.

A. W. TOZER

If the Lord be with us, we have no cause of fear. His eye is upon us, His arm over us, His ear open to our prayer—His grace sufficient, His promise unchangeable.

JOHN NEWTON

Yes, pine for thy God, fainting soul!
  ever pine;
O languish mid all that life brings thee of mirth;
Famished, thirsty, and restless—
  let such life be thine—
For what sigh is to heaven, desire is to earth.

God loves to be longed for, He loves to be sought,
For He sought us Himself with such longing and love;
He died for desire of us, marvelous thought!
And He yearns for us now to be with Him above.
FREDERICK WILLIAM FABER

All people that on earth do dwell
Sing to the Lord with cheerful voice. . . .
For why? the Lord our God is good:
His mercy is for ever sure;
His truth at all times firmly stood,
And shall from age to age endure.
WILLIAM KETHE

O God, our help in ages past
Our hope for years to come,
Our shelter from the stormy blast,
And our eternal home.

A thousand ages in Thy sight
Are like an evening gone,
Short as the watch that ends the night
Before the rising sun.

Time, like an ever-rolling stream,
Bears all its sons away;
They fly forgotten, as a dream
Dies at the opening day.
ISAAC WATTS

The trouble with our modern thinking is that we have a conception that God is a haphazard God with no set rules of life and salvation. Ask the astronomer if God is a haphazard God. He will tell you that every star moves with precision in its celestial path. Ask the scientist if God is a haphazard God. He will tell you that His formulas and equations are fixed, and that to ignore the laws of science would be a fool's folly. If the laws in the material realm are so fixed and exact, is it reasonable that God could afford to be haphazard in the spiritual realm when eternal destinies of souls are at stake? Just as God has equations and rules in the material realm, God has equations and rules in the spiritual.

BILLY GRAHAM

Dios tarda pero no olvida—God delays but doesn't forget.
SPANISH PROVERB

GOD'S WILL

I find that doing the will of God leaves me no time for disputing about His plans.

GEORGE MACDONALD

I was frustrated out of my mind, trying to figure out the will of God. I was doing everything but getting into the presence of God and asking Him to show me.

PAUL LITTLE

Some people think that God peers over the balcony of heaven trying to find anybody who is enjoying life. And when He spots a happy person, He yells, "Now cut that out!" That concept of God should make us shudder because it's blasphemous!

PAUL LITTLE

In His will is our peace.

DANTE ALIGHIERI

Others think it's a choice between doing what we want to do and being happy, and doing what God wants us to do and being miserable.

PAUL LITTLE

Thy way, not mine, O Lord,
However dark it be!
Lead me by thine own hand;
Choose thou the path for me.

Smooth let it be or rough,
It will be still the best;
Winding or straight, it leads
Right onward to thy rest.

I dare not choose my lot;
I would not if I might;
Choose thou for me, my God:
So shall I walk aright.

Take thou my cup and it
With joy or sorrow fill,
As best to thee may seem;
Choose thou my good and ill.

Choose thou for me my friends,
My sickness or my health;
Choose thou my cares for me,
My poverty or wealth.

Not mine, not mine the choice,
In things or great or small:
Be thou my guide, my strength,
My wisdom, and my all.

HORATIUS BONAR

I like to interpose in all of my appointments, if the Lord wills.
A. B. SIMPSON

Can you think of a father who has no will or plan for the life of his son? Can you imagine a mother who has no clear will or definite ambition for her daughter? Can you imagine a man who has no special desire or pattern in the one he chooses to be his wife? Can you conceive of a king or ruler who has no will or desire or law to govern the conduct of his people? A captain who has no plan for his soldiery? An employer who has no plan or pattern to guide the labor of his workers? If so, then you may also think that God does not have a plan for your life, for every one of these symbols is used in the Bible to represent the relation the Christian bears to his Lord.

G. CHRISTIAN WEISS,
THE PERFECT WILL OF GOD

To know the will of God is the greatest knowledge! To do the will of God is the greatest achievement!

GEORGE W. TRUETT

If God gives you a watch, are you honoring Him more by asking Him what time it is or by simply consulting the watch?

A. W. TOZER

In almost everything that touches our everyday life on earth, God is pleased when we're pleased. He wills that we be as free as birds to soar and sing our maker's praise without anxiety.

A. W. TOZER

Has it ever struck you that the vast majority of the will of God for your life has already been revealed in the Bible? That is a crucial thing to grasp.

PAUL LITTLE

When we want to know God's will, there are three things which always concur: the inward impulse, the Word of God and the trend of circumstances. . . . Never act until these three things agree.

F. B. MEYER

Perhaps some of our teaching about God's will could be made more helpful if we supplemented it by additional figures of speech. It is useful . . . for example, to think of God's will as an area in a television wave guide or tube. As I understand it, the waves in this tube bounce back anywhere within the tube that they "want" to go, completely free so long as they remain in the tube. They are not channeled to a thin line—they just can't go outside of the wave guide.

KENNETH PIKE

My Jesus, as Thou wilt: O may Thy will be mine!
Into Thy hand of love I would my all resign.
Through sorrow or thro' joy, Conduct me as Thine own,
And help me still to say, "My Lord, Thy will be done!"

My Jesus, as Thou wilt: All shall be well for me;
Each changing future scene I gladly trust with Thee.
Straight to my home above I travel calmly on,
And sing in life or death, "My Lord, Thy will be done!"

BENJAMIN SCHMOLCK

The man or woman who is wholly or joyously surrendered to Christ can't make a wrong choice—any choice will be the right one.

A. W. TOZER

The history of all the great characters of the Bible is summed up in this one sentence: They acquainted themselves with God, and acquiesced His will in all things.

RICHARD CECIL

Man proposes, but God disposes.

THOMAS À KEMPIS

Blessed is the man who finds out which way God is moving and then gets going in the same direction.

ANONYMOUS

Six Steps to Knowing God's Will

1. *I seek at the beginning to get my heart into such a state that it has no will of its own in regard to a given matter. Nine-tenths of the trouble with people is just here. Nine-tenths of the difficulties are overcome when our hearts are ready to do the Lord's will, whatever it may be. When one is truly in this state, it is usually but a little way to the knowledge of what His will is.*
2. *Having done this, I do not leave the result to feeling or simple impression. If I do so, I make myself liable to great delusions.*
3. *I see the will of the Spirit of God through, or in connection with, the Word of God. The Spirit and the Word must be combined. If I look to the Spirit alone without the Word, I lay myself open to great delusions also. If the Holy Spirit guides us at all, He will do so according to the Scriptures and never contrary to them.*
4. *Next I take into account providential circumstances. These often plainly indicate God's will in connection with His Word and Spirit.*
5. *I ask God in prayer to reveal His will to me aright.*
6. *Thus, through prayer to God, the study of His Word, and reflection, I come to a deliberate judgment according to the best of my ability and knowledge; and if my mind is thus at peace, and continues so after two or three more petitions, I proceed accordingly. In trivial matters, and in transactions involving more important issues, I have found this method always effective.*

GEORGE MUELLER

That the Almighty does make use of human agencies and directly intervenes in human affairs is one of the plainest statements in the Bible. I have had so many evidences of His direction, so many instances when I have been controlled by some other power than my own will, that I cannot doubt that this power comes from above.

ABRAHAM LINCOLN

GOSPEL

The glory of the gospel is that when the church is absolutely different from the world, she invariably attracts it.

D. MARTYN LLOYD-JONES

The gospel is neither a discussion or a debate. It is an announcement.

PAUL S. REES

The inclusive gospel cannot be shared by an exclusive people.

G. S.

The gospel is not merely a message of deliverance, it is also a rule of conduct. It is not merely theology, it is also ethics. Like some of the ancient municipal charters, the grant of privileges and proclamation of freedom is also the sovereign code which imposes duties and shapes life.

ALEXANDER MACLAREN

Each generation of the church in each setting has the responsibility of communicating the gospel in understandable terms, considering the language and thought-forms of that setting.

FRANCIS SCHAEFFER, *ESCAPE FROM REASON*

If they had a social gospel in the days of the prodigal son, somebody would have given him a bed and a sandwich and he never would have gone home.

VANCE HAVNER

Men may not read the gospel in sealskin, or the gospel in morocco, or the gospel in cloth covers, but they can't get away from the gospel in shoe leather.

DONALD GREY BARNHOUSE

The gospel to me is simply irresistible.

BLAISE PASCAL

Philosophical argument has sometimes shaken my reason for the faith that was in me; but my heart has always assured me that the Gospel of Jesus Christ must be reality.

DANIEL WEBSTER

The real truth is that while He came to preach the gospel, His chief object in coming was that there might be a gospel to preach.

R. W. DALE

GOSSIP AND SLANDER
· ·

He who hunts for flowers will find flowers; and he who loves weeds will find weeds.

HENRY WARD BEECHER

The secret of a governable tongue is not self-control but Christ-control.

G. S.

Thy friend has a friend, and thy friend's friend has a friend; be discreet.

THE TALMUD

Remember, every time you open your mouth to talk, your mind walks out and parades up and down the words.

EDWIN H. STUART

I am more deadly than the screaming shell from the howitzer. I win without killing. I tear down homes, break hearts, and wreck lives. I travel on the wings of the wind. No innocence is strong enough to intimidate me, no purity pure enough to daunt me. I have no regard for truth, no respect for justice, no mercy for the defenseless. My victims are as numerous as the sands of the sea, and often as innocent. I never forget and seldom forgive. My name is Gossip.

MORGAN BLAKE, ATLANTA JOURNAL

So live that you wouldn't be ashamed to sell the family parrot to the town gossip.

WILL ROGERS

Language is the apparel in which your thoughts parade before the public. Never clothe them in vulgar or shoddy attire.

GEORGE CRANE

The tongue can be a beautiful angel or a hideous demon. The tongue can be as honey or vinegar. The tongue can be pure or vile. The tongue can caress or cut. The tongue can rouse men to act as well as it can subdue their emotions. A false whisper can infuriate a nation, but the power of eloquence can quell the fury of a multitude. A word of anger can wound while a word of kindness can win. Words of hate can kill and words of love can kiss. God says: "Death and life are in the power of the tongue" (Proverbs 18:21).

G. S.

Girl like her mother: Clip off the old soundtrack.

G. S.

Three boys were playing when one noticed a large gossipy man coming down the sidewalk. "Clear the roadway," said one. "Here comes the sound truck."

G. S.

There's only one thing as difficult as unscrambling an egg, and that's unspreading a rumor.

G. S.

I would rather play with forked lightning, or take in my hand living wires with their fiery current, than speak a reckless word against any servant of Christ, or idly repeat the slanderous darts which thousands of Christians are hurling on others, to the hurt of their own souls and bodies.

A. B. SIMPSON

GRACE

"The grace of God," says Luther, "is like a flying summer shower." It has fallen upon more than one land, and passed on. Judea had it, and lies barren and dry. These Asiatic coasts had it, and flung it away.

ALEXANDER MACLAREN

Grace is but glory begun, and glory is but grace perfected.

JONATHAN EDWARDS

I remember a rough parable of Luther's, grafted on an older legend, which runs somewhat in this fashion:—A man's heart is like a foul stable. Wheelbarrows and shovels are of little use, except to remove some of the surface filth, and to litter all the passages in the process. What is to be done with it? "Turn the Elbe into it," says he. The flood will sweep away all the pollution. Not my own efforts, but the influx of that pardoning, cleansing grace which is in Christ will wash away the accumulations of years, and the ingrained evil which has stained every part of my being.

ALEXANDER MACLAREN

There, but for the grace of God, goes John Bradford.

JOHN BRADFORD

Grace means the free, unmerited, unexpected love of God, and all the benefits, delights, and comforts which flow from it. It means that while we were sinners and enemies we have been treated as sons and heirs.

R. P. C. HANSON

Salvation is from our side a choice, from the divine side it is a seizing upon, an apprehending, a conquest by the Most High God. Our "accepting" and "willing" are reactions rather than actions. The right of determination must always remain with God.

A. W. TOZER

[Grace is] free sovereign favor to the ill-deserving.

BENJAMIN B. WARFIELD

The law tells me how crooked I am. Grace comes along and straightens me out.

D. L. MOODY

GROWTH

· ·

The unexamined life is not worth living.

SOCRATES

The strongest principle of growth lies in human choice.

GEORGE ELIOT

> *How does the soul grow? Not all in a minute!*
> *Now it may lose ground, and now it may win it;*
> *Now it resolves, and again the will faileth;*
> *Now it rejoiceth, and now it bewaileth;*
> *Now its hopes fructify, then they are blighted;*
> *Now it walks sullenly, now gropes benighted;*
> *Fed by discouragements, taught by disaster;*
> *So it goes forward, now slower, now faster,*
> *Till all the pain is past, and failure made whole,*
> *It is full grown, and the Lord rules the soul.*
>
> SUSAN COOLIDGE

The story is told of a young sixteenth-century artist who worked hard and long on a statue of an angel. The famous Michelangelo was invited to view the finished masterpiece. As Michelangelo studied it, he commented, "It lacks only one thing . . . and that is life. *If it had* life, *it would be as perfect as God could make it."*

God's life *is the starting place and the first requisite for growth.*

G. S.

Robert Browning said, "Man was made to grow, not stop." The apostles Peter and Paul believed the same thing. Peter challenged all Christians to "grow in the grace and knowledge of our Lord and Savior Jesus Christ" (2 Peter 3:18 NKJV).

G. S.

Dead things cannot grow. Before there can be spiritual growth, there must be spiritual life. When a child is born, his first cry indicates life. If there is life, a world of possibilities beckons to this new baby. If there is no life, there is no hope. A fence post placed in the ground will not grow, but a little seed will grow spontaneously. Drop a stone into the richest soil and it will be exactly the same size years later. Place a seed into the ground, and it will spring up and produce a stalk and flowers. The difference is plain: one has life while the other does not.

G. S.

Building yourselves up on your most holy faith.

JUDE 20 NKJV

The harvest of old age is the memory and rich store of blessings laid up earlier in life.

CICERO

If God can make of an ugly seed,
With a bit of earth and air
And dew and rain, sunshine and shade,
A flower so wondrous and fair,
What can He make of a soul like you,
With the Bible and faith and prayer,
And the Holy Spirit, if you do His will
And trust in His love and care.

AUTHOR UNKNOWN

GUIDANCE
. . . .

Trust in the Lord with all thine heart; and lean not unto thine own understanding. In all thy ways acknowledge him, and he shall direct thy paths.

PROVERBS 3:5-6

Lead, kindly Light, amid the encircling gloom
Lead thou me on;
The night is dark, and I am far from home;
Lead thou me on.

JOHN HENRY NEWMAN

You can't drive straight on a twisting lane.

RUSSIAN PROVERB

Men give advice; God gives guidance.

LEONARD RAVENHILL

Teach me thy way, O Lord, and lead me in a plain path.

PSALM 27:11

It is difficult to steer a parked car, so get moving.

HENRIETTA MEARS

Day by day I turned to my Bible. Almost every day a verse seemed to speak to me and I began to write that verse against one of the arguments. At the end of a year, every argument in favor of staying in business had been wiped out. It took over a year, but I was not in a hurry. I was willing to wait; I wanted it to be in God's time. Too much was at stake to dash into the thing. I wanted to intelligently find the will of God. And I found it as I sought the Lord through my daily reading and meditation. I committed it all to the Lord and step by step, the way opened.

ALAN REDPATH

Abide with me, fast falls the eventide;
The darkness deepens; Lord, with me abide!
When other helpers fail, and comforts flee,
Help of the helpless, O abide with me.

Swift to its close ebbs out life's little day;
Earth's joys grow dim; its glories pass away;
Change and decay in all around I see;
O thou who changest not, abide with me.

I need Thy presence every passing hour;
What but Thy grace can foil the tempter's power?
Who like Thyself my guide and stay can be?
Through cloud and sunshine, O abide with me!

I fear no foe, with Thee at hand to bless;
Ills have no weight, and tears no bitterness.
Where is death's sting? Where, grave, thy victory?
I triumph still, if Thou abide with me.

Hold Thou Thy word before my closing eyes;
Shine through the gloom, and point me to the skies;
Heaven's morning breaks, and earth's vain shadows flee—
In life, in death, O Lord, abide with me.

HENRY FRANCIS LYTE

As you walk through the valley of the unknown, you will find the
footprints of Jesus both in front of you and beside you.

CHARLES STANLEY

Guide me, O thou great Redeemer
Pilgrim through this barren land;
I am weak, but thou art mighty,
Hold me with thy powerful hand;
Bread of heaven,
Feed me till I want no more.

WILLIAM WILLIAMS

Often guidance in the will of God will come to us in the normal cir-cumstances of life, through open and closed doors. But be careful not to give this area more consideration than it deserves. Satan can also open and shut doors of opportunity. Gather all the facts, and prayer-fully seek the mind of God.

G. S.

HAPPINESS (SEE CHEERFULNESS)

Happiness is a perfume you cannot pour on others without getting a few drops on yourself.

ANONYMOUS

I can say that I never knew what joy was like until I gave up pursuing happiness, or cared to live until I chose to die. For these two discoveries I am beholden to Jesus.

MALCOLM MUGGERIDGE

God cannot give us a happiness and peace apart from Himself, because it is not there. There is no such thing.

C. S. LEWIS, *MERE CHRISTIANITY*

Holiness, not happiness, is the chief end of man.

OSWALD CHAMBERS

No man should desire to be happy who is not at the same time holy. He should spend his efforts in seeking to know and do the will of God, leaving to Christ the matter of how happy he should be.

A. W. TOZER

HEART

The eyes see what the heart loves. If the heart loves God and is single in this devotion, then the eyes will see God whether others see Him or not.

WARREN WIERSBE, *LIVE LIKE A KING*

In making our decisions, we must use the brains that God has given us. But we must also use our hearts which He also gave us.
                                                                FULTON OURSLER

There never was any heart truly great and generous, that was not also tender and compassionate.
                                                                ROBERT FROST

The widest thing in the universe is not space; it is the potential capacity of the human heart. Being made in the image of God, it is capable of almost unlimited extension in all directions.
                                                                A. W. TOZER

HEAVEN

> *There is a land of pure delight,*
> *Where saints immortal reign;*
> *Infinite day excludes the night,*
> *And pleasures banish pain.*
>   ISAAC WATTS

We talk about heaven being so far away. It is within speaking distance to those who belong there. . . . Heaven is a prepared place for a prepared people.

                                                                D. L. MOODY

I would rather go to heaven alone than go to hell in company.
                                                                R. A. TORREY

Christ's grave was the birthplace of an indestructible belief that death is vanquished and there is life eternal.
                                                                ADOLPH HARNACK

Those are dead even for this life who hope for no other.
                                                                JOHANN WOLFGANG VON GOETHE

What is heaven going to be like? Just as there is a mystery to hell, so there is a mystery to heaven. Yet, I believe the Bible teaches that heaven is a literal place. Is it one of the stars? I don't know. I can't even speculate. The Bible doesn't inform us. I believe that out there in space where there are one thousand million galaxies, each a hundred thousand light years or more in diameter, God can find some place to put us in heaven. I'm not worried about where it is. I know it is going to be where Jesus is. Christians don't have to go around discouraged and despondent with their shoulders bent. Think of it—the joy, the peace, the sense of forgiveness that He gives you, and then heaven too.

BILLY GRAHAM

I had a million questions to ask God: but when I met Him, they all fled my mind; and it didn't seem to matter.

CHRISTOPHER MORLEY

In heaven after "ages of ages" of growing glory, we shall have to say, as each new wave of the shoreless, sunlit sea bears us onward, "It doth not yet appear what we shall be."

ALEXANDER MACLAREN

If you read history you will find that the Christians who did most for the present world were precisely those who thought most of the next. It is since Christians have largely ceased to think of the other world that they have become so ineffective in this.

C. S. LEWIS, *MERE CHRISTIANITY*

Aim at heaven and you will get earth thrown in. Aim at earth and you will get neither.

C. S. LEWIS, *LIVING QUOTATIONS*

Has this world been so kind to you that you should leave with regret? There are better things ahead than any we leave behind.

C. S. LEWIS, *LIVING QUOTATIONS*

I believe there is a heaven. One day, when I was a little boy in west-
ern North Carolina, I carved an inscription on one of the bricks of the
old-fashioned chimney of my home. It read, "Heaven I hope to win."
I had been told at home and in the little country church and at
Sunday school about a beautiful city. They had read Pilgrim's
Progress *to me, and I had made up my mind to head heavenward.*

Not long ago I visited that old spot where the plain little house
and the old chimney still stand. I searched for that inscription on the
worn old brick, and to my delight I found it. Carved over half a cen-
tury ago, most of it had been erased by the rains and the snows and
the steady erosion of heat and cold. But I could still make out clearly
two words—heaven and hope.

I, too, have stood the gales, the summers, the winters of all those
years, but the ravages of life's seasons have not removed the hope of
heaven from my heart. It is embedded there more securely than my
boyish fingers ever carved it into that old brick. The infidels have
blown their blast, and Bible critics even in pulpits and seminary
chairs have tried to dim that hope. But it burns brighter than ever
before.

When I wrote that inscription, most of my loved ones were living
here. Now most of them have taken up their residence over there. But
best of all, I have my Savior's word about it: "If it were not so, I
would have told you" (John 14:2). That settles it. If it weren't true,
He would let us know. And on that rock I stand.

VANCE HAVNER

Paul had a rough time of it. He never stayed in a Riviera cottage
writing his memoirs. He sat in a dingy Roman prison waiting to have
his head chopped. But he had fought a good fight, finished his course,
and kept the faith. He was waiting for a crown, anxious to depart
and be with Christ, which is far, far better.

I find the last miles to be the best. When it's twilight on the trail,
remember that the other side of the sunset is sunrise. The other side of
evening is morning; beyond death is life. One hour in heaven, and
we shall be ashamed that we ever grumbled.

VANCE HAVNER

230

When I started out as a boy preaching, Father went along. Then when I got old enough to go by myself, he'd meet me at the little rail-road station in Newton, North Carolina. I can see him standing there by that old Ford roadster, in that old blue serge suit that hadn't been pressed since the day he bought it.

When I'd go up to him, the first thing he'd ask me would be, "How did you get along?

It's been a long time, and one of these days when my train rounds into Grand Central Station in glory, I think he'll be there—not in the old blue serge suit, but in robes of glory. I wouldn't be sur-prised if the first thing he'd say would be, "How did you get along?"

I think I'll say, "Pretty well, and I owe a lot to you for it." Then I think I'd say, "You remember back in the country when I was a little boy, no matter where I was in the afternoon I was supposed to be back by sundown. It's been a long trip, Dad, but here I am by the grace of God, home before dark."

VANCE HAVNER

HELL
· ·

Hell is the highest reward that the devil can offer you for being a ser-vant of his.

BILLY SUNDAY

It does not require a decision to go to hell.

ANONYMOUS

When I pastored a country church, a farmer didn't like the sermons I preached on hell. He said, "Preach about the meek and lowly Jesus."
I said, "That's where I got my information about hell."

VANCE HAVNER

Hell is where everyone is doing his own thing. Paradise is where everyone is doing God's thing.

THOMAS HOWARD

On one occasion Colonel Robert G. Ingersoll, the agnostic lecturer of the last century, was announced to give an address on hell. He declared he would prove conclusively that hell was a wild dream of some scheming theologians who invented it to terrify credulous people. As he was launching into his subject, a half-drunken man arose in the audience and exclaimed, "Make it strong, Bob. There's a lot of us poor fellows depending on you. If you are wrong, we are all lost. So be sure you can prove it clear and plain."

No amount of reasoning can nullify God's sure Word. He has spoken as plainly of a hell for the finally impenitent as of a heaven for those who are saved.

G. S.

The safest road to Hell is the gradual one—the gentle slope, soft underfoot, without sudden turnings, without milestones, without signposts.

C. S. LEWIS, *THE SCREWTAPE LETTERS*

The vague and tenuous hope that God is too kind to punish the ungodly has become a deadly opiate for the consciences of millions.

A. W. TOZER

One of the horrors of hell is the undying memory of a misspent life— "Son, remember" (Luke 16:25).

ANONYMOUS

HERITAGE
· ·

Wisdom is to be gained only as we stand upon the shoulders of those who have gone before.

LEARNED HAND

What from your fathers' heritage is lent,
Earn it anew to really possess it.

JOHANN WOLFGANG VON GOETHE

The young, whether they know it or not, live on borrowed property.
RICHARD W. LIVINGSTONE

I desire no future that will break the ties of the past.
GEORGE ELIOT

HISTORY
· ·

All history is incomprehensible without Christ.
JOSEPH ERNEST RENAU

How shall we labour with any effect to build up the Church, if we have no thorough knowledge of her history, or fail to apprehend it from the proper point of observation? History is, and must ever continue to be, next to God's Word, the richest foundation of wisdom, and sweet guide to all successful practical activity.
PHILIP SCHAFF

History is a story written by the finger of God.
C. S. LEWIS

In Guatemala and southern Mexico one can observe the Indians who are without doubt the lineal descendants of those who created the Mayan civilization. Today they are a humble people, not asking much of themselves or of the world, and not getting much. A light went out.
JOHN W. GARDNER

Rome remained great as long as she had enemies who forced her to unity, vision, and heroism. When she had overcome them all, she flourished for a moment and then began to die.
WILL DURANT, *CAESAR AND CHRIST*

Those who disregard the past are bound to repeat it.
GEORGE SANTAYANA

Consciousness of the past alone can make us understand the present.
HERBERT LUETHY

History is a bucket of ashes.

CARL SANDBURG

History is indeed little more than the register of the crimes, follies, and misfortunes of mankind.
EDWARD GIBBON

Jesus Christ is everywhere; He is behind everything we see if only we have eyes to see Him; and He is the Lord of history if only we penetrate deep enough beneath the surface.
CHARLES HABIB MALIK

. . . a page of history is worth a volume of logic.
OLIVER WENDELL HOLMES, JR.

HOBBIES AND LEISURE
· ·

It is a sad thing when a man has only a vocation, with no avocation whatsoever. An avocation can very well save the situation if we are condemned to the monotonous work which may be the by-product of some large productive process. Then our sense of creativity should be derived from our avocation or hobby. If a man can have a hobby, he can retain vigor and vitality.
HAROLD OCKENGA

Every now and then go away, have a little relaxation. For when you come back to your work, your judgment will be surer, since to remain constantly at work, you lose power of judgment. Go some distance away because then the work appears smaller, and more of it can be taken in at a glance, and a lack of harmony or proportion is more readily seen.
LEONARDO DA VINCI

No man is really happy or safe without a hobby, and it makes precious little difference what the outside interest may be—botany, beetles or butterflies, roses, tulips or irises; fishing, mountaineering or antiquities—anything will do so long as he straddles a hobby and rides it hard.

SIR WILLIAM OSLER

One ought, every day at least, to hear a little song, read a good poem, see a fine picture, and, if it were possible, to speak a few reasonable words.

JOHANN WOLFGANG VON GOETHE

HOLINESS

The greatest contribution anyone can make is the example of a holy life.

UNKNOWN

There's a price to pay to be a holy man of God. You have to buck the current because the tide's running the other way.

VANCE HAVNER

The true Christian ideal is not to be happy but to be holy.

A. W. TOZER, *THE DIVINE CONQUEST*

HOLY SPIRIT

God commands us to be filled with the Spirit; and if we aren't filled, it's because we're living beneath our privileges.

D. L. MOODY

If you have been born of the Holy Spirit, you will not have to serve God . . . it will become the natural thing to do.

D. L. MOODY

How would you like to live with somebody who was everlastingly grieving your heart by his conduct?

G. CAMPBELL MORGAN

The Spirit of God was the spirit of conviction while sin worked itself out from Fall to Flood; He was a Spirit of detailed service while the people of God were being organized into a nationality; He was a Spirit of strength while the people were fighting for the land, and were casting out those who had deeply sinned; and He became a Spirit of hope when the peculiar people had passed into a condition of apostasy and wandering. He lit the horizon with the glow of approaching day.

G. CAMPBELL MORGAN,
THE SPIRIT OF GOD

It is impossible for that man to despair who remembers that his Helper is omnipotent.

JEREMY TAYLOR

When the Spirit presents Christ to our inner vision it has an exhilarating effect on the soul much as wine has on the body. The Spirit-filled man may literally dwell in a state of spiritual fervour amounting to a mild and pure inebriation. God dwells in a state of perpetual enthusiasm. He pursues His labours always in a fullness of holy zeal.

A. W. TOZER, *OF GOD AND MEN*

When we rely on organization, we get what organization can do. When we rely upon education, we get what education can do. When we rely on eloquence, we get what eloquence can do. But when we rely on the Holy Spirit, we get what God can do.

A. C. DIXON

Watch out for any ministry or person who claims to be led by the Holy Spirit but acts contrary to the Word of God. And beware of any movement or group whose focus is the Holy Spirit. The Holy Spirit points not to Himself but to Jesus Christ.

G. S.

The doctrine of the Spirit as it relates to the believer has over the last half-century been shrouded in a mist such as lies upon a mountain in stormy weather. A world of confusion has surrounded this truth. This confusion has not come by accident. An enemy has done this. Satan knows that Spiritless evangelicalism is as deadly as Modernism or heresy, and he has done everything in his power to prevent us from enjoying our true Christian heritage.

A. W. TOZER

There must be an emptying before there can be a filling. Your life may be powerless because you have never given complete control to God's Spirit.

G. S.

It is curious to remark, that wherever the Holy Ghost is spoken of in the Bible, He is spoken of in terms of gentleness and love. We often read of "the wrath of God" the Father, as Romans 1:18; and we read of the wrath of God the Son, as Psalms 2:12, but we nowhere read of the wrath of God the Holy Ghost.

ROBERT M. MCCHEYNE

Notice three important facts about Ephesians 5:18. First, it is in the imperative mood. It is not a suggestion or an appeal, but a command. Anything less than the fullness of the Spirit is disobedience to the Word of God.

Second, it is a present tense verb. We are to be filled with the Holy Spirit now. And it is a continuous action verb. It could be translated, "Be being filled with the Spirit." We must be filled daily, constantly, moment by moment. Yesterday's blessings are not sufficient for today or tomorrow.

Third, it is a passive verb. That means that being filled with the Spirit is not something we do, but something that is done for us. We must be yielded. We must be willing. We must be believing. But God does the filling. We simply receive it by faith.

G. S.

Imagine, if you will, a brand-new factory filled with the finest modern equipment—everything that is needed to manufacture quality products.

Then suppose a visitor enters the factory and comments on the beauty of the machines but wonders why the machines are not running. No one is sure, he is told. "Why not oil the machines?" the man suggests. They do. But still nothing happens.

A little later another visitor comes in and comments on the splendid layout of the facilities. But there is no action. "I think you need some drapes and a few pictures on the wall," he says. So these are added. The place looks better, but still none of the equipment moves.

Other suggestions follow one by one—stained glass windows, an organ, even a steeple, but nothing works. The machinery still remains idle.

Finally, someone asks, "Did anyone turn on the power?"

Turn on the power? Of course, that's it! Sure enough, when the master control panels are switched on, the machines begin to roll. Soon the materials are fashioned and processed and the factory begins to produce.

"How simple," you say. You are absolutely right. But what the power was to the factory, the Holy Spirit is in the life of each believer. Just as the factory must have power to produce, so we need the Holy Spirit and the power He gives to live successfully in the Christian life.

G. S.

I believe firmly that the moment our hearts are emptied of pride and selfishness and ambition and everything that is contrary to God's law, the Holy Spirit will fill every corner of our hearts. But if we are full of pride and conceit and ambition and the world, there is no room for the Spirit of God.

D. L. MOODY

Though every believer has the Holy Spirit, the Holy Spirit does not have every believer.

A. W. TOZER

The world has yet to see what God can do with and for and through and in a man who is fully and wholly consecrated to Him.
HENRY VARLEY

We do not use the Holy Spirit; He uses us.
WARREN WIERSBE

HOME
· ·

An ideal wife is any woman who has an ideal husband.
BOOTH TARKINGTON

The little child digs his well in the seashore sand, and the great Atlantic, miles deep, miles wide, is stirred all through and through to fill it for him.
PHILLIPS BROOKS

The happiness of the domestic fireplace is the first boon of heaven.
THOMAS JEFFERSON

Home is where the heart is.
PLINY THE ELDER

Home should be a place of mutual responsibility and respect, of encouragement and cooperation and counsel, of integrity, of willingness to work, of discipline when necessary, with the tempering quality of love added to it, with a sense of belonging, and with someone to talk to.
RICHARD L. EVANS

Home that our feet may leave, but not our hearts.
ANONYMOUS

HONESTY
· ·

Ay, sir; to be honest, as the world goes, is to be one man picked out of ten thousand.

WILLIAM SHAKESPEARE, *HAMLET*

"Honesty is the best policy," but he who acts on that principle is not an honest man.

RICHARD WHATELY, *APOPHTHEGMS*

I hope I shall possess firmness and virtue enough to maintain what I consider the most enviable of all titles, the character of an honest man.

GEORGE WASHINGTON

A jug is never carried under one's coat for an honest reason.

LATIN PROVERB

The louder he talked of his honor, the faster we counted our spoons.

RALPH WALDO EMERSON

HOPE
· ·

It has been said that man can live about forty days without food, about three days without water, and about eight minutes without air—but only one second without HOPE.

ANONYMOUS

"Totally without hope one cannot live." To live without hope is to cease to live. Hell is hopelessness. It is no accident that above the entrance to Dante's hell is the inscription: "Leave behind all hope, you who enter here."

FYODOR DOSTOYEVSKY

Hope means expectancy when things are otherwise hopeless.

G. K. CHESTERTON

In Man's Search for Meaning, *Dr. Victor Frankl, an Austrian psychiatrist, observed that a prisoner did not continue to live very long after hope was lost. But even the slightest ray of hope—the rumor of better food, a whisper about an escape—helped some of the camp inmates to continue living even under systematic horror.*

G. S.

The word hope *in Scripture is a term of certainty. To say that we hope for the return of the Lord is not to say that we are uncertain about His coming. His coming for His own is certain.*

The Greek word translated "hope" in the New Testament is elpizo, *which means "to anticipate with confident expectation." Elpizo is also translated "trust" in several New Testament verses. Hope is one of the three evidences of salvation—faith, hope, and love—referred to by the apostle Paul throughout the epistles (see 1 Corinthians 13:13; Colossians 1:4-5; 1 Thessalonians 1:3).*

G. S.

The world is full of experiments for bringing deliverance to the race, but on the authority of the New Testament and in the light of nineteen centuries of history, I declare my conviction that the only hope of this world is the return of Christ to reign over the earth and to establish universal peace.

A. J. GORDON

Hope is wishing for a thing to come true; faith is believing that it will come true.

NORMAN VINCENT PEALE

He who plants a tree plants a hope.

LUCY LARCOM

There is not enough darkness in all the world to put out the light of one small candle.

ANONYMOUS

HUMANISM, SECULAR
· ·

No morality can be founded on authority even if the authority were divine.

A. J. AYER, *ESSAYS ON HUMANISM*

The New Testament is certainly not a blue-print for twentieth-century Christian behavior.

F. R. BARRY,
CHRISTIAN ETHICS AND SECULAR SOCIETY

Humanism asserts that the nature of the universe depicted by modern science makes unacceptable any supernatural or cosmic guarantees of human values.

THE HUMANIST MANIFESTO I

The cosmos is all that is or ever was or ever will be.

CARL SAGAN,
IN THE PUBLIC TELEVISION SHOW "COSMOS"

What marks our own generation? It is the fact that modern man thinks there is nobody home in the universe.

FRANCIS SCHAEFFER, *DEATH IN THE CITY*

Humanism, man beginning only from himself, had destroyed the old basis of values, and could find no way to generate with certainty any new values. In the resulting vacuum the impoverished values of personal peace and affluence had come to stand supreme.

FRANCIS SCHAEFFER,
HOW SHOULD WE THEN LIVE?

Man can will nothing unless he has first understood that he must count on no one but himself; that he is alone, abandoned on earth in the midst of his infinite responsibilities, without help, with no other aim than the one he sets himself, with no other destiny than the one he forges for himself on this earth.

JEAN-PAUL SARTRE

We have grasped the mystery of the atom and rejected the Sermon on the Mount. . . . Ours is a world of nuclear giants and ethical infants.
OMAR BRADLEY

As in 1933 (the date of The Humanist Manifesto I) humanists still believe that traditional theism, especially faith in the prayer-hearing God, assumed to love and care for persons, to hear and understand their prayers, and to be able to do something about them, is an unproved and outmoded faith. Salvationism, based on mere affirmation, still appears as harmful, diverting people with false hopes of heaven hereafter. Reasonable minds look to other means for survival.
THE HUMANIST MANIFESTO II

HUMILITY

· ·

Do you want to enter what people call "the higher life"? Then go a step lower down.
ANDREW MURRAY

The ears of barley that bear the richest grain always hang the lowest.
ANONYMOUS

They that know God will be humble, and they that know themselves, cannot be proud.
JOHN FLAVEL

The meek man is not a human mouse afflicted with a sense of his own inferiority. Rather he may be in his moral life as bold as a lion and as strong as Samson; but he has stopped being fooled about himself. He has accepted God's estimate of his own life. He knows he is as weak and helpless as God declared him to be, but paradoxically, he knows at the same time that he is in the sight of God of more importance than angels. In himself, nothing; in God, everything. That is his motto.

A. W. TOZER, *THE PURSUIT OF GOD*

Humility is as scarce as an albino robin.
A. W. TOZER

I used to think that God's gifts were on shelves one above the other, and that the taller we grew in Christian character the easier we could reach them. I now find that God's gifts are on shelves one beneath the other. It is not a question of growing taller, but of stooping down, to get His best gifts.
F. B. MEYER, *ALLIANCE WEEKLY*

The higher a man is in grace, the lower he will be in his own esteem.
CHARLES HADDON SPURGEON

"Become nothing if you would become something." In His rules of success, you must stoop to rise, go down to get up, and shrink to grow.
ANONYMOUS

I have never accepted what many people have kindly said, namely that I inspired the nation. It was the nation and the race dwelling all round the globe that had the lion heart. I had the luck to be called upon to give the roar.
WINSTON CHURCHILL

Humility is to make a right estimate of one's self.
CHARLES HADDON SPURGEON

To be poor in spirit means knowing yourself, accepting yourself, and being yourself to the glory of God.
WARREN WIERSBE, *LIVE LIKE A KING*

Life is a long lesson in humility.
JAMES M. BARRIE

I believe the first test of a truly great man is his humility.
JOHN RUSKIN

A cartoon in The Anglican Digest *pictures a rector standing outside his study door, contemplating his name plate on which his name was followed by four impressive doctor's degrees, which in turn was followed by the words in large prints: AND YOUR HUMBLE SERVANT.*

HUNGER

We cannot exist as a little island of well-being in a world where two-thirds of the people go to bed hungry every night.

ELEANOR ROOSEVELT

Hungry bellies have no ears.

FRANÇOIS RABLEAIS

They that die by famine, die by inches.

MATTHEW HENRY

Our policy is not directed against any country or doctrine, but against hunger, poverty, desperation, and chaos.

GEORGE C. MARSHALL

Is it only the mouth and belly which are injured by hunger and thirst? Men's minds are also injured by them.

MENCIUS

A hungry man is not a free man.

ADLAI E. STEVENSON

HYPOCRISY

May God deliver us from a ho-hum attitude. Young people can read their parents. They can see right through their teachers, and they turn away in disgust from a make-believe faith.

G. S.

I am afraid we modern Christians are long on talk and short on conduct. We use the language of power but our deeds are the deeds of weakness. We settle for words in religion because deeds are too costly. It is easier to pray, "Lord, help me to carry my cross daily" than to pick up the cross and carry it; but since the mere request for help to do something we do not actually intend to do has a certain degree of religious comfort, we are content with repetition of the words.

A. W. TOZER, *BORN AFTER MIDNIGHT*

Honey in his mouth, knives in his heart.

CHINESE PROVERB

HUMOR

He who laughs . . . lasts.

D. L. Moody was a man of wholesome humor, and even occasionally, practical jokes. Often he would tell stories with such gusto that he would laugh 'til he cried. He enjoyed gathering his associates about him at the close of the day, to see who could tell the best stories. When asked how he could laugh so fully, after preaching so seriously, he once answered, "If I didn't laugh, I would have a nervous breakdown, at the pace at which I live."

John Wesley occasionally reminded his hearers that "Sour godliness is the devil's religion."

Leslie B. Flynn writes, "Though people know about the prodigious labors of David Livingstone in opening up Africa for missionary endeavor, few know that in the midst of their lonely life, he and his wife often acted like jolly school kids on an excursion. Mirth saturated their lives so much that Livingstone more than once said to his wife, 'Really, my dear, we ought not to indulge in so many jokes. We are getting too old. It is not becoming. We must be more staid.'"

I have discovered that humor is like divine medicine. It cheers the mind, enlightens the message, and relieves the listener. "A merry heart doeth good like a medicine" (Proverbs 17:22).

Suffice it to say, appropriate humor is like medicine.

G. S.

The more one suffers, the more, I believe, one has a sense of the comic. It is only by the deepest suffering that one acquires the authority, in the art of the comic.

SØREN KIERKEGAARD

Pleasant words are as an honeycomb, sweet to the soul, and health to the bones.

PROVERBS 16:24

A merry heart makes a cheerful countenance . . . a merry heart has a continual feast.

PROVERBS 15:13-15 NKJV

A chuckle a day may not keep the doctor away, but it sure does make those times in life's waiting room a little more bearable.

ANNE WILSON SCHAEF

Be amusing; never tell unkind stories; above all, never tell long ones.

BENJAMIN DISRAELI

The art of medicine consists of amusing the patient, while nature cures the disease.

VOLTAIRE

Comedy is essentially a miracle. I believe I'm as important to society as a doctor; to create laughter creates magic!

KATHLEEN FREEMAN

Humor breaks down walls.

GOLDIE HAWN

Give us, Lord,
A bit of sun,
A bit of work,
And a bit of fun.

ENGLISH PRAYER

God writes a lot of comedy . . . the trouble is, He's stuck with so many bad actors who don't know how to play funny.

GARRISON KEILLOR

Everyone only goes around the track once in life, and if you don't enjoy that trip, it's pretty pathetic.

GARY ROGERS

What is funny about us is precisely that we take ourselves too seriously.

REINHOLD NIEBUHR

One of the best things people can have up their sleeves, is a funny bone.

RICHARD L. WEAVER II

Once you have them by the funny bone, their hearts and minds will follow.

ROBERT WIEDER

Care to our coffin adds a nail, no doubt,
And every grin so merry draws one out.
JOHN WOLCOT

It is often just as sacred to laugh as it is to pray.
CHARLES SWINDOLL

Happiness is a warm puppy.

CHARLES SCHULZ

Happiness is like a cat. If you try to coax it or call it, it will avoid you. It will never come. But if you pay no attention to it and go about your business, you'll find it rubbing against your legs and jumping into your lap.

WILLIAM BENNETT

The Constitution only guarantees the American people the right to pursue happiness. You have to catch it yourself.
BENJAMIN FRANKLIN

The happiness of life is made up of minute fractions—the little, soon-forgotten charities of a kiss or smile, a kind look or heartfelt compliment.

SAMUEL TAYLOR COLERIDGE

Happiness is your dentist telling you it won't hurt, and then having him catch his hand in the drill.

JOHNNY CARSON

It is not the level of prosperity that makes for happiness but the kinship of heart to heart and the way we look at the world. Both attitudes are within our power, so that a man is happy so long as he chooses to be happy, and no one can stop him.

ALEKSANDR SOLZHENITSYN

Happiness is a butterfly, which, when pursued, is always just beyond your grasp, but which, if you will sit down quietly, may alight upon you.

NATHANIEL HAWTHORNE

Laugh, and the world laughs with you;
Weep, and you weep alone;
For the sad old earth must borrow its mirth,
It has trouble enough of its own.
ELLA WHEELER WILCOX

One thing I know: the only ones among you, who will be really happy, are those who will have sought and found how to serve.
ALBERT SCHWEITZER

One of the things I keep learning, is that the secret of being happy is doing things for other people.

DICK GREGORY

A sense of humor can help you overlook the unattractive, tolerate the unpleasant, cope with the unexpected, and smile through the unbearable.

MOSHE WALDOKS

You don't stop laughing because you grow old, you grow old because you stop laughing.
  I see humor as food. I don't think that the only time people should eat food is when they're ill. An adequate share of humor and laughter represent an essential part of the diet of the healthy person.
NORMAN COUSINS

Humor is a healthy way of feeling "distance" between one's self and the problem, a way of standing off and looking at one's problems with perspective.

ROLLO MAY

Humor is not a trick, not jokes. Humor is a presence in the world— like grace—and shines on everybody.

GARRISON KEILLOR

If humor is something like a sword, maybe it has to be strapped on, but nobody should go around without it in any period of time. . . . Since one of its chief constituents is taste, it should be used sparingly sometimes and left in its sheath at other times, but it should always be handy.

JAMES THURBER

A sense of humor is part of the art of leadership, of getting along with people, of getting things done.

DWIGHT D. EISENHOWER

Humor is my sword and my shield. It protects me. You can open a door with humor and drive a truck right through.

ALAN SIMPSON

Humor is a great thing, the saving thing, after all. The minute it crops up, all our hardnesses yield, all our irritations and resentments flit away, and a sunny spirit takes their place.

MARK TWAIN

Like a welcome summer rain, humor may suddenly cleanse and cool the earth, the air and you.

LANGSTON HUGHES

A person without a sense of humor, is like a wagon without springs—jolted by every pebble in the road.

HENRY WARD BEECHER

Good humor is the health of the soul, sadness its poison.
I. V. STANISLAUS

To every thing there is a season, and a time to every purpose under the heaven: A time to be born, and a time to die; . . . . A time to weep, and a time to laugh.
ECCLESIASTES 3:1-2, 4

I found people looked better when they laughed.
MORT SAHL

Laugh and the world laughs with you. Cry and you get all wet.
ANONYMOUS

Laugh and the world laughs with you. Snore and you sleep alone.
ANTHONY BURGESS

If I get big laughs, I'm a comedian. If I get little laughs, I'm a humorist. If I get no laughs, I'm a singer.
GEORGE BURNS

The person who can bring the spirit of laughter into a room is indeed blessed.
BENNETT CERF

Man is distinguished from all other creatures by the faculty of laughter.
JOSEPH ADDISON

Laughter is like changing a baby's diaper—it doesn't permanently solve any problems, but it makes things more acceptable for a while.
ANONYMOUS

Gentlemen, why don't you laugh? With the fearful strain that is upon me night and day, if I did not laugh, I should die. You need this medicine as much as I do.
ABRAHAM LINCOLN

His laughter tinkled among the teacups.
T. S. ELIOT

Seven days without laughter makes one weak.
JOEL GOODMAN

If you laugh a lot, when you get older your wrinkles will be in the right places.
ANDREW MASON

Ten minutes of genuine belly laughter had an anesthetic effect and would give me at least two hours of pain-free sleep.
NORMAN COUSINS

Laughter is a form of internal jogging.
NORMAN COUSINS

It is bad to suppress laughter. It goes back down and spreads your hips.
FRED ALLEN

A person who belly-laughs, doesn't bellyache.
SUSAN THURMAN

Laughter is the shortest distance between two people.
VICTOR BORGE

To get 'em listening, get 'em laughing.
ALLEN KLEIN

'Tis easy enough to be pleasant,
When life flows along like a song;
But the man worth while is the one who will smile
When everything goes dead wrong.
ELLA WHEELER WILCOX

If I were given the opportunity to present a gift to the next generation, it would be the ability for each individual to learn to laugh at himself.

CHARLES SCHULZ

I have seen what a laugh can do. It can transform almost unbearable tears into something bearable, even hopeful.

BOB HOPE

It is pleasing to God whenever thou rejoicest or laughest from the bottom of thy heart.

MARTIN LUTHER

A little levity will save many a good heavy thing from sinking.

SAMUEL BUTLER

He who is of a merry heart has a continual feast.

PROVERBS 15:15 NKJV

Barking dogs may occasionally bite, but laughing men hardly ever shoot!

KONRAD LORENZ

To laugh often and much; to win respect of intelligent people and the affection of children . . . to leave the world a better place . . . to know even one life has breathed easier because you have lived. This is to have succeeded.

RALPH WALDO EMERSON

Mirth is like a flash of lightning that breaks through a gloom of clouds and glitters for a moment.

JOSEPH ADDISON

God Almighty first planted a garden; and, indeed, it is the purest of human pleasures.

FRANCIS BACON

Mirth is God's medicine. Everybody ought to bathe in it. Grim care, moroseness, anxiety—all this rust of life—ought to be scoured off by the oil of mirth.

HENRY WARD BEECHER

The true object of all human life is play. Earth is a task garden; heaven is a playground.

G. K. CHESTERTON

One of the many pleasures of old age, is giving things up.

MALCOLM MUGGERIDGE

A laugh is a smile that bursts.

MARY H. WALDRIP

The world always looks brighter from behind a smile.

ANONYMOUS

*Better by far you should forget and smile
Than that you should remember and be sad.*

CHRISTINA ROSSETTI

A smile costs nothing but gives much. It enriches those who receive without making poorer those who give. It takes but a moment, but the memory of it sometimes lasts forever. None is so rich or mighty that he can get along without it and none is so poor that he cannot be made rich by it. A smile creates happiness in the home, fosters good will in business and is the countersign of friendship. It brings rest to the weary, cheer to the discouraged, sunshine to the sad and is nature's best antidote for trouble. Yet it cannot be bought, begged, borrowed, or stolen, for it is something that is of no value to anyone until it is given away. Some people are too tired to give you a smile. Give them one of yours, as none needs a smile so much as he who has no more to give.

ANONYMOUS

No matter how grouchy you're feeling,
You'll find the smile more or less healing.
It grows in a wreath
All around the front teeth—
Thus preserving the face from congealing.
ANTHONY EUWER

A smile is the universal welcome.
MAX EASTMAN

A smile is an inexpensive way to improve your looks.
CHARLES GORDY

You're never fully dressed without a smile.
MARTIN CHARNIN

It takes seventeen muscles to smile and forty-three muscles to frown.
ANONYMOUS

The fruit of love is service. The fruit of service is peace. And peace
begins with a smile.
MOTHER TERESA

A smile is a light on your face to let someone know you are at home.
ANONYMOUS

There are no language barriers when you are smiling.
ALLEN KLEIN

When people are smiling they are most receptive to almost anything
you want to teach them.
ALLEN FUNT

Wit is a sword; it is meant to make people feel the point as well as see
it.

G. K. CHESTERTON

All wit rests on a cheerful awareness of life's incongruities.
GEORGE WILL

You can turn painful situations around through laughter. If you can find humor in anything—even poverty—you can survive it.
BILL COSBY

There is a thin line that separates laughter and pain, comedy and tragedy, humor and hurt. And how do you know laughter if there is no pain to compare it with?
ERMA BOMBECK

A man hath no better thing under the sun, than to eat, and to drink, and to be merry.
ECCLESIASTES 8:15

In the beginning God made a man and a woman and set them on earth. Then the man and woman looked at each other and burst out laughing.
AFRICAN MYTH

We act as though comfort and luxury were the chief requirements of life, when all that we need to make us really happy is something to be enthusiastic about.
CHARLES KINGSLEY

All nature wears one universal grin.
HENRY FIELDING

A person will be called to account on Judgment Day for every permissible thing he might have enjoyed but did not.
TALMUD

Before I got married I had six theories about bringing up children. Now I have six children—and no theories.
LORD ROCHESTER

There are two things to aim at in life: first, to get what you want; and, after that, to enjoy it. Only the wisest of mankind achieve the second.

LOGAN PEARSALL SMITH

Comedy is simply a funny way of being serious.
PETER USTINOV

The only way to get a serious message across is through comedy.
WOODY HARRELSON

Will the party who picked up the black cocker spaniel puppy Saturday on Wendell Road either return him or come back and get the three-year-old boy he belongs to?

ANDERSON (IND.) DAILY BULLETIN

Hermann Adler, a British rabbi, was sitting beside Cardinal Herbert Vaughan at an official luncheon. "Now, Dr. Adler," said the cardinal mischievously, "when may I have the pleasure of helping you to some ham?" "At Your Eminence's wedding," was the reply.

When the main portion of a banquet was finished, the presiding person whispered to the first speaker, "Shall we let the people enjoy themselves a little longer, or would you like to deliver the speech now?"

While on the subway, I got up and gave my seat to a lady who was holding a strap. She was surprised and said to me, "Why did you do that?" Seeing that she was incapable of understanding a spiritual reason, I said to her, "Ma'm, I tell you, ever since I was a little boy, I have had an infinite respect for a woman with a strap in her hand."

After the Fall in the Garden of Eden, Adam was walking with his two boys, Cain and Abel. They passed by the wrecked ruins of the once beautiful Garden of Paradise, and Adam pulled the two boys to him and looked in and said, "Boys, that's where your mother ate us out of house and home."

If you copy anything out of one book, it is plagiarism. If you copy it out of two books, it is research. If you copy it out of six books, you are a professor!

In response to an audience's prolonged applause, the speaker responded, "Applause before a speaker begins his talk is an act of faith. Applause during the speech is an act of hope. Applause after he has concluded is an act of charity."

An eternally feminine problem is always: "What will I wear?" It probably began the day after the initial rebellion, when Eve looked up at the leaves of the fig tree and said: "I wonder which one I will wear today?"

A little girl was always lying. She was given a St. Bernard dog, and this little girl went out and told all the neighbors that she had been given a lion. The mother called her and said, "I told you not to lie. You go upstairs and tell God you are sorry. Promise God you will not lie again."

She went upstairs and said her prayers and then came down. Her mother said, "Did you tell God you are sorry?"

The little girl said, "Yes, I did. And God said that sometimes He finds it hard to tell my dog from a lion, too."

Jack Benny was invited to visit the White House. A guard stopped him and asked what he had in the violin case he was carrying. "A machine gun," said Benny solemnly. With the same solemnity, the guard said, "Oh, okay enter. I was afraid for a moment that it was your violin."

JACK BENNY

One of the major embarrassments to which lecturers are submitted is the audience's looking at their watches. I once asked John Erskine if he found the ordeal particularly trying.

"No," he replied, "not until they start shaking them!"

FRANK CROWNINSHIELD, IN *VOGUE*

The toastmaster introduced the speaker with great fervor, stressing her years of faithful service to the club and eulogizing her ability and charm. Somewhat overwhelmed, the speaker faded into the audience. "After such an introduction," she said disarmingly, "I can hardly wait to hear what I'm going to say."

ADNELLE H. HESKETT

After-dinner speaker's remark: "Now before I start I want to say something."

Meek little man in a florist shop: "I'd like something in the nature of a peace feeler for my wife."

ANGELO, IN *ESQUIRE*

On a lecture tour, Louis Untermeyer told a Texas audience all his best stories. After the lecture he was presented with his check, which he realized had been rather a burden on the committee. With a wave of his hand, he offered it back to be put to some good use. The committee faltered. They retired to a back room to decide what to do. The problem settled, they returned, accepted the check, and said that it would be the beginning of a special fund. "And the purpose of this fund?" asked Mr. Untermeyer. Their eyes fluttered unhappily. "It's a fund to get better lecturers next year," they said.

THE STAGE

Church notice from the Parkersburg, W. Va., News: "'Change Your Wife Through Prayer' will be the sermon subject Sunday."

Letter to the editor of a correspondence column: "I am only 19 and I stayed out till two the other night. My mother objects. Did I do wrong?"

The answer: "Try to remember."

CECIL HUNT, *LAUGHING GAS* (METHUEN)

A hearse in Norwich, Conn., has this gentle reminder as a license plate number: U-2.

Keep your temper. Do not quarrel with an angry person, but give him a soft answer. It is commanded by the Holy Writ and, furthermore, it makes him madder than anything else you could say.
ANONYMOUS

Motorist's definition of a split second: The interval of time between the change of a stop light to green and the fellow behind you tooting his horn.

Just before Christmas a college professor read the following on an examination paper: "Only God knows the answer to this question. Merry Christmas." Across the paper the professor wrote: "God gets an A; you get an F. Happy New Year."

Upon entering a room in a Washington hotel, a woman recognized a well-known Government official pacing up and down and asked what he was doing there.

"I am going to deliver a speech," he said.

"Do you usually get very nervous before addressing a large audience?"

"Nervous?" he replied. "No, I never get nervous."

"In that case," demanded the lady, "what are you doing in the Ladies' Room?"

FLOORCRAFT

Church bulletin, Seaford, N.Y.: "Come In and Have Your Faith Lifted."

Traffic warning, New Rochelle, N.Y.: "Go slow. This is a one-hearse town."

A woman, pricing a hat, gasped when told it was $75. "Why, there isn't anything on that hat!" "You are paying for the restraint," the saleswoman replied quietly.

RAYMOND C. MAYER,
HOW TO DO PUBLICITY (HARPER)

261

A pat on the back develops character, if administered young enough, often enough, and low enough.

RUSSELL COUNTY NEWS

An insurance agent, writing a policy for a cowpuncher, asked if he had ever had any accidents.

"No," said the cowboy, then added, trying to be helpful, "a bronc kicked in a couple of my ribs and a rattlesnake bit me a couple of years ago."

"Well!" said the agent. "Don't you call those accidents?"

"No," replied the knight of the branding iron, "they done it a-purpose."

GRIT

When Calvin Coolidge was in the Massachusetts legislature, another member asked him whether the people where he came from said, "A hen lays, or a a hen lies."

"The people where I come from," Mr. Coolidge replied, "lift her up to see."

WILLIAM LYON PHELPS

One very angry skunk to another skunk: "So do you!"

HANK KETCHAM, IN LIBERTY

President Coolidge once invited some Vermont friends to dine at the White House. They were worried about their table manners, so decided to do everything Coolidge did. The meal passed smoothly until coffee was served and Coolidge poured his into a saucer. The guests followed suit. Then he added sugar and cream. The visitors did likewise. Then Coolidge leaned over and gave his to the cat.

HENRY CHARLES SUTER

A mother had been lecturing her small son, stressing that we are in this world to help others. He considered this, then asked somberly: "What are the others here for?"

GRACE PERKINS OURSLER

In Northampton, Mass., a Smith College freshman scrawled as her denominational preference: "I like to be called Betty."
TIME

On the front window of a Louisville, Ky. grocery store was written: "Boy Wanted." Below was scribbled: "I want one, too, Jeanne."
HELYNE S. PINCUS

Sir Arthur Conan Doyle once sent a telegram to each of 12 friends, all men of great virtue and of considerable position in society. The message was worded: "FLY AT ONCE; ALL IS DISCOVERED." Within 24 hours, the story runs, all 12 had left the country.
F. L. WELLMAN,
GENTLEMEN OF THE JURY

Bear, standing at the door of his cave, reminds a bird: "Remember now—call us about half past April."
ED NOFZIGER, IN PM

A professor of Greek tore his suit and took it to a tailor named Acidopolus, from Athens. Mr. Acidopolus examined the suit, and asked, "Euripides?" "Yes," said the professor. "Eumenides?"
CARLYN COFFIN, QUOTED BY BENNETT CERF,
THE SATURDAY REVIEW OF LITERATURE

Repentance was perhaps best defined by a small girl: "It's to be sorry enough to quit."
C. H. KILMER IN THE NEW ILLUSTRATOR

A Negro preacher began his sermon by saying: "Brethren and sisters, here you is comin' to pray for rain. I'd like to ask you just one question—where is yo' umbrellas?"
HARPER GARCIA SMYTH,
LET'S ADVENTURES IN PERSONALITY

I like work; it fascinates me. I can sit and look at it for hours.
JEROME K. JEROME

A young Scottish preacher lived seven miles up the river from his church. There came a Sunday when the snowdrifts made the road impassable, and he skated down the river to his church service. Hauled before the bar of his presbytery for breaking the Sabbath, his defense was that skating was the only way he could get there. "Young man," said the moderator, "there is just one question. Did ye, or did ye not, enjoy the skatin'?"

C. F. WISHART

Said a Quaker spinster who was asked why she had never married: "It takes a mighty good husband to be better than none."

IRVIN AND RUTH POLEY,
FRIENDLY ANECDOTES

A Scotsman was told by his doctor that his wife should have had her tonsils taken out when she was a little girl. He had the operation performed—and sent the bill to his father-in-law!

SCOTCH, EDITED BY GREGORY
HARTSWICK

The chain of wedlock is so heavy that it takes two to carry it—sometimes three.

ALEXANDER DUMAS

Bookstore clerk to couple: "Here's a practical book on child training written by an authority—a sitter."

CARTOON, *NEW ORLEANS TIMES-PICAYUNE*

A Londoner shared the train-carriage with an elderly Scot. At each stop the old man rushed out, ran down the platform, then rushed back, panting. The curious Londoner finally asked why. "Well," said the Scot, "I saw a specialist in London about my heart. He says I might drop dead anytime; so I'm just booking from station to station."

LEIGH MITCHELL HODGES

Conscience: The still small voice that makes you feel still smaller.

JAMES A. SANAKER

Max Schling, a New York florist, ran a whole advertisement in short-hand to the New York Times. *Many a businessman cut it out and handed it to his secretary to translate. The ad asked secretaries to think of Schling when the boss wanted flowers for his wife.*

MODERN SELLING

A young lady after a broken engagement returned all the gent's letters marked, "Fourth Class Male."

WILLIE D. HERBERT

A gentle Quaker, hearing a strange noise in his house one night, got up and discovered a burglar busily at work. So he went and got his gun, then came back and stood quietly in the doorway. "Friend," he said, "I would do thee no harm for the world, but thee standest where I am about to shoot."

THE KELLOGG MESSENGER

Little Claude's mother had reluctantly allowed her precious child to attend public school. She gave the teacher a long list of instructions. "My Claude is so sensitive," she explained. "Don't ever punish him. Just slap the boy next to him. That will frighten Claude."

PHILADELPHIA BULLETIN

Poise: The art of raising the eyebrows instead of the roof.

HOWARD W. NEWTON
IN *REDBOOK MAGAZINE*

George Bernard Shaw was poring over a secondhand bookstall of volumes much marked down, when he came across a volume containing his own plays. The book was inscribed, moreover to a friend, beneath whose name on the flyleaf G.B.S. saw, written in his own hand, "With the compliments of George Bernard Shaw." Buying the book, Mr. Shaw wrote under the inscription, "With renewed compliments. G.B.S.," and sent it back to the early recipient.

In three days guests, like fish, begin to stink.

BENJAMIN FRANKLIN

Conscience: Something that feels terrible when everything else feels swell.

Perhaps the wittiest and most graceful tribute ever spoke by a man of his wife was said by Joseph H. Choate.
Someone asked him: "Mr. Choate, if you could not be yourself, who would you rather be?"
Instantly came the reply: "Mrs. Choate's second husband."
WILLIAM I. JONES

George Bernard Shaw once remarked: "I often quote myself. It adds spice to my conversation."

From the Mt. Carmel, Ill., Republican-Register: "The fifth grade chorus sang, 'Nobody Knows the Trouble I've Been.'"

Small boy to father: "Here's my report card and one of yours I found in the attic."
HOFF, IN THE SATURDAY EVENING POST

Introducing Thomas Alva Edison at dinner, the toastmaster mentioned his many inventions, dwelling at length on the talking machine. The aged inventor then rose to his feet, smiled and said gently: "I thank the gentleman for his kind remarks but I must insist upon a correction. God invented the talking machine. I only invented the first one that can be shut off."
LOUIS SOBOL, KING FEATURES

A friend of George Bernard Shaw tells of an evening he spent with them. While G.B.S. told stories, Mrs. Shaw busied herself knitting. "What are you knitting?" asked the guest in an aside.
"Oh, nothing, nothing at all," whispered Mrs. Shaw. "It's just that I've heard these stories of his 2000 times, and if I didn't do something with my hands, I'd choke him."
LEONARD LYONS

Bud Abbott and Lou Costello were discussing an actor they knew.
"Nice guy," said Abbott, "but have you noticed how he always lets his friends pick up the dinner check?"
"Yes," said Costello. "He has a terrible impediment in his reach!"
ANDREW B. HECHT

A male customer approached the sales lady in a bookstore and asked, "Where can I find the book, Man Is the Head of the Home?" *to which she responded, "In the fiction department."*

The Diet Club will meet Thursday night at 7:30 p.m. Please use the large double door at the side entrance.

IDEALS

Sometimes a person's mind is stretched by a new idea and never does go back to its old dimensions.

OLIVER WENDELL HOLMES, SR.

Never tell a young person that something cannot be done. God may have been waiting for countless centuries for somebody ignorant enough of the impossibility to do that thing.

ANONYMOUS

The power of ideals is incalculable. We see no power in a drop of water. But let it get into a crack in the rock and be turned to ice, and it splits the rock; turned into steam, it drives the pistons of the most powerful engines. Something has happened to it which makes active and effective the power that is latent in it.

ALBERT SCHWEITZER

I know of no more encouraging fact than the unquestionable ability of man to elevate his life by a conscious endeavor.

HENRY DAVID THOREAU

Character is singularly contagious.

SAMUEL A. ELIOT

IDEAS

A fair idea put to use is better than a good idea kept on the polishing wheel.

ALEX OSBORN

False ideas are the greatest obstacles to the reception of the gospel. We may preach with all the fervor of a reformer and yet succeed only in winning a straggler here and there, if we permit the whole collective thought of the nation or of the world to be controlled by ideas which, by the resistless force of logic, prevent Christianity from being regarded as anything more than a harmless delusion. Under such circumstances, what God desires us to do is to destroy the obstacle at its root. . . . What is today a matter of academic speculation begins tomorrow to move armies and pull down empires.

J. GRESHAM MACHEN

Nothing is as powerful as an idea whose time has come.

VICTOR HUGO

Ideas rule life and in the long run shape the ages.

ANONYMOUS

There is something inevitable about an idea whose hour has struck.

JOHANN WOLFGANG VON GOETHE

IDOLATRY
· ·

The worship of the false in any form is idolatry.

WILLIAM PURCELL

You don't have to go to heathen lands today to find false gods. America is full of them. Whatever you love more than God is your idol.

D. L. MOODY

*Indeed the Idols I have loved so long
Have done my credit in the World much wrong:
Have drown'd my Glory in a shallow Cup
And sold my reputation for a Song.*

OMAR KHAYYAM, *RUBYAIYAT*,
FITZGERALD TRANSLATION

270

*... the triumph of my art is in thoroughly examining whether the
thought which the mind of the young man brings forth is a false idol
or a noble and true birth.*

PLATO

*How glad the heathens would have been,
That worship idols, wood and stone,
If they the book of God had seen.*

ISAAC WATTS

*Man is certainly stark mad; he cannot make a worm, and yet he will
be making gods by dozens.*

MICHEL DE MONTAIGNE

IMAGINATION
· ·

*The soul without imagination is what an observatory would be with-
out a telescope.*

HENRY WARD BEECHER

*When I could not sleep for cold
I had fire enough in my brain,
And builded with roofs of gold
My beautiful castles in Spain!*

JAMES RUSSELL LOWELL

The human race is governed by its imagination.

NAPOLEON BONAPARTE

Imagination is the air of the mind.

PHILIP JAMES BAILEY

IMMORTALITY

I perceived that in kinship with wisdom lies immortality.
ANONYMOUS

God created man for immortality, and made him the image of his own eternal self.
WISDOM OF SOLOMON 2:23 NEB

A few years ago when I was in Northfield, Massachusetts, to conduct evangelistic services, I visited "Roundtop" where D.L. Moody is buried. As I knelt in prayer, I recalled vividly Mr. Moody's eloquent words:

> *Someday you will ready in the papers that D.L. Moody is dead. Don't you believe a word of it. At that moment I shall have gone up higher; that is all; out of this old clay tenement, into a house that is immortal—a body that death cannot touch, that sin cannot taint; a body fashioned like unto His glorious body. I was born of the flesh in 1837. I was born of the spirit in 1856. That which is born of the flesh may die. That which is born of the spirit will live forever.*

Mr. Moody was right. And I expect to meet him one day in a glorified body that will never die.
G. S.

INCARNATION

For in Christ all the fullness of the Deity lives in bodily form.
COLOSSIANS 2:9 NIV

Jesus' coming is the final and unanswerable proof that God cares.
WILLIAM BARCLAY

The Incarnation would be equally a miracle however Jesus entered the world.
P. T. FORSYTH

He was made what we are, that He might make us what He is Himself.

SAINT IRENAEUS

Whoever thinks God is most freely revealed in the impersonal movements of the stellar galaxies must reckon yet with Jesus Christ as the incarnation of righteousness, goodness and love, and with the well-nigh irresistible impression that the eternal God is best seen in His personality and life.

CARL F. H. HENRY

INFLUENCE

Let no man imagine that he has no influence.

HENRY GEORGE

The good person increases the value of every other person whom he influences in any way.

ANONYMOUS

Young people set their watches, for right time or wrong, by the watches of their elders.

ANONYMOUS

But evil men and seducers shall wax worse and worse, deceiving, and being deceived.

2 TIMOTHY 3:13

The serene, silent beauty of a holy life is the most powerful influence in the world, next to the might of God.

BLAISE PASCAL

The length and breadth of our influence upon others depends upon the depth of our concern for others.

ANONYMOUS

You cannot antagonize and influence at the same time.
JOHN KNOX

I am a part of all that I have met.
ALFRED, LORD TENNYSON

INTELLIGENCE

He [Christ] wants a child's heart, but a grown-up's head. He wants us to be simple, single-minded, affectionate, and teachable, as good children are; but He also wants every bit of intelligence we have to be alert at its job, and in first-class fighting trim.
C. S. LEWIS, MERE CHRISTIANITY

Anyone who is honestly trying to be a Christian will soon find his intelligence being sharpened: one of the reasons why it needs no special education to be a Christian is that Christianity is an education itself. That is why an uneducated believer like Bunyan was able to write a book that has astonished the whole world.
C. S. LEWIS, MERE CHRISTIANITY

If you are thinking of becoming a Christian, I warn you, you are embarking on something which is going to take the whole of you, brains and all.
C. S. LEWIS

I do not feel obliged to believe that that same God who has endowed us with sense, reason, and intellect has intended us to forego their use.
GALILEO

I tremble for my country when I think that schools may be sending forth into government people who are too proudly "practical" to take ideas seriously.
GEORGE WILL,
STATECRAFT AS SOULCRAFT

Every powerful movement has had its philosophy which has gripped the mind, fired the imagination and captured the devotion of its adherents.

JOHN STOTT, *YOUR MIND MATTERS*

Ideas have consequences.

RICHARD WEAVER, *IDEAS HAVE CONSEQUENCES*

There is no longer a Christian mind. It is common place that the mind of modern man has been secularized. . . . But unfortunately the Christian mind has succumbed to the secular drift with a degree of weakness and nervelessness unmatched in Christian history.

HARRY BLAMIRES, *THE CHRISTIAN MIND*

JESUS

Jesus has not lost a battle yet—not one.

RICHARD ROBERTS

Follow me; I am the way, the truth, and the life.
Without the way there is no going;
Without the truth there is no knowing;
Without the life there is no living.

THOMAS À KEMPIS

Napoleon was right when he said, "I know men, and I tell you, Jesus
is more than a man. Comparison is impossible between Him and any
other human being who ever lived, because He was the Son of God."
Emerson was right when he replied to those who asked him why he
did not include Jesus among his Representative Men, "Jesus was not
just a man." Arnold Toynbee was right when he said, "As we stand
and gaze with our eyes fixed upon the farther shore, a simple figure
rises from the flood and straightaway fills the whole horizon of histo-
ry. There is the Savior."

BILLY GRAHAM

The hand that holds the seven stars is as loving as the hand that was
laid in blessing upon the little children; the face that is as the sun
shining in its strength beams with as much love as when it drew
publicans and harlots to His feet. The breast that is girt with the gold-
en girdle is the same breast upon which John leaned his happy head.

ALEXANDER MACLAREN

Jesus clothes the Beatitudes with His own life.

CARL F. H. HENRY

Jesus is all we have; He is all we need and all we want. We are ship-wrecked on God and stranded on omnipotence!

VANCE HAVNER

Jesus is not one of many ways to approach God, nor is He the best of several ways; He is the only way.

A. W. TOZER, *THAT INCREDIBLE CHRISTIAN*

"I'm ready to accept Jesus as a great moral teacher, but I don't accept His claim to be God." That is the one thing we must not say. A man who was merely a man and said the sort of things Jesus said would not be a great moral teacher. He would either be a lunatic—on a level with the man who says he is a poached egg—or else he would be the Devil of Hell. You must make your choice. Either this man was, and is, the Son of God; or else a madman or something worse. You can shut Him up for a fool, you can spit at Him and kill Him as a demon, or you can fall at His feet and call Him Lord and God. But let us not come with any patronizing nonsense about His being a great human teacher. He has not left that open to us. He did not intend to.

C. S. LEWIS, *MERE CHRISTIANITY*

His zeal never degenerated into passion, nor His constancy into obstinacy, nor His benevolence into weakness, nor His tenderness into sentimentality. His unworldliness was free from indifference and unsociability, His dignity from pride and presumption, His affectability from undue familiarity, His self-denial from moroseness, His temperance from austerity. He combined child-like innocency with manly strength, absorbing devotion to God with untiring interest in the welfare of man, tender love to the sinner with uncompromising severity against sin, commanding dignity with winning humility, fearless courage with wise caution, unyielding firmness with sweet gentleness!

PHILIP SCHAFF

I have one passion only: It is He! It is He!

NIKOLAUS LUDWIG VON ZINZENDORF

To tie Jesus Christ to the very best human system is to tie a star, light years distant, to a dead horse here on earth. Neither star nor Christ will thus be bound.

JOE BAYLY

JEWS

There is a bright and exciting future for the nation of Israel. Jeremiah 31:10 says, "He that scattered Israel will gather him." God is going to continue bringing the people of Israel back to their land for the fulfillment of the promises He made to Abraham many years ago. The Jewish nation, despite the stated intentions of many of her enemies, is indestructible. This is God's promise: "I am with thee, saith the Lord, to save thee: though I make a full end of all nations whither I have scattered thee, yet will I not make a full end of thee" (Jeremiah 30:11).

No nation is more significant in the future of world politics than the nation of Israel. That is a meaningful statement in light of the fact that less than fifty years ago some believed that the Jewish people could never again hope to return to their land as a sovereign nation. Today the headlines show that what was once scoffed at as a ludicrous idea has indeed taken place. Israel has returned to the world scene and is now more important, more strategic, and more crucial to future events than ever seemed possible. The rebirth of the nation Israel has been like the key piece of a jigsaw puzzle, enabling the other pieces to fall quickly in place.

G. S.

Certainly as Israel's promises are being fulfilled before our eyes other aspects of prophecy such as the resurrection of the dead in Christ and the translation of living saints become a real and an imminent possibility.

JOHN F. WALVOORD

More than any other of the world's races and nations, the Jewish people can trace their history with accuracy. The origin of most nations is wrapped in surmise and conjecture, but Scripture clearly records the beginning of the Hebrews. In Genesis 12, the Lord said to Abraham, "Get thee out of thy country, and from thy kindred, and from thy father's house, unto a land that I will shew thee: and I will make of thee a great nation, and I will bless thee, and make thy name great; and thou shalt be a blessing: and I will bless them that bless thee, and curse him that curseth thee: and in thee shall all families of the earth be blessed" (vv. 1–3 emphasis added).

G. S.

"Can you give me one single irrefutable proof of God?"
"Yes, your majesty, the Jews."

MARQUIS D'ARGENS
TO FREDERICK THE GREAT

Religious or secularized, the Jew remains a Jew—malgré lui— a voluntary or involuntary witness to the truth that is symbolized in the story of God's covenant with Abraham.

ALAN RICHARDSON, CHRISTIAN APOLOGETICS

JOY
· ·

Joys are always on the way to us. They are always traveling to us through the darkness of the night. There is never a night when they are not coming.

AMY CARMICHAEL

Joy is the gigantic secret of the Christian

G. K. CHESTERTON

There is more joy in Jesus in twenty-four hours than there is in the world in 365 days. I have tried them both.

R. A. TORREY

Joy, in Nature's wide dominion,
Mightiest cause of all is found;
And 'tis joy that moves the pinion
When the wheel of time goes round.
JOHANN VON SCHILLER

Joy is never in our power and pleasure often is.
C. S. LEWIS, *SURPRISED BY JOY*

This is the land of sin and death and tears . . . but up yonder is unceasing joy.
D. L. MOODY

There is a sweet joy which comes to us through sorrow.
CHARLES HADDON SPURGEON

Any man can again have the joy of his first meeting with God if he will go back over the same road.
ROY L. SMITH

Cheerfulness and contentment are great beautifiers and are famous preservers of youthful looks.
CHARLES DICKENS

Love, in the divine alchemy of life, transmutes all duties into privileges, all responsibilities into joys.
WILLIAM GEORGE JORDAN

Nothing great was ever achieved without enthusiasm.
RALPH WALDO EMERSON

If you have no joy, there's a leak in your Christianity somewhere.
BILLY SUNDAY

JUDGMENT
· ·

> *Heaven is above all yet; there sits a judge*
> *That no king can corrupt.*
>
> WILLIAM SHAKESPEARE, *HENRY VIII*

The time was the 19th of May 1780. The place was Hartford, Connecticut. The day has gone down in New England history as a terrible foretaste of Judgment Day. For at noon the skies turned from blue to grey and by mid-afternoon had blackened over so densely that, in that religious age, men fell on their knees and begged a final blessing before the end came. The Connecticut House of Representatives was in session. And as some of the men fell down and others clamored for an immediate adjournment, the speaker of the House, one Colonel Davenport, came to his feet. He silenced them and said these words: "The day of judgment is either approaching or it is not. If it is not, there is no cause for adjournment. If it is, I choose to be found doing my duty. I wish therefore that candles may be brought."

ALISTAIR COOKE

Though the mills of God grind slowly, yet they grind exceedingly
> *small;*
Though with patience He stands waiting, with exactness grinds He
> *all.*

FRIEDRICH VON LOGAU, TRANSLATED BY
HENRY WADSWORTH LONGFELLOW

At the day of Doom men shall be judged according to their fruits. It will not be said then, Did you believe? but, Were you doers, or talkers only?

JOHN BUNYAN

Sometimes those of us who hold that the Lord Jesus Christ is coming again are spoken of as pessimists. I think it can be truly said that we are really the only ones who have any right to be optimistic.

WILLIAM CULBERTSON

I shall tell you a great secret, my friend. Do not wait for the last judgment, it takes place every day.

ALBERT CAMUS

The final chapter of human history is solely God's decision, and even now He is everywhere active in grace or judgment. Never in all history have men spoken so much of end-time, yet been so shrouded in ignorance of God's impending doomsday.

CARL F. H. HENRY

One of the greatest paintings of all time is Michelangelo's The Last Judgment. *The action of the painting centers on Christ as He raises His arm in a gesture of damnation. Though some elements of the painting appear unbiblical, at that time its message reminded people of God's holy presence, which had been forgotten in the humanism of the day.*

The painting pictures the dead as they are resurrected to be judged. As hell releases its captives, the Judge of Heaven reviews their works. The entire painting reflects the despair of that generation.

When the painting was unveiled, a storm of conviction fell upon the viewers. All Europe trembled as the story of the power of The Last Judgment *traveled from city to city.*

G. S.

God gives Jesus Christ authority to judge all men because of who He is. *Jesus is uniquely qualified to judge because He is God and has existed from eternity (John 1:1). As God, He knows everything, can be everywhere at once, and has unlimited power and authority. He knows everything we think and sees everything we do. Thus He can judge perfectly, with wisdom and full understanding and without error or partiality.*

Christ is also uniquely qualified to judge because of what He has done. *By dying for our sins on the cross, He demonstrated perfect love for all men. Thus, when He judges, His perfect righteousness is balanced by His perfect love.*

G. S.

[About Andrew Jackson] I have great respect for the President but all men need to be restored, and unless our good President repents of his sin, he will be judged by God.

PETER CARTWRIGHT

Some seem to think that if we are Christians, God is not going to bring up anything done in this life. It is all under the blood. Put everything on Jesus and live anyway you please. Surely that cannot be right.

KEITH L. BROOKS

JUSTICE
· ·

. . . the Christian's goal is not power, but justice. We are to seek to make the institutions of power just, without being corrupted by the process necessary to do this.

CHARLES COLSON

I will look, your Honor, and endeavor to find a precedent, if you require it; though it would seem to be a pity that the Court should lose the honor of being the first to establish so just a rule.

RUFUS CHOATE

There is no virtue so truly great and godlike as justice.

JOSEPH ADDISON

If we have to choose between making men Christian and making the social order more Christian, we must choose the former. But there is no such antithesis. . . . There is no hope of establishing a more Christian social order except through the labour and sacrifice of those in whom the Spirit of Christ is active, and the first necessity for progress is more and better Christians taking full responsibility as citizens for the political, social and economic system under which they and their fellows live.

WILLIAM TEMPLE

JUSTIFICATION
· ·

Now the article of justification, which is our sole defense, not only against all the force and craft of man, but also against the gates of hell, is this: that by faith only in Christ, and without works, we are pronounced righteous and saved.

MARTIN LUTHER

To say that God justifies the ungodly means quite simply that God in His amazing love treats the sinner as if he were a good man. Again, to put it very simply, God loves us, not for anything we are, but for what He is.

WILLIAM BARCLAY

KINDNESS

> The heart benevolent and kind
> The most resembles God.
>> ROBERT BURNS

Kindness is a language which the blind can see and the deaf can hear.

ANONYMOUS

Kindness is the golden chain by which society is bound together.

JOHANN WOLFGANG VON GOETHE

Be kind; everyone you meet is fighting a hard battle.

IAN MACLAREN

Humanitarianism is a grand-sounding word, but it can sometimes mean something very much thinner than human kindness.

A. C. CRAIG

There is a grace of kind listening, as well as a grace of kind speaking.

FREDERICK WILLIAM FABER

Getting money is not all a man's business: to cultivate kindness is a valuable part of the business of life.

SAMUEL JOHNSON

> That best portion of a good man's life,
> His little, nameless, unremembered acts
> Of kindness and love.
>> WILLIAM WORDSWORTH,
>> *LINES ABOVE TINTERN ABBEY*

The best place to find a good helping hand is at the end of your arm.
MARTIN VANBEE

KINGDOMS
· ·

He has rescued us out of the darkness and gloom of Satan's kingdom and brought us into the Kingdom of his dear Son.
COLOSSIANS 1:13 TLB

And if thou be not in the kingdom of Christ, it is certain that thou belonged to the kingdom of Satan, which is this evil world.
MARTIN LUTHER

Goodness is a realm; and there is a realm of evil. Each is spiritually against the other. If the other world has a king, there is also a prince of this world; and there can be no peace except in a complete victory, so that such a war shall never be again.
P. T. FORSYTH

The fundamental biblical opposition is not between flesh and Spirit, creature and Creator, but between the Creator of the flesh and its destroyer, between God and the devil, Christ and Satan, the Holy Spirit and the Unholy.
PHILIP S. WATSON

KNOWLEDGE
· ·

We must observe that the knowledge of God which we are invited to cultivate is not that which, resting satisfied with empty speculation, only flutters in the brain, but a knowledge which will prove substantial and fruitful whenever it is duly perceived and rooted in the heart.
JOHN CALVIN

Knowledge comes by eyes always open and working hands, and there is no knowledge that is not power.

JEREMY TAYLOR

Knowledge is indispensable to Christian life and service. If we do not use the mind that God has given us, we condemn ourselves to spiritual superficiality and cut ourselves off from many of the riches of God's grace.

JOHN R. STOTT

LAST WORDS

. . . .

See in what peace a Christian can die.
JOSEPH ADDISON

Et tu, Brute fili—*You also, O son Brutus.*
JULIUS CAESAR (ATTRIBUTED)

Turn up the lights; I don't want to go home in the dark.
O. HENRY

I am about to take my last voyage, a great leap in the dark.
THOMAS HOBBES

How were the circus receipts at Madison Square Garden?
P. T. BARNUM

. . . the fog is rising.
EMILY DICKINSON

On Friday, December 22, 1899, D. L. Moody awoke to his last winter dawn. Having grown increasingly weak during the night, he began speaking in slow measured words: "Earth recedes, heaven opens before me!" Son Will, who was nearby, hurried across the room to his father's side.

"Father, you are dreaming," he said.

"No. This is no dream, Will," said the elder Moody. "It is beautiful. It is like a trance. If this is death it is sweet. God is calling me and I must go. Don't call me back."

Let us cross over the river and rest under the shade of the trees.
THOMAS J. "STONEWALL" JACKSON

Just before his death on March 2, 1791, John Wesley opened his eyes and exclaimed in a strong, clear voice, "The best of it is, God is with us."
G. S.

LAUGHTER

· ·

Laugh, and the world laughs with you;
Weep, and you weep alone.
For the sad old earth must borrow its mirth,
But has troubles enough of its own.
ELLA WHEELER WILCOX

I laugh because I must not cry. . . . With the fearful strain that is on me night and day, if I did not laugh I should die.
ABRAHAM LINCOLN

He who laughs—lasts.

NORWEGIAN PROVERB

People who laugh actually live longer than people who don't laugh. Few persons realize that health actually varies according to the amount of laughter.
JAMES S. WALSH

A man isn't poor if he can still laugh.
RAYMOND HITCHCOCK

One should take good care not to grow too wise for so great a pleasure of life as laughter.
JOSEPH ADDISON

I am not in the show business alone to make money. I feel it my mission, as long as I live, to provide clean, moral, and healthful recreation for the public to which I have so long catered.
P. T. BARNUM

LAZINESS
· ·

We have so many labor-saving devices today that we go broke keeping them repaired. Everything is easier, but requires greater maintenance.

LORNE SANNY

Absorption in ease is one of the most reliable signs of present or impending decay.

RICHARD WEAVER

Laziness grows on people; it begins in cobwebs and ends in iron chains. The more one has to do, the more he is able to accomplish.

THOMAS BUXTON

The lazier a man is, the more he plans to do tomorrow.

NORWEGIAN PROVERB

He also that is slothful in his work is brother to him that is a great waster.

PROVERBS 18:9

The sluggard will not plow by reason of the cold; therefore shall he beg in harvest, and have nothing.

PROVERBS 20:4

Not slothful in business; fervent in spirit; serving the Lord.

ROMANS 12:11

LEADERS
· ·

Do you wish to rise? Begin by descending. You plan a tower that will pierce the clouds? Lay first the foundation of humility.

SAINT AUGUSTINE

We need a baptism of clear seeing. We desperately need seers who can see through the mist—Christian leaders with prophetic vision. Unless they come soon it will be too late for this generation. And if they do come we will no doubt crucify a few of them in the name of our worldly orthodoxy.

A. W. TOZER, *THE ROOT OF THE RIGHTEOUS*

A true and safe leader is likely to be one who has no desire to lead, but is forced into a position of leadership by the inward pressure of the Holy Spirit and the press of the external situation.

A. W. TOZER

> *A leader is best*
> *When people barely know that he exists,*
> *Not so good when people obey and acclaim him,*
> *Worse when they despise him.*
> *"Fail to honor people,*
> *They fail to honor you";*
> *But of a good leader, who talks little,*
> *When his work is done, his aim fulfilled,*
> *They will all say, "We did this ourselves."*

LAO-TZU

The penalty of leadership is loneliness.

H. WHEELER ROBINSON

Energy is the dynamo, the power plant of personality, the driving force upon which all other traits depend. It is the Alpha but not the Omega of leadership.

E. S. BOGARDUS

George Washington, kneeling in prayer at Valley Forge, tells something about the heartbeat of the founders of America. We need to remember that the method of all leadership is humble, modest service. What else makes a nation great?

G. S.

A great leader never sets himself above his followers except in carry-ing responsibilities.

JULES ORMONT

LEARNING
· ·

Our safety does not lie in the present perfection of our knowledge of the will of God, but in our sincerity in obeying the light we have, and in seeking for more.

EDWARD WORSDELL

The greatest discovery of my generation is that human beings can alter their lives by altering their attitudes of mind.

WILLIAM JAMES

The doorstep to the temple of wisdom is the knowledge of our own ignorance.

CHARLES HADDON SPURGEON

Teaching that would lay any claim at all to distinction, if not to actu-al greatness, is the influence of personality upon personality, rather than the mere imparting of a set of facts.

FRANK E. GAEBELEIN

I grow old learning something new every day.

SOLON

Whosoever would understand what he hears must hasten to put into practice what he has heard.

SAINT GREGORY

There are no foolish questions and no man becomes a fool until he has stopped asking questions.

CHARLES P. STEINMETZ

As we acquire more knowledge, things do not become more comprehensible but more mysterious.

ALBERT SCHWEITZER

Of the two purposes of education—to make a person fit for the world as it is and to make him able to change it—the second is the more important.

C. DELISLE BURNS

LIES
· ·

Slander, lies, character assassination—these things are a threat to every single citizen everywhere in this country. When even one American—who has done nothing wrong—is forced by fear to shut his mind and close his mouth, then all Americans are in peril. It is the job of all of us—of every American who loves his country and his freedom—to rise up and put a stop to this terrible business.

HARRY S. TRUMAN,
SPEECH ON MCCARTHYISM

There are people who exaggerate so much that they can't tell the truth without lying.

H. W. SHAW

As ten millions of circles can never make a square, so the united voice of myriads cannot lend the smallest foundation to falsehood.

OLIVER GOLDSMITH

So near is falsehood to truth that a wise man would do well not to trust himself on the narrow edge.

CICERO

And he that does one fault at first,
And tries to hide it, makes it two.
ISAAC WATTS

Who is not sure of his memory should not attempt lying.
MICHEL DE MONTAIGNE

LIFE

It is not how many years we live, but rather what we do with them.
EVANGELINE CORY BOOTH

Living is licking honey off a thorn.

Optimism: a cheerful frame of mind that enables a tea kettle to sing though in hot water up to its nose.

Life can never be wholly dark or futile once the key to its meaning is in our hands.
J. B. PHILLIPS

LIFE VIEWS

Always take hold of things by the smooth handle.
THOMAS JEFFERSON

Life is like riding a bicycle. You don't fall off until you stop pedaling.
CLAUDE PEPPER

Life is not a spectacle or a feast; it is a predicament.
GEORGE SANTAYANA

Life is an onion and one cries while peeling it.
FRENCH PROVERB

We are born crying, live complaining, and die disappointed.
THOMAS FULLER

All I maintain is that on this earth there are pestilences and there are victims, and it's up to us, as far as possible, not to join forces with the pestilences.

ALBERT CAMUS

Life at the longest is amazingly short. The Bible uses several metaphors to convey just how brief it is.

Job says, "My life is wind" (Job 7:7), and "My days are swifter than a weaver's shuttle" (Job 7:6). Have you ever watched a weaver's shuttle? It moves so fast that you can't distinguish its movement. It's just a blur.

The psalmist compares life to a fading flower or a falling leaf: "As for man, his days are as grass; as a flower of the field, so he flourisheth. For the wind passeth over it, and it is gone" (Psalm 103:15-16).

The writer of Chronicles says, "Our days on the earth are as a shadow, and there is none abiding" (I Chronicles 29:15).

And Psalm 90:9 reminds, "We spend our years as a tale that is told."

James (4:14) asks, "What is your life? It is even a vapor, that appeareth for a little time, and then vanisheth away."

Life is so short that the wood of the cradle rubs up tight against the marble of the tomb.

G. S.

In the land of lobelian and tennis flannels
The rabbit shall burrow and the thorn revisit,
The nettle shall flourish on the gravel court,
And the wind shall say: "Here were decent godless people:
Their only monument the asphalt road
And a thousand lost golf balls."

T. S. ELIOT

Life is the art of drawing sufficient conclusions from insufficient premises.

SAMUEL BUTLER

We can fly like the bird,
And swim like the fish,
If we could only learn
To behave like men—we'd
Be doing something.

VANCE HAVNER

Life is one long process of getting tired.

SAMUEL BUTLER

Life is made up of sobs, sniffles, and smiles, with sniffles predomi-
nating.

O. HENRY

There is such a thing as the very perfection of arrangement without
life, like cabinets in a museum, where all the specimens are duly clas-
sified and dead.

ALEXANDER MACLAREN

Farewell! a long farewell, to all my greatness!
This is the state of man: today he puts forth
The tender leaves of hope; tomorrow blossoms,
And bears his blushing honors thick upon him;
The third day comes a frost, a killing frost;
And when he thinks, good easy man, full surely
His greatness is a-ripening, nips his root,
And then he falls, as I do.

WILLIAM SHAKESPEARE,
WOLSEY IN *HENRY VIII*

Life is a hard fight, a struggle, a wrestling with the principle of evil,
hand to hand, foot to foot. Every inch of the way is disputed. The
night is given us to take breath, to pray, to drink deep at the fountain
of power. The day, to use the strength which has been given us, to go
forth to work with it till the evening.

FLORENCE NIGHTINGALE

Any twenty-year-old who isn't a liberal doesn't have a heart, and any forty-year-old who isn't a conservative doesn't have a brain.

WINSTON CHURCHILL

A man is rich in proportion to the number of things which he can afford to let alone.

HENRY DAVID THOREAU

The great thing is to be found at one's post as a child of God, living each day as though it were our last, but planning as though our world might last a hundred years.

C. S. LEWIS, *GOD IN THE DOCK*

When I consider the short duration of my life, swallowed up in the eternity before and after, the little space which I fill, and even can see, engulfed in the infinite immensity of space of which I am ignorant, and which knows me not, I am frightened, and am astonished being here rather than there, why now rather than then.

BLAISE PASCAL

Without Christ life is as the twilight with dark night ahead; with Christ, it is the dawn of morning with the light and warmth of a full day ahead.

PHILIP SCHAFF

LITTLE THINGS

Regarding the lever: "Give me a firm place to stand, and I will move the earth."

ARCHIMEDES

If you add a little to a little and do this often, soon the little will become great.

HESIOD, *WORKS AND DAYS*

Little words are the sweetest to hear; little charities fly furthest and stay longest on the wing; little lakes are the stillest; little hearts are the fullest, and little farms are the best tilled. Little books are read the most and little songs are the dearest loved. And when Nature would make anything especially rare and beautiful, she makes it little; little pearls, little diamonds, little dews. Agar's is a model prayer but then it is a little one; and the burden of the petition is for but the little. The Sermon on the Mount is little, but the last dedication discourse was an hour long. Life is made up of little things that count, and death is what remains of them all. Day is made up of little beams, and night is glorious with little stars.

ANONYMOUS

Little pots soon boil over.

ANONYMOUS

Better to light one small candle than to curse the darkness.

CHINESE PROVERB

LONELINESS
· ·

Few of us have reached middle life who do not, looking back, see our track strewed with the gaunt skeletons of dead friendships, and saddened by footprints striking away from the line of march, and leaving us the more solitary for their departure.

ALEXANDER MACLAREN

Loneliness is the first thing which God's eye named, not good.

JOHN MILTON

Cannot the heart in the midst of crowds feel frightfully alone?

CHARLES LAMB

People are lonely because they build walls instead of bridges.

JOSEPH FORT NEWTON

Didst thou give me this inescapable loneliness so that it would be easier for me to give thee all.

DAG HAMMARSKJÖLD

One of the prominent symptoms of our times . . . is loneliness. Isn't it ironic that in an age of the greatest population explosion the world has ever known, more people are desperately lonely than ever before? . . . Even the high-rise apartments in our big cities are monuments to loneliness. There is aching loneliness behind those doors for many people. I know of those, both in the city and in the suburb, who go to the large shopping centers simply for the opportunity to talk to somebody in the store. At least the checker will speak to them as they go out. Loneliness is one of the desperate problems of our age.

PAUL LITTLE

The central purpose of Christ's life . . . is to destroy the life of loneliness and to establish here on earth the life of love.

THOMAS WOLFE

Loneliness is stamped on the American face; it rises like an exhalation from the American landscape.

VAN WYCK BROOKS

LOST MAN
· ·

All man's miracles derive from not being able to sit quiet in a room alone.

BLAISE PASCAL

There is a God-shaped vacuum in every heart.

BLAISE PASCAL

> *I cannot find my way: there is no star*
> *In all the shrouded heavens anywhere.*

EDWIN ARLINGTON ROBINSON

There is no exit from the human dilemma.
JEAN-PAUL SARTRE

*Man is lost because he is separated from God, his true reference point,
by true moral guilt. But he never will be nothing. Therein lies the
horror of his lostness. For man to be lost, in all his uniqueness and
wonder, is tragic.*
FRANCIS SCHAEFFER

*Man is the product of causes which had no provision of the end they
were achieving . . . his origin, his growth, his hopes and fears, his
loves and his beliefs, are but the outcome of accidental collocations of
atoms . . . no fire, no heroism, no intensity of thought and feeling, can
preserve an individual life beyond the grave . . . and the whole temple of man's achievement must inevitably be buried beneath the
debris of a universe in ruins.*
BERTRAND RUSSELL

The mass of men live lives of quiet desperation.
HENRY DAVID THOREAU

I am a fallen, lost creature.
SAMUEL COLERIDGE

> *I fled Him, down the nights and down the days;*
>   *I fled Him down the arches of the years;*
> *I fled Him, down the labyrinthine ways*
>   *Of my own mind; and in the midst of tears*
> *I hid from Him, and under running laughter.*
>   *Up vistaed hopes, I sped;*
>   *And shot, precipitated,*
> *Adown Titanic glooms of chasmed fears,*
>   *From those strong Feet that followed, followed after.*
FRANCIS THOMPSON,
THE HOUND OF HEAVEN

All my life I have been seeking to climb out of the pit of my besetting sins and I cannot do it and I never will unless a hand is let down to draw me up.

SENECA

The world is . . . a kind of spiritual kindergarten where millions of bewildered infants are trying to spell "God" with the wrong blocks.
EDWIN ARLINGTON ROBINSON

Mock on, mock on, Voltaire, Rousseau;
Mock on, mock on; 'tis all in vain!
You throw the sand against the wind,
And the wind blows it back again.
WILLIAM BLAKE

God does not die on the day when we cease to believe in a personal deity, but we die on the day when our lives cease to be illuminated by the steady radiance, renewed daily, of a wonder, the source of which is beyond all reason.

DAG HAMMARSKJÖLD

Modern writers depict the pessimism of our time and many of them throw up their hands in despair and say, "There is no answer to man's dilemma." Hemingway once said, "I live in a vacuum that is as lonely as a radio tube when the batteries are dead, and there is no current to plug into." Eugene O'Neill in "Long Day's Journey Into Night" typifies the philosophical attitude of our day. He says, "Life's only meaning is death." I say to Hemingway and O'Neill, who have already gone on, "There is more to life than death." There is more to life than a radio tube that needs a place to plug into. Jesus taught us the dignity and importance of being a person. God put us on this earth for a purpose, and our purpose is fellowship with God and to glorify God.

BILLY GRAHAM

Dr. Rollo May in his book, Man's Search for Himself, *quotes Friedrich Nietzsche who wrote a parable about the "death of God." It is a haunting story about a madman who ran into the village square shouting, "Where is God?"*

The people around him did not believe in God; they laughed and said that perhaps God had gone on a voyage or emigrated. The madman then shouted: "Where is God? I shall tell you! We have killed Him—you and I—yet how have we done this? . . . Who gave us the sponge to wipe away the whole horizon? What did we do when we unchained the earth from its sun? . . . Whither shall we move now? Away from all suns? Do we not fall incessantly? Backward, sideward, forward, in all directions? Is there yet any up and down?"

G. S.

LOVE
· ·

You called, you cried, you shattered my deafness, you sparkled, you blazed, you drove away my blindness, you shed your fragrance, and I drew in my breath, and I pant for you.

SAINT AUGUSTINE

For though thou didst know the whole Bible by heart and the sayings of the philosophers, what doth it profit thee without the love of God? . . . Surely a humble husbandman that serveth God is better than a proud philosopher who, neglecting himself, labours to understand the movements of the heavens.

THOMAS À KEMPIS

A wise lover values not so much the gift of the lover as the love of the giver.

THOMAS À KEMPIS

What a vast distance there is between knowing God and loving Him!

BLAISE PASCAL

Let everyone understand that real love of God does not consist in tear-shedding, nor in that sweetness and tenderness for which we usually long, just because they console us, but in serving God in justice, fortitude of soul and humility.

SAINT THERESA OF AVILA

You wish to hear from me why and how God is to be loved? My answer is: the reason for loving God is God Himself, and the measure in which we should love Him is to love Him without measure.

SAINT BERNARD OF CLAIRVAUX

Love so amazing, so divine, demands my soul, my life, my all.

ISAAC WATTS

I never knew up to that time that God loved us so much. This heart of mine began to thaw out; I could not keep back the tears. I just drank it in. . . . I tell you there is one thing that draws above everything else in the world and that is love.

D. L. MOODY

Satan separates; God unites; love binds us together.

D. L. MOODY

Love is the best thing in the world, and the thing that lives longest.

HENRY VAN DYKE

I have decided to stick with love. Hate is too great a burden to bear.

MARTIN LUTHER KING, JR.

Yes, love is the magic key of life—not to get what we want but to become what we ought to be.

EILEEN GUDER

No cord nor cable can so forcibly draw, or hold so fast, as love can do with a twined thread.

ROBERT BURTON

Only the loving will have any understanding of love—just as only the good will understand goodness. When one has gotten only a little way into loving, one learns that what understanding we do attain, poor and partial as it must be, is not gotten by thinking about it. It comes by receiving and giving love, as a part of the process of living.

EILEEN GUDER

Love is exclusively a Person.

NORMAN GRUBB

For where love is wanting, the beauty of all virtue is mere tinsel, is empty sound, is not worth a straw, nay more, is offensive and disgusting.

JOHN CALVIN

And the moral of that is "Oh, 'tis love, 'tis love, that makes the world go round!"

LEWIS CARROLL,
ALICE'S ADVENTURES IN WONDERLAND

Respect is what we owe; love, what we give.

PHILIP JAMES BAILEY

I think true love is never blind,
But rather brings an added light,
An inner vision quick to find
The beauties hid from common sight.

PHOEBE CARY

A friendship like love is warm;
A love like friendship steady.

THOMAS MOORE

If you haven't love in your heart, you should throw your hope to the four winds, and go and get a better one.

D. L. MOODY

Music is Love in search of a word.

SIDNEY LANIER

Required in every good lover . . . the whole alphabet . . . Agreeable, Bountiful, Constant, Dutiful, Easy, Faithful, Gallant, Honourable, Ingenious, Joyful, Kind, Loyal, Mild, Noble, Officious, Prudent, Quiet, Rich, Secret, True, Understanding, Valiant, Wise . . . Young and Zealous.

MIGUEL DE CERVANTES

Across the gateway of my heart
I wrote "No Thoroughfare,"
But love came laughing by, and cried:
"I enter everywhere."

HERBERT SHIPMAN

How vast a memory has Love!

ALEXANDER POPE

God, from a beautiful necessity, is Love.

MARTIN FARQUHAR TUPPER

Love is ever the beginning of Knowledge, as fire is of light!

THOMAS CARLYLE

I think that love is the only spiritual power that can overcome the self-centeredness that is inherent in being alive. Love is the thing that makes life possible, or, indeed, tolerable.

ARNOLD TOYNBEE

Real love is the universal language—understood by all. You may have every accomplishment or give your body to be burned; but, if love is lacking, all this will profit you and the cause of Christ nothing.

HENRY DRUMMOND

Love would put a new face on this weary old world in which we dwell as pagans and enemies too long, and it would warm the heart to see how fast the vain diplomacy of statesmen, the impotence of armies, and navies, and lines of defense, would be superseded by this unarmed child. Love will creep where it cannot go, will accomplish that by imperceptible methods—being its own level, fulcrum, and power—which force could never achieve.

RALPH WALDO EMERSON

Infantile love follows the principle: "I love because I am loved." Mature love follows the principle: "I am loved because I love." Immature love says: "I love you because I need you." Mature love says: "I need you because I love you."

ERICH FROMM

The desire of power in excess caused the angels to fall; the desire of knowledge in excess caused man to fall, but in love there is no excess, neither can angel or man come in danger by it.

FRANCIS BACON

Love does not die easily. It is a living thing. It thrives in the face of all life's hazards, save one—neglect.

JAMES D. BRYDEN

Do you know the world is dying
For a little bit of love?
Everywhere we hear them sighing,
For a little bit of love.

ANONYMOUS

I took up that word Love, and I do not know how many weeks I spent in studying the passages in which it occurs, till at last I could not help loving people. I had been feeding on love so long that I was anxious to do everybody good I came in contact with. I got full of it. It ran out my fingers. You take up the subject of love in the Bible! You will get so full of it that all you have to do is to open your lips, and a flood of the Love of God flows out.

D. L. MOODY

I visited the 110-story, 1,454-foot Sears Tower, the tallest man-made structure on earth. It is a fantastic architectural feat, but someday its tons of concrete will be broken and its designer's name will be forgotten. And yet a cup of cold water, given in love, will break on the shores of eternity. In a world gone mad with greed and hate, how wonderful to know that love never dies! Love is never obsolete.

G. S.

It is possible to have compassion without love, and it is possible to have kindness without love; but it is impossible for one who has put on love to be unkind and without compassion, for love itself is not just an accessory garment. Love is the complete garment that has all the others built into it, so that love is a total way of life.

RAY ANDERSON

Love is appealing, but its practice is appallingly difficult.

ANONYMOUS

The churches would soon be filled if outsiders could find that people in them loved them when they came. This love draws sinners! We must win them to us first, then we can win them to Christ. We must get people to love us, and then turn them over to Christ.

D. L. MOODY

Persons are to be loved; things are to be used.

REUEL HOWE

People don't go where the action is, they go where love is.

JESS MOODY

*Blest be the tie that binds
Our hearts in Christian love;
The fellowship of kindred minds,
Is like to that above.*

JOHN FAWCETT

310

O, there is nothing holier, in this life of ours, than the first conscious-ness of love—the first fluttering of its silken wings.
                                        HENRY WADSWORTH LONGFELLOW

This "first love" seeks not people, but a Person, the One who alone merits our first love. The "first love" is the intimate personal relation-ship of love which one has with our Lord Jesus Christ.
                                        M. BASILEA SCHLINK

No one can live without being a debtor; no one should live without being a creditor.
                                        N. J. PANIN

No single factor has so limited the Christian church down through the years as man's inhumanity to man—sometimes outright cruelty, but far more often, sheer lovelessness.
                                        G. S.

Without God's help, our other loves cannot even remain what they start out to be, or become what they promise.
                                        G. S.

Life minus love equals zero!
Five steps in knowing how to love:
1. *Receive Christ as your Saviour. He is God's gift of love to you. "God is love" (1 John 4:8).*
2. *Experience the power of God's love in your life. "The love of God is shed abroad in our hearts" (Romans 5:5).*
3. *Seek the fruit of the Spirit (Galatians 5:22).*
4. *Pray for an abounding love (Philippians 1:9).*
5. *Begin to love by faith. Believe God for the love you cannot muster in yourself.*
                                        G. S.

Love is not big-headed; it is big-hearted.
                                        G. S.

Living without loving is merely existing!

G. S.

The call to love is not for the halfhearted. It is a full-time, life-long vocation.

G. S.

First love looks at the grand possibilities, not the weight of the problems. . . . First love is warm, radiant, and real.

G. S.

> *I asked a river, "What is love?"*
> *And it replied: "The sea."*
> *I asked the question of the trees:*
> *"The wind," they answered me.*
> *I asked a mountain and it cried:*
> *"The stars!" And I asked a field of grain;*
> *It quickly sang: "The rain! The rain!"*
> *The shore told me it was the tide.*
> *And when I asked my soul, it said:*
> *"Love is the shining key*
> *To that fair golden temple*
> *Of my immortality."*
>
> ADELAIDE P. LOVE

Our Lord told His disciples that love and obedience were organically united. The final test of love is obedience.

A. W. TOZER, *THAT INCREDIBLE CHRISTIAN*

Love is the only fire that is hot enough to melt the iron obstinancy of a creature's will.

ALEXANDER MACLAREN

Love is optimistic; it looks at people in the best light. Love thinks constructively as it senses the grand possibilities in other people.

G. S.

Young people talk a lot about love. Most of their songs are about love. . . . "The supreme happiness of life," Victor Hugo said long ago, "is the conviction that we are loved." "Love is the first requirement for mental health," declared Sigmund Freud. The Bible teaches that "God is love" and that God loves you. To realize that is of paramount importance. Nothing else matters so much. And loving you, God has wonderful plans for your life. Who else could plan and guide your life so well?

BILLY GRAHAM

Love and a cough cannot be hid.

GEORGE HERBERT

Our souls, by reason of sin, are "like sweet bells jangled, harsh and out of tune." Love's master hand laid upon them restores to them their part in "the fair music that all creatures make to their great Lord," and brings us into such accord with God that "We on earth with undiscording voice, May rightly answer" even the awful harmonies of His lips.

ALEXANDER MACLAREN

What does love look like? It has the hands to help others. It has the feet to hasten to the poor and needy. It has the eyes to see misery and want. It has the ears to hear the sighs and sorrows of men. That is what love looks like.

SAINT AUGUSTINE

If monotony tries me, and I cannot stand drudgery; if stupid people fret me and little ruffles set me on edge; if I make much of the trifles of life, then I know nothing of Calvary love.

AMY CARMICHAEL

Love for the Lord is not an ethereal, intellectual, dreamlike thing; it is the intensest, most vital, most passionate love of which the human heart is capable.

OSWALD CHAMBERS

He prayeth best, who loveth best
All things both great and small;
For the dear God who loveth us,
He made and loveth all.

SAMUEL T. COLERIDGE

A part of kindness consists in loving people more than they deserve.

JOSEPH JOUBERT

Our heart oft times wakes when we sleep, and God can speak to that,
either by words, by proverbs, by signs and similitudes, as well as if
one was awake.

JOHN BUNYAN

MAN

Man appears for a little while to laugh and weep, to work and play, and then to go to make room for those who shall follow him in the never ending cycle.

A. W. TOZER

Man is but a reed, the most weak in nature, but he is a thinking reed.

BLAISE PASCAL

The more I see of man, the more I like dogs.

MADAME DE STAËL

"Slightly lower than the angels" is a whole lot better than slightly higher than the apes. Let's get the order straight. God, angelic beings, man, animals, and vegetables.

STUART BRISCOE

God tells man who he is. God tells us that He created man in His image. So man is something wonderful.

FRANCIS SCHAEFFER,
ESCAPE FROM REASON

There is nothing autonomous—nothing apart from the lordship of Jesus Christ and the authority of the Scriptures. God made the whole man and is interested in the whole man, and the result is a unity.

FRANCIS SCHAEFFER,
ESCAPE FROM REASON

It is not a world out of joint that makes our problem but rather the shipwrecked souls in it. It is Hamlet, not his world, that is wrong.

P. T. FORSYTH

Man has two great spiritual needs. One is for forgiveness. God answered that at Calvary. The other is for goodness. God answered that at Pentecost.

BILLY GRAHAM

The true measure of a man comes when all the chips are down.

JOSEPH STOWELL

The release of atom power has changed everything except our way of thinking, and thus we are being driven unarmed towards a catastrophe. . . . The solution of this problem lies in the heart of humankind.

ALBERT EINSTEIN

If we let ourselves believe that man began with divine grace, that he forfeited this by sin, and that he can be redeemed only by divine grace through the crucified Christ then we shall find a peace of mind never granted to philosophers. He who cannot believe is cursed, for he reveals by his unbelief that God has not chosen to give him grace.

BLAISE PASCAL

*It's easy enough to be pleasant
when life flows along like a song.
But the man worthwhile
is the man who can smile
when everything goes wrong.*

ELLA WHEELER WILCOX, "WORTHWHILE"

*Life isn't fair to us men.
When we are born, our mothers get the compliments and the flowers.
When we are married, our brides get the presents and the publicity.
When we die, our widows get the life insurance and winters in
    Florida.
What do women want to be liberated from?*

APPARENTLY THE MAN WHO WROTE THIS
WAS AFRAID TO SIGN HIS NAME

A man asked a female clerk in the bookstore, "Have you a book enti-
tled Man, Master of the Home?" *She looked at him for a moment*
and then replied, "Try the fiction department, please."

Until Eve arrived, this was a man's world.

What a piece of work is a man! how noble in reason! how infinite in
faculty! in form, and moving how express and admirable! in action
how like an angel! in apprehension how like a god! the beauty of the
world! the paragon of animals! And yet, to me, what is this quintes-
sence of dust? man delights not me: no, nor woman neither.
WILLIAM SHAKESPEARE, *HAMLET*

Up till now, man derived his coherence from his Creator. But from the
moment that he consecrates his rupture with him, he finds himself
delivered over to the fleeting moment, to the passing days, and to
wasted sensibility.
ALBERT CAMUS

Man's chief end is to glorify God, and to enjoy Him forever.
SHORTER WESTMINSTER CATECHISM

MARRIAGE

Wives, submit to your own husbands, as is fitting in the Lord.
Husbands, love your wives and do not be bitter toward them.
COLOSSIANS 3:18–19 NKJV

Let the wife make her husband glad to come home and let him make
her sorry to see him leave.
MARTIN LUTHER

One of the mysteries of life is how the boy who wasn't good enough to
marry the daughter can be the father of the smartest grandchild in
the world.

Think of all the squabbles Adam and Even must have had in the course of their nine hundred years. Eve would say, "You ate the apple," and Adam would retort, "You gave it to me."
MARTIN LUTHER

To keep your marriage brimming,
With love in the loving cup,
Whenever you're wrong, admit it,
Whenever you're right, shut up.
OGDEN NASH

Marriage is never finished. The lesson is never learned. The effort is never at an end. Marriage, like life, is a matter of solving the little things. The big ones generally take care of themselves. It is a matter of surrendering small, personal preferences.
RANDOLPH RAY

By all means marry. If you get a good wife, you will become very happy; if you get a bad one, you will become a philosopher—and that is good for any man.
SOCRATES

Two friends met after many years. One was married, the other single. The married man asked the other, "How have you managed to stay single all this time?" "It's not difficult," replied the bachelor. "Every time I watch a commercial on television I learn about women—that they are anemic, have stringy and broken hair, large pores, wrinkles, rough hands, underarm odor, and are overweight."

Success in marriage consists not only in finding the right mate, but also in being the right mate.
ANONYMOUS

A bachelor is a fellow who doesn't think the bonds of matrimony are a good investment.
MAURICE SEITTER

Three Guidelines for a Christian Marriage

First of all, and foundational to a biblical understanding of marriage, is the truth that marriage is a permanent relationship. *In Mark 10:6-7, Jesus said, "From the beginning of the creation God made them male and female. For this cause shall a man leave his father and mother, and cleave to his wife." And then in verse nine we read, "What therefore God hath joined together, let not man put asunder."*

A second biblical guideline is that marriage is a harmonious partnership. *The Bible speaks of the union of the husband and wife as harmonious. Jesus said, "And they twain shall be one flesh: so then* they are no more twain, *but one flesh" (Mark 10:8, emphasis added).*

I have never known of a broken marriage where the husband and wife had enjoyed a true partnership that had been harmonious and mutually sacrificial. But God established marriage to be just that, and His Word gives guidelines about how to keep harmony in the home.

But there is a truth that is even greater than the truths that marriage is a permanent relationship and a harmonious partnership. And that is the biblical teaching that marriage is a spiritual companionship.

Christian marriage should be a companionship where each helps the other to grow in Christ. The Bible tells us that in the marriage relationship, the husband and wife become one. It is my conviction that that speaks not only of a physical union, but of a spiritual union as well.

G. S.

They divorce in order to remarry. They marry in order to divorce.
SENECA

It is not marriage that fails; it is people that fail. All that marriage does is show people up.

ANONYMOUS

319

MEANING
· ·

If God exists and we are made in His image we can have real meaning, and we can have real knowledge through what He has communicated to us.

> FRANCIS SCHAEFFER,
> *THE GOD WHO IS THERE*

There is a land of the living and a land of the dead and the bridge is love, the only survival, the only meaning.

> THORNTON WILDER

Eternal truths will be neither true nor eternal unless they have fresh meaning for every new social situation.

> FRANKLIN D. ROOSEVELT

Hold every moment sacred. Give each clarity and meaning, each the weight of thine awareness, each its true and due fulfillment.

> THOMAS MANN

You must lie upon the daisies and discourse in novel phrases of your complicated state of mind,
The meaning doesn't matter if it's only idle chatter of a transcendental kind.

> WILLIAM S. GILBERT, *PATIENCE*

Dare to err and to dream. Deep meaning often lies in childish plays.

> JOHANN VON SCHILLER

> *A voice in the wind I do not know;*
> *A meaning on the face of the high hills*
> *Whose utterance I cannot comprehend.*
> *A something is behind them: that is God.*
>
> GEORGE MACDONALD

THE MEDIA
· ·

Journalism largely consists in saying "Lord Jones is Dead" to people who never knew Lord Jones was alive.
G. K. CHESTERTON

Newspaper editors are men who separate the wheat from the chaff, and then print the chaff.
ADLAI STEVENSON

Journalism is literature in a hurry.
MATTHEW ARNOLD

We're in the same position as a plumber laying a pipe. We're not responsible for what goes through the pipe.
DAVID SARNOFF

I keep reading between the lies.
GOODMAN ACE

MEDIOCRITY
· ·

There are no dull subjects, only dull writers.
H. L. MENCKEN

MEDITATION
· ·

Now in the morning, having risen a long while before daylight, He went out and departed to a solitary place; and there He prayed.
MARK 1:35 NKJV

A man of meditation is happy, not for an hour or a day, but quite round the circle of all his years.
ISAAC TAYLOR

John Wesley preached over 44,000 sermons in his lifetime. He traveled by horseback and carriage nearly 300,000 miles, wrote grammar and theological textbooks in four languages, and yet always had time for a quiet time. While still in his childhood, Wesley resolved to dedicate an hour each morning and evening to Bible study and prayer.

G. S.

If we have not quiet in our minds, outward comfort will do no more for us than a golden slipper on a gouty foot.

JOHN BUNYAN

The longest journey is the journey inward. . . . The road of holiness necessarily passes through the world of action.

DAG HAMMARSKJÖLD

Andrew Bonar, a great man of God, had three rules that he lived by. Rule 1—Not to speak to any person before speaking to Jesus Christ. Rule 2—Not to do anything with his hands until he had been on his knees. Rule 3—Not to read the papers until he had read his Bible.

G. S.

Dorothy Haskins tells the story of a noted concert artist who was asked the secret of her mastery of the violin. "Planned neglect," she replied and then explained, "There were many things which used to demand my time. When I went to my room after breakfast, I made my bed, straightened the room, dusted, and did whatever seemed necessary. When I finished my work, I turned to my violin practice. That system failed, however, to accomplish what I should on the violin, so I reversed things. I deliberately planned to neglect everything else until my practice period was complete. And that program of planned neglect is the secret of my success.

MEMORY
· ·

A man's real possession is his memory. In nothing else is he rich, in nothing else is he poor.

ALEXANDER SMITH

A retentive memory is a good thing, but the ability to forget is the true token of greatness.

ELBERT HUBBARD

Own only what you can always carry with you: know languages, know countries, know people. Let your memory be your travel bag.

ALEXSANDR SOLZHENITSYN

When I was younger I could remember anything, whether it had happened or not.

MARK TWAIN

A couple was sitting in the worship service when the wife suddenly remarked, "Oh, how awful! I forgot to turn off the electric iron before I left home!"

"Don't worry, dear," the husband said cheerfully. "It won't burn long. I just remembered I forgot to turn off the faucet in the bathtub."

G. S.

We have committed the Golden Rule to memory; now let us commit it to life.

EDWIN MARKHAM

When saving for old age, be sure to put away a few pleasant thoughts.

ANONYMOUS

Like a bird singing in the rain, let grateful memories survive in time of sorrow.

ROBERT LOUIS STEVENSON

There are few greater treasures to be acquired in youth than great poetry—and prose—stored in the memory. At the time one may resent the labor of storing. But they sleep in the memory and awake in later years, illuminated by life and illuminating it.

RICHARD W. LIVINGSTONE

The advantage of a bad memory is that one enjoys several times the same good things for the first time.

FRIEDRICH NIETZSCHE

MIND
· ·

The mind is like the stomach. It is not how much you put into it that counts, but how much it digests.

A. J. NOCK

Nothing relieves and ventilates the mind like a resolution.

JOHN BURROUGHS

Little minds are interested in the extraordinary; great minds in the commonplace.

ELBERT HUBBARD

The mind of man is like a clock that is always running down, and requires to be as constantly wound up.

WILLIAM HAZLITT

MISSIONS
· ·

"I can't get interested in missions," remarked a young lady.

"No," was the reply given to her, "you can hardly expect to. It is just like getting interest at a bank: you have to put in a little something first and the more you put in—time or money or prayer—the more the interest grows."

ANONYMOUS

Some wish to live within the sound of church and chapel bells. I want to run a rescue shop within a yard of hell.

C. T. STUDD

When the Spirit of God comes into a man, He gives him a world-wide view.

OSWALD CHAMBERS

The Spirit of Christ is the spirit of missions, and the nearer we get to Him the more intensely missionary we must become.

HENRY MARTYN

Let's stop routing Christ through western Europe and the United States. Let's abandon the folly of dressing Him in Western clothes, imputing to Him a Western life-style, implying to the world His message was born in the West. Let's take Him directly from Jerusalem to the point of action. Better still, let's bring Him directly from heaven to the area of human need.

JOHN HAGGAI

In 1956 Life *magazine told of the shocking death of five missionaries in the jungles of Ecuador. For several months these men had tried to make contact with the primitive Auca Indians. On their first attempt to establish a camp, they were brutally murdered!*

Today these same Auca tribesmen are all Christians. They are leaders of a small congregation that worships near the spot where the missionaries died. Many educators and government leaders have expressed astonishment at the miraculous change in these Indians. How did it happen? The answer lies in the love of God expressed to these people by the sister of Nate Saint and the wife of Jim Elliot, two of the martyred missionaries. Led by God who is love and not vengeance, these women were able to break down the walls of distrust. In time they were able to share the gospel with these tribesmen and see the love of Christ transform their lives.

G. S.

All the world is my parish.

JOHN WESLEY

Attempt great things FOR God and expect great things FROM God.
WILLIAM CAREY

"I am going down into the pit; you hold the ropes," said Carey the pioneer missionary. They that hold the ropes, and the daring miner that swings away down in the darkness, are one in work, may be one in the motive, and, if they are, shall be one in the reward.
ALEXANDER MACLAREN

John Currier, a man who could not read or write, was found guilty of murder and sentenced to prison for life in 1949. Later he was transferred from prison and paroled to work for a wealthy farmer near Nashville, Tennessee.

In 1968, however, his sentence was terminated. State Correction Department records show that a letter was written to the convict and the farmer for whom he worked. The letter said he was free.

But Currier never saw the letter or even knew it had been written. One year went by . . . then two . . . then five, and finally, ten; and still he did not know that he was free.

By this time, the farmer to whom he had been paroled was dead, but Currier kept working, serving out his sentence. He was given a little money for personal needs—five dollars a week at first, then a little more, and finally twenty dollars weekly.

But life was hard and filled with labor. He slept in a drafty trailer, taking baths in a horse trough with a garden hose. Life held very little joy and no promise.

This went on till just a few years ago. Then a state parole officer learned of his plight and told him of the missing letter, according to the Chicago Tribune, *February 7, 1979.*

Would it matter to you if someone sent you an important message—the most important of your life, but year after year the urgent message was never delivered?

G. S.

I look upon foreign missionaries as the scaffolding around a rising building. The sooner it can be dispensed with, the better; or rather, the sooner it can be transferred to other places, to serve the same temporary use, the better.

HUDSON TAYLOR

I have four sons whom I love dearly. Suppose our lawn needed to be cut. I could say, "Boys, can you see the need? The grass is high. It's above my knees. Soon I will not be able to get to the garage. Don't you see the desperate need?" But in the final analysis, they get out the mower because their father says, "Mow the grass!" World evangelization is an imperative because Jesus said so.

G. S.

The story is told that during the reign of Oliver Cromwell, there was a shortage of currency in the British Empire. Representatives carefully searched the nation in hope of finding silver to meet the emergency.

After one month, the committee returned with its findings. "We have searched the empire in vain seeking to find silver," it reported. "To our dismay, we found none anywhere except in the cathedrals where the saints are carved from choice silver."

To this, Oliver Cromwell eloquently answered, "Let's melt down the saints and put them into circulation." Why not ask the Lord to melt us down for greater spiritual circulation?

G. S.

Our supreme task is world evangelization in this generation.

D. L. MOODY AND JOHN R. MOTT

MISTAKES
· ·

The man who is incapable of making a mistake is incapable of anything.

ABRAHAM LINCOLN

The man who makes no mistakes does not usually make anything.
EDWARD JOHN PHELPS

I have my faults, but being wrong ain't one of them.
JAMES RIDDLE HOFFA

When Henry Ward Beecher was preaching in Brooklyn, he carried a handful of flowers into the pulpit one Lord's Day and placed them in a vase that they might adorn the stand from which he spoke. The newspapers, the next day, carried lengthy articles condemning Beecher for desecrating the pulpit with flowers.

And when Morse was trying to get money from Congress for a telegraph line from Baltimore to Washington, he had to endure the adverse criticisms of the press for eleven years.

And when, in 1845, Mr. Adam Thompson got up the first bathtub in America, the newspapers said he was "going to spoil the democratic simplicity of the republic."

And when Cyrus Field was trying to lay the Atlantic cable, the newspapers denounced his cable as "a mad freak of stubborn ignorance."
ROBERT G. LEE

Sometimes we may learn more from a man's errors than from his virtues.
HENRY WADSWORTH LONGFELLOW

The sages do not consider that making no mistakes is a blessing. They believe, rather, that the great virtue of man lies in his ability to correct his mistakes and continually to make a new man of himself.
WANG YANG-MING

MODERN CULTURE
· ·

Secularism has this age by the throat.
WALTER LOWRIE

We live in the kind of world in which the only constant factor is change, and some of the changes are unhappy ones. . . . What do we do when the roof falls in?

EILEEN GUDER

We are living in a culture that is secular. Religion does not play the role that it used to play. This is particularly true for people under forty years of age in this society. When a strong religious bond is missing, there are few things that can hold the culture together.

RICHARD HOFSTADTER

Ours is an age without heroes . . . today no one bestrides our narrow world like a colossus.

ARTHUR M. SCHLESINGER, JR.

We ourselves were sure that at long last a generation had arisen keen and eager, to put this disorderly earth to right . . . and fit to do it . . . we meant so well, we tried so hard, and look what we have made of it. We can only muddle in the muddle. What is required is a new kind of man.

WALTER LIPPMANN

The greatest difficulty with the world is not its ability to produce, but its unwillingness to share.

ROY L. SMITH

We face the twin enemies of crime and Communism. Crime and moral decay are eating at us from within. And Communism stands ready to pick up the pieces.

J. EDGAR HOOVER

The greatest question of our time is not communism versus individualism, not Europe versus America, not even the East versus the West; it is whether men can bear to live without God. Can civilization hold together if man abandons his faith in God?

WILL DURANT

It is scarcely possible in most places to get anyone to attend a meeting where the only attraction is God.

A. W. TOZER, MAN, THE DWELLING PLACE OF GOD

What on earth will today's younger generation be able to tell their children they had to do without?

CHICAGO DAILY NEWS

The midnight oil that modern students burn is gasoline.

ANONYMOUS

One of our great historians, Arnold Toynbee, writes of nineteen major civilizations that have existed since man began to structure governments. Of the nineteen, no more than five remain. Our Western civilization is among them. Today we are asking with growing concern, "Will it survive?"

G. S.

Whoever marries the spirit of this age will find himself a widower in the next.

WILLIAM R. INGE

MONEY

I hate money, but it soothes my nerves.

JOE LOUIS

Whoever said money can't buy happiness didn't know where to shop.

I don't like money. I don't like aspirin. But, it seems, I always need both, sometimes for the same reason.

When a fellow says, "It ain't the money, but the principle of the thing," it's the money.

ELBERT HUBBARD

I carry a rabbit's foot in my pocket because it saves me a lot of money. . . . Every time my wife sticks her hand in, she thinks it's a mouse.
ED FORD

After Clarence Darrow had solved a client's legal problem, the client asked, "How can I ever show my appreciation?" The lawyer replied, "My good friend, ever since the Phoenicians invented money, there has been only one answer to that question."
CLARENCE S. DARROW

Someone who's obsessed with making money to the exclusion of other goals in life has likely forgone the possibility of the acceptance in God's kingdom.
JIMMY CARTER

That money talks
I'll not deny,
I heard it once:
It said, "Goodbye."
RICHARD ARMOUR

During a serious illness, I had an unaccountable fit of anxiety about money matters. One of the brethren, after trying to comfort me, went straight home, and came back to me bringing all the stocks and shares and deeds and available funds he had, putting them down on the bed: "There, dear Pastor, I owe everything I have in the world to you, and you are quite welcome to all I possess." Of course I soon got better and returned it all to my dear friend.
C.HARLES HADDON SPURGEON

To be clever enough to get a great deal of money, one must be stupid enough to want it.
G. K. CHESTERTON

A man's treatment of money is the most decisive test of his character—how he makes it and how he spends it.
JAMES MOFFATT

331

Money reveals where our interests lie; it can direct our attitudes; it ever exposes us to the danger of worshiping it; and it represents value. Money not only talks; it screams.

LESLIE B. FLYNN

The Bible is very clear on the point that if we have money enough to live well, and do not share with others in need, it is questionable whether God's love is in us at all.

G. S.

In seventeen of His thirty-seven parables, Jesus dealt with property and man's responsibility for using it wisely.

G. S.

Writer Bert Bacharach tells us that the highest income made in any year was Al Capone's "take" in 1927—reputed to have been one hundred and five million dollars. But his "take" when he died was nothing—zero. No money was in his shroud—his hands were empty—even as the hands of all the poor and all the rich are empty when burial is accomplished.

ROBERT G. LEE

How we use our money demonstrates the reality of our love for God. In some ways it proves our love more conclusively than depth or knowledge, length of prayers or prominence of service. These things can be feigned, but the use of our possessions shows us up for what we actually are.

CHARLES CALDWELL RYRIE,
BALANCING THE CHRISTIAN LIFE

Material wealth is either a window through which we see God or a mirror in which we see ourselves.

WARREN WIERSBE, *LIVE LIKE A KING*

Money is a means, not an end—a tool to provide people with opportunities to hear and accept the gospel of Christ.

CHARLES STANLEY

Each of us will eventually give away all our earthly possessions. How we choose to do so, however, is a reflection of our commitment to the kingdom of God.

CHARLES STANLEY

Fortune does not change men. It only unmasks them.

MUSIC

· ·

He did not see any reason why the devil should have all the good tunes.

FROM E. W. BROOM, OF ROWLAND HILL

Christianity is the only religion that abounds in song. Atheism is songless; agnosticism has nothing to sing about; the various forms of idolatry are not tuneful; but Judaism said, "O come, let us sing unto the Lord"; and when Christ came, the angels greeted His birth with praise, and since then Christian song has gained in fullness and strength of voice with each century.

ANONYMOUS

Without music life would be a mistake.

FRIEDRICH NIETZSCHE

Bach almost persuaded me to be a Christian.

ROGER FRY

A friend once asked the great composer Haydn why his church music was always so full of gladness. He answered, "I cannot make it otherwise. I write according to the thoughts I feel. When I think upon my God, my heart is so full of joy that the notes dance and leap from my pen; and since God has given me a cheerful heart, it will be pardoned me that I serve Him with a cheerful spirit."

HENRY VAN DYKE

I know that the twelve notes in each octave and the varieties of rhythm offer me opportunities that all of human genius will never exhaust.

IGOR STRAVINSKY

There will be no song on our lips if there be no anguish in our hearts.

KARL BARTH

Music is the only language in which you cannot say a mean or sarcastic thing.

JOHN ERSKINE

NATION

National honor is national property of the highest value.
JAMES MONROE

It is not desirable to cultivate a respect for the law, so much as for the right.
HENRY DAVID THOREAU

The test of a nation is the growth of its people intellectually and spiritually. Money and so-called prosperity are of very little account! Babylon, Persia, Greece, Rome, Spain and France all had their turn in being the richest in the world. And instead of saving them, their so-called prosperity proved to be the ruin of them. Our nation is now the richest, but it could easily become a second-class nation and head downward. Money will not save us. Only a sane, spiritual revival which changes the desires of our people will save us.
ROGER BABSON

America! America!
God shed His grace on thee
And crown thy good with brotherhood
From sea to shining sea!
KATHERINE LEE BATES

When any nation has become overly pleasure-seeking, history has already begun its epitaph.
HOWARD WHITMAN

No nation has ever failed to prosper when its people put God first and their country second.
HAROLD LINDSELL,
THE WORLD, THE FLESH AND THE DEVIL

NATURE
· ·

Nature is the art of God.

SIR THOMAS BROWNE

The art of seeing nature is a thing almost as much to be acquired as the art of reading the Egyptian hieroglyphics.

JOHN CONSTABLE

One touch of nature makes the whole world kin.

WILLIAM SHAKESPEARE,
TROILUS AND CRESSIDA

Nature's laws affirm instead of prohibit. If you violate her laws you are your own prosecuting attorney, judge, jury, and hangman.

LUTHER BURBANK

Nothing is more beautiful than the loveliness of the woods before sunrise.

GEORGE WASHINGTON CARVER

The man who has seen the rising moon break out of the clouds at midnight has been present like an archangel at the creation of light and of the world.

RALPH WALDO EMERSON

No sight is more provocative of awe than is the night sky.

LLEWELYN POWYS

Doth not all nature around me praise God? If I were silent, I should be an exception to the universe. Doth not the thunder praise Him as it rolls like drums in the march of the God of armies? Do not the mountains praise Him when the woods upon their summits wave in adoration? Doth not the lightning write His name in letters of fire? Hath not the whole earth a voice? And shall I, can I, silent be?

CHARLES HADDON SPURGEON

NEGLECT
· ·

When I was in the hospital in Hawaii, I read again of the shocking events which led up to the destruction of the United States fleet at Pearl Harbor. On that fateful day of December 7, 1941, the Japanese attacked. We know now that the attack was invited by our failure to be always vigilant. The result was the destruction of our fleet—the cause was tragic indifference. When comfort and ease and pleasure are put ahead of duty and conviction, progress is always set back. What makes us Christians shrug our shoulders when we ought to be flexing our muscles? What makes us apathetic in a day when there are loads to lift, a world to be won, and captives to be set free? Why are so many bored, when the times demand action? Christ told us that in the last days there would be an insipid attitude toward life.

BILLY GRAHAM

All that is necessary for the forces of evil to win in the world is for enough good men to do nothing.

EDMUND BURKE

Some of us are as dead to the perception of God's gracious call, just because it has been sounded on uninterruptedly, as are the dwellers by a waterfall to its unremitting voice.

ALEXANDER MACLAREN

The untended garden will soon be overrun with weeds; the heart that fails to cultivate truth and root out error will shortly be a theological wilderness.

A. W. TOZER, *MAN, THE DWELLING PLACE OF GOD*

NEIGHBORS
· ·

Good fences make good neighbors.

ROBERT FROST

No one is rich enough to do without a neighbor.
DANISH PROVERB

Because we cannot see Christ we cannot express our love to Him; but our neighbors we can always see, and we can do to them what, if we saw Him, we would like to do to Christ.
MOTHER TERESA

The Bible tells us to love our neighbors, and also to love our enemies; probably because generally they are the same people.
G. K. CHESTERTON

> *To love the whole world*
> *For me is no chore;*
> *My only real problem's*
> *My neighbor next door.*
C. W. VANDERBERGH

NEW BIRTH

I find you grow more and more famous in the learned world. As you have made a pretty considerable progress in the mysteries of electricity, I would now humbly recommend to your diligent, unprejudiced pursuit and study, the mystery of the new birth. It is a most important, interesting study; and, when mastered, will richly answer and repay you for all your pains. One, at whose bar we are shortly to appear, hath solemnly declared, without it we cannot enter the kingdom of heaven. You will excuse this freedom. I must have something of Christ in all my letters.
GEORGE WHITEFIELD,
LETTER TO BENJAMIN FRANKLIN, 17 AUGUST 1752

Every story of conversion is the story of a blessed defeat.
C. S. LEWIS

Man's efforts to make himself personally and collectively happy in earthly terms are doomed to failure. He must indeed, as Christ said, be born again, be a new man, or he's nothing. So at least I have concluded, having failed to find . . . any alternative proposition. As far as I am concerned, it is Christ or nothing.

MALCOLM MUGGERIDGE

The sense of newness is simply delicious. It makes new the Bible, and friends, and all mankind, and love, and spiritual things, and Sunday, and church, and God Himself. So I've found.

TEMPLE GARDNER OF CAIRO

O Lord, convert the world—and begin with me.

A CHINESE STUDENT'S PRAYER

On January 12, 1723, I made a solemn dedication of myself to God, and wrote it down; giving up myself, and all that I had to God; to be for the future, in no respect, my own; to act as one that had no right to be himself, in any respect. And solemnly vowed to take God for my whole portion and felicity; looking on nothing else, as any part of my happiness, nor acting as if it were; and his law for the constant rule of my obedience: engaging to fight against the world, the flesh and the devil, to the end of my life.

JONATHAN EDWARDS,
PERSONAL NARRATIVE

When by the Spirit of God, I understood these words, "The just shall live by faith," I felt born again like a new man: I entered through the open doors into the very Paradise of God!

MARTIN LUTHER

Napoleon believed that the fate of every battle was decided in the space of five minutes. All his maneuvering and planning led to that strategic moment of crisis, the moment of action and decision.

So with you, my friend. Your future, your eternal welfare is decided in but a few moments of decision.

G. S.

Someone else, describing his new life in Christ, said, "Everything seems new—the Bible, my friends, my love for others, even Sunday itself. I have a new desire for spiritual things, a desire to know more about God and His church."

We must begin by acknowledging that we need God's help, God's power and God's life. Dead things cannot grow; and without Christ, we are spiritually dead. We are powerless and defeated.

G. S.

OPINIONS

* *

The foolish and the dead, never change their opinions.
JAMES RUSSELL LOWELL

As for the differences of opinion upon speculative questions, if we wait till they are reconciled, the action of human affairs must be suspended forever. But neither are we to look for perfection in any one man, nor for agreement among many.
JUNIUS

Opinions cannot survive if one has no chance to fight for them.
THOMAS MANN

We hardly find any persons of good sense save those who agree with us.
FRANÇOIS DUC DE LA ROCHEFOUCAULD

Some praise at morning what they blame at night,
But always think the last opinion right.
ALEXANDER POPE

"That was excellently observed," say I when I read a passage in another where his opinion agrees with mine. When we differ, then I pronounce him to be mistaken.
JONATHAN SWIFT

OPPORTUNITY
· ·

> *There is a tide in the affairs of men,*
> *Which, taken at the flood, leads on to fortune;*
> *Omitted, all the voyage of their life*
> *Is bound in shallows and in miseries.*
> *On such a full sea are we now afloat;*
> *And we must take the current when it serves,*
> *Or lose our ventures.*
>
> WILLIAM SHAKESPEARE, BRUTUS,
> IN *JULIUS CAESAR*

Small opportunities are often the beginning of great enterprises.
DEMOSTHENES

Opportunities multiply as they are seized; they die when neglected.
ANONYMOUS

A pessimist is one who makes difficulties of his opportunities; an optimist is one who makes opportunities of his difficulties.
REGINALD B. MANSELL

> *To each is given a bag of tools,*
> *A shapeless mass, and a book of rules,*
> *And each must make, ere life is flown,*
> *A stumbling-block or a stepping-stone.*
>
> ANONYMOUS

The reason so many people never get anywhere in life is because, when opportunity knocks, they are out in the backyard looking for four-leaf clovers.
WALTER P. CHRYSLER

Four things come not back—the spoken word, the sped arrow, the past life, and the neglected opportunity.
ARABIC PROVERB

The morning hour has gold in its mouth.
BENJAMIN FRANKLIN

When one door closes, another opens; but we often look so long and so regretfully upon the closed door that we do not see the one which has opened for us.
ALEXANDER GRAHAM BELL

Wherever there is danger, there lurks opportunity; whenever there is opportunity, there lurks danger. The two are inseparable; they go together.
EARL NIGHTINGALE

A man must make his opportunity as oft as find it.
FRANCIS BACON

When written in Chinese, the word "crisis" is composed of two characters—one represents danger and the other represents opportunity.
JOHN F. KENNEDY

Opportunities are often disguised as hard work, so most people fail to recognize them.
ANN LANDERS

PAIN

But may the God of all grace, who called us to His eternal glory by Christ Jesus, after you have suffered a while, perfect, establish, strengthen, and settle you.

1 PETER 5:10 NKJV

God whispers to us in our pleasures, speaks in our conscience, but shouts in our pain: it is His megaphone to rouse a deaf world.

C. S. LEWIS

If God exempted Christians from pain, pastors and ministers could stop preaching. TV preachers could cancel their air time, and lay people could stop witnessing. Nonbelievers would throng to the church and wear out the carpeted aisles to the altar, for Christianity would be the modern-day panacea, a gold-plated insurance policy for happiness.

However, that is not God's plan. No conversion decision will ever shield a person from suffering, though some individuals seem to accept Christ on the basis of a mythical theology, which they base on such promises as, "Beloved, I pray that you may prosper in all things and be in health, just as your soul prospers" (3 John 2 NKJV). These new believers are either soon disillusioned or grow into an understanding that God doesn't promise us a rose garden, He just helps us exist in the brown, dried-out pasture in which we sometimes find ourselves.

G. S.

Great sufferers do the world's work; a crown of loftiest achievement is a crown of thorns like our Savior's.

THEODORE EPP

Many a sick, weakly soul cowers within a healthy body, while many a hopeless sufferer is perfectly whole in heart. . . . A healthy soul is a greater gift than a healthy body, and this is something that none of us need lack.

MARGARET CLARKSON

PASSION
· ·

Mostly, we authors must repeat ourselves—that's the truth! We have two or three great moving experiences in our lives—experiences so great and moving that it doesn't seem at the time that anyone else has been caught up and pounded and dazzled and astonished and beaten and broken and rescued and illuminated and rewarded and humbled in just that way ever before.

F. SCOTT FITZGERALD

A poem is never a put-up job so to speak. It begins as a lump in the throat, a sense of wrong, a homesickness, a love sickness. It is never a thought to begin with.

ROBERT FROST

PAST
· ·

> *Here lies my past*
> *Good-bye I have kissed it;*
> *Thank you, kids,*
> *I wouldn't have missed it.*

OGDEN NASH, *YOU CAN'T GET THERE FROM HERE.*

You cannot change the past, but the past can change you, either for better or for worse. It all depends on how you look at it. The past can be a rudder that guides you or an anchor that hinders you. Leave your past mistakes with God, and look to the future by faith.

WARREN WIERSBE

I tell you the past is a bucket of ashes.

CARL SANDBURG

PASTORS
· ·

*God is on the lookout for a man whose heart is perfect toward Him.
Will you be quiet enough to hear Him, brave enough to proclaim
Him, and honest enough to obey Him?*

VANCE HAVNER

*Senator Robert S. Kerr of Oklahoma was a member of the First
Baptist Church of Oklahoma City. He was a long-time Sunday school
teacher and Christian philanthropist. He gave more than one million
dollars to Baptist institutions in Oklahoma.*

*His pastor, Dr. H. H. Hobbs, in his tribute to his friend at the
memorial service in the church, quoted a prayer the senator had published many years before called "A Prayer for My Pastor":*

*"Our Father, let me be a pillar of strength to help hold him up
and not a thorn in his back to pull him down. Let me support him
without striving to possess him. Let me lift his hands without placing
shackles around them. Let me give him help that he may devote more
time in working for the salvation of others and less time in gratifying
my vanity. Let me work for him as the pastor of all the members and
not compel him to spend precious time in bragging on me. Let me be
unselfish in what I do for him and not selfish in demanding that he
do more for me. Let me strive to serve him and the church much and
be happy as he serves me less and the church and others more."*

ROBERT G. LEE

*The one thing no church can stand is a pastor who really wants to be
something else. The men who really want out ought to be helped out,
for the Christian ministry is no place for a man who wants to be
something else. It is a place for men who can give counsel, not the
place for men who need counsel.*

DUKE K. MCCALL

PATIENCE
· ·

Patience overcomes everything. The world is his who has patience.
PROVERB

Patience often gets the credit that belongs to fatigue.
ANONYMOUS

John Wesley, the founder of Methodism, used to recall that as a youth his behavior often displeased his father. His mother was more forbearing. "How can you have the patience," exploded the elder Wesley, "to tell that blockhead John the same thing twenty times over?"

"Why," replied Mrs. Wesley, "if I had told him but nineteen times I had wasted my breath!"
G. S.

The faith of Christ offers no buttons to push for quick service. The new order must wait the Lord's own time, and that is too much for the man in a hurry. He just gives up and becomes interested in something else.
A. W. TOZER, MAN, THE DWELLING PLACE OF GOD

A doctor was once asked by a patient who had met with a serious accident, "Doctor, how long shall I have to lie here?"

"Only a day at a time," was his answer.

This taught the patient a valuable lesson. It was the same lesson God had recorded for His people for all ages. If we are faithful a day at a time, the long years will take care of themselves.
ANDREW MURRAY

The most useful virtue is patience.
JOHN DEWEY

He that can have patience can have what he will.
BENJAMIN FRANKLIN

*Prayer of the modern American: "Dear God, I pray for patience. And
I want it right now!"*

 OREN ARNOLD

*New England preacher Phillips Brooks was known for his calmness
and poise. His intimate friends, however, knew that he, too, suffered
moments of frustration and irritability. One day a friend saw him
pacing the floor like a caged lion. "What is the trouble, Dr. Brooks?"
asked the friend. "The trouble is," replied Brooks, "that I'm in a
hurry, but God isn't." Have you ever felt that way?*

G. S.

> *Did the leaves of the trees say something to you*
>   *as you passed them today?*
> *They were not created this spring, but months ago.*
>   *(And right now others are being fashioned*
>   *for another year.)*
> *At the bottom of every leaf is a cradle, and in it*
>   *is an infant germ:*
> *The winds will rock it and the birds will sing to it*
>   *all summer long and next spring it will unfold.*

ANONYMOUS

PATRIOTISM
· ·

I should like to be able to love my country and to love justice.

ALBERT CAMUS

If I added to their pride of America, I am happy.

CARL SANDBURG

*"My country, right or wrong," is a thing no patriot would think of
saying except in a desperate case. It is like saying, "My mother, drunk
or sober!"*

G. K. CHESTERTON, *THE DEFENDANT.* 1901

Abandon your animosities and make your sons Americans!
ROBERT E. LEE

I venture to suggest that patriotism is not a short and frenzied out-burst of emotion but the tranquil and steady dedication of a lifetime.
ADLAI STEVENSON

PEACE
· ·

In life troubles will come which seem as if they never will pass away. The night and the storm look as though they will last forever; but calm and the morning cannot be stayed; the storm in its very nature is transient. The effort of nature, as that of the human heart, is to return to its repose, for God is peace.
GEORGE MACDONALD

The sea was beating against the rocks in huge, dashing waves. The lightning was flashing, the thunder was roaring, the wind was blow-ing; but the little bird was asleep in the crevice of the rock, its head serenely under its wing, sound asleep. That is peace—to be able to sleep in the storm! In Christ, we are relaxed and at peace in the midst of the confusions, bewilderments, and perplexities of this life. The storm rages, but our hearts are at rest. We have found peace—at last!
BILLY GRAHAM

Drop Thy still dews of quietness,
Till all our strivings cease;
Take from our souls the strain and stress,
And let our ordered lives confess,
The beauty of Thy peace.
JOHN GREENLEAF WHITTIER

Peace, perfect peace, in this dark world of sin?
The blood of Jesus whispers peace within.
EDWARD HENRY BICKERSTETH

When each earthly prop gives under,
And life seems a restless sea,
Are you then a God-kept wonder,
Satisfied and calm and free?

ANONYMOUS

The winter's day has had its melancholy grey sky, with many a bitter dash of snow and rain—but it has stormed itself out, and at eventide a rent in the clouds reveals the sun, and it closes in peaceful clearness of night.

ALEXANDER MACLAREN

There is an end to all "the weary oar, the weary, wandering fields of barren foam." On the shore stands the Christ; and there is rest there.

ALEXANDER MACLAREN

PEOPLE

I was so shy, I was like an ingrown toenail.

BARBARA RUSH

The pressure of public opinion is like the pressure of the atmosphere; you can't see it—but, all the same, it is sixteen pounds to the square inch.

JAMES RUSSELL LOWELL

All the world is queer save thee and me, and even thou art a little queer.

ROBERT OWEN

There is no such thing [as great people]! The greatest man or woman is 99 percent just like yourself.

GEORGE BERNARD SHAW

The more I get to know people, the more I love my dog.
                                        FREDERICK THE GREAT

PERSEVERANCE, PERSISTENCE
· ·

Perseverance is the most overrated of traits if it is unaccompanied by talent; beating your head against a wall is more likely to produce a concussion in the head than a hole in the wall.
                                        SYDNEY HARRIS

The Man Who Quits

The man who quits has a brain and hand
As good as the next, but lacks the sand
That would make him stick, with a courage stout,
To whatever he tackles, and fight it out.

He starts with a rush, and a solemn vow
That he'll soon be showing the other how;
Then something new strikes his roving eye,
And his task is left for the bye-and-bye.

It's up to each man what becomes of him;
He must find in himself the grit and vim
That brings success; he can get the skill
If he brings to the task a steadfast will.

No man is beaten till he gives in;
Hard luck can't stand for a cheerful grin;
The man who fails needs a better excuse,
Than the quitter's whining, "What's the use?

For the man who quits lets his chances slip,
Just because he's too lazy to keep his grip.
The man who sticks goes ahead with a shout,
While the man who quits joins the "Down and out."
                                        ANONYMOUS

It was among the Parthians the custom that none were to give their children any meat in the morning before they saw the sweat on their faces. . . . You shall find this to be God's usual course: not to give His children the taste of His delights till they begin to sweat in seeking after them.

RICHARD BAXTER

Oh, the little more, and how much it is!
And the little less, and what worlds away!
ROBERT BROWNING

Feather by feather the goose is plucked.
JOHN RAY

The difference between perseverance and obstinacy is, that one often comes from a strong will, and the other from a strong won't.
HENRY WARD BEECHER

The great composer does not set to work because he is inspired, but becomes inspired because he is working. Beethoven, Wagner, Bach and Mozart settled down day after day to the job in hand with as much regularity as an accountant settles down each day to his figures. They didn't waste time waiting for an inspiration.
ERNEST NEWMAN

Perseverance: a lowly virtue whereby mediocrity achieves an inglorious success.

AMBROSE BIERCE

Mon centre cède, ma droite recule, situation excellente, j'attaque—My center is giving way, my right is retreating. Situation excellent. I shall attack.
FIELD MARSHALL FERDINAND FOCH

Inspiration without perspiration leads to frustration and stagnation.
BILL BRIGHT

Nothing in the world can take the place of persistence. Talent will not; nothing is more common than unsuccessful men with talent. Genius will not; unrewarded genius is almost a proverb. Education will not; the world is full of educated derelicts. Persistence and determination alone are omnipotent.

CALVIN COOLIDGE

We have all a few moments in life of hard, glorious running; but we have days and years of walking—the uneventful discharge of small duties.

ALEXANDER MACLAREN

For all your days prepare,
And meet them ever alike:
When you are the anvil, bear—
When you are the hammer, strike.
EDWIN MARKHAM

It is more important to gird ourselves for the grind of life than it is to throw ourselves into high gear only for the grandiose affairs of life.
CHARLES CALDWELL RYRIE

PLEASURE

A perpetual holiday is a good working definition of hell.
GEORGE BERNARD SHAW

Human nature is indeed in the grip of an overwhelming army of occupation. Its natural aim, it can truthfully be said, is pleasure; and when we consider the amount of time, energy, money, interest and enthusiasm that men and women give to the satisfaction of this aim we can appreciate the accuracy of James' diagnosis; and Christians can use it as a reliable yardstick by which to measure the sincerity of their religion. Is God or pleasure the dominant concern of their life?
R. V. G. TASKER

America rocks from a pleasure explosion. Every week, twelve million golfers vie for tee-off times, nine million tennis players compete across the nets; while four million skiers spend millions of dollars on equipment and resorts. Each year twenty-three million fishermen and hunters search for game in the woodlands of our nation.

G. S.

But pleasures are like poppies spread—
You seize the flow'r, its bloom is shed;
Or like the snow falls in the river—
A moment white, then melts forever.

ROBERT BURNS

Here are two tests to evaluate our pleasure:

First, do these pleasures encourage Christian development? "All things are lawful unto me, but all things are not expedient" (1 Corinthians 6:12). "Expedient" means profitable. Many activities may be legitimate, but do they help me to glorify my Lord and Savior Jesus Christ?

Second, do these pleasures endanger Christian maturity? "All things are lawful for me," said Paul, "but I will not be brought under the power of any" (1 Corinthians 6:12b). Seemingly innocent pleasures can choke out our spiritual lives.

God's Word talks about another kind of pleasure: eternal pleasure, lasting pleasure, pleasures forevermore. David said, "Thou wilt shew me the path of life: in thy presence is fulness of joy; at thy right hand there are pleasures for evermore" (Psalm 16:11).

G. S.

Satan is not such a fool as to fish without bait.

ANONYMOUS

The only path to pleasure is in pleasing God.

RICHARD OWEN ROBERTS

POETRY

Poetry is a way of taking life by the throat.

ROBERT FROST

POLITICS

Man's capacity for justice makes democracy possible, but his inclination to injustice makes democracy necessary.

REINHOLD NIEBUHR,
*THE CHILDREN OF LIGHT AND THE CHILDREN OF
DARKNESS*, 1944

Winston Churchill was asked why he got into politics. He replied, "Ambition, pure ambition." Then asked what made him stay in politics, he replied, "Anger, pure unadulterated anger."

WINSTON CHURCHILL

Have you ever seen a candidate talking to a rich person on television?

ART BUCHWALD

A man of few words, Calvin Coolidge explained why: "I found out early in life that you never have to explain something you haven't said."

CALVIN COOLIDGE

In 1958, when he was speaking to members of the Gridiron Club in Washington, and it was known he would seek the Democratic nomination, John F. Kennedy said, "I have just received the following wire from my generous Daddy: 'Dear Jack—Don't buy a single vote more than is necessary. I'll be hanged if I am going to pay for a landslide.'"

JOHN F. KENNEDY

He serves his party best who serves the country best.

RUTHERFORD B. HAYES

I know that when things don't go well, they like to blame the president, and that is one of the things presidents are paid for.
JOHN F. KENNEDY

I tell you, Folks, all Politics is Apple Sauce.
WILL ROGERS

Whenever a man has cast a longing eye on offices, a rottenness begins in his conduct.
THOMAS JEFFERSON

But the future lies with those wise political leaders who realize that the great public is interested more in government than in politics.
FRANKLIN DELANO ROOSEVELT

Politics has got so expensive that it takes lots of money to even get beat with.
WILL ROGERS

Politics are almost as exciting as war, and quite as dangerous. In war you can only be killed once, but in politics many times.
WINSTON CHURCHILL

Politics is the art of the possible, not the art of the ideal.
RUSSELL KIRK

POVERTY

Poverty is not dishonorable in itself, but only when it comes from idleness, intemperance, extravagance, and folly.
PLUTARCH

No society can surely be flourishing and happy, of which the far greater part of the members are poor and miserable.
ADAM SMITH

For every talent that poverty has stimulated it has blighted a hundred.
JOHN W. GARDNER

Not he who has little, but he who wishes more, is poor.
SENECA

This Administration here and now declares unconditional war on poverty in America.
LYNDON B. JOHNSON

If you spend all your time collecting money for fear of poverty, you are practicing poverty already.
ANONYMOUS

You don't have to look for distress; it is screaming at you!
SAMUEL BECKETT

POWER
· ·

Responsibility gravitates toward him who gets ready for it, and power flows to him and through him who can use it.
GEORGE WALTER FISKE

Self-reverence, self-knowledge, self-control
These three alone lead life to sovereign power.
ALFRED, LORD TENNYSON

It is the magician's bargain: give up our souls, get power in return. But once our souls, that is, our selves, have been given up, the power thus conferred will not belong to us. We shall in fact be the slaves and puppets of that to which we have given our souls.
C. S. LEWIS

Meekness is power under control.
WARREN WIERSBE, LIVE LIKE A KING

PRAISE (SEE THANKS AND PRAISE)

PRAYER
· ·

The moment you wake up each morning, all your wishes and hopes for the day rush at you like wild animals. And the first job each morning consists in shoving it all back; in listening to that other voice, taking that other point of view, letting that other, larger, stronger, quieter life come flowing in.

C. S. LEWIS

To be a Christian without prayer is no more possible than to be alive without breathing.

MARTIN LUTHER

The principal cause of my leanness and unfruitfulness is owing to an unaccountable backwardness to pray. I can write or read or converse or hear with a ready heart; but prayer is more spiritual and inward than any of these, and the more spiritual any duty is the more my carnal heart is apt to start from it.

RICHARD NEWTON

Prayer is not something to be added after other approaches in our search for the will of God have been tried and have failed. No, we should pray as we use the personal resources God has given us.

T. B. MASTON

Do not pray for tasks equal to your powers. Pray for powers equal to your tasks.

PHILLIPS BROOKS

More things are wrought by prayer than this world dreams of.

ALFRED, LORD TENNYSON

Prayer is the key of the morning and the bolt of the evening.

MATTHEW HENRY

If you pray for bread and bring no basket to carry it, you prove the doubting spirit which may be the only hindrance to the gift you ask.
D. L. MOODY

Prayer is the preface to the book of Christian living, the text of the new life sermon, the girding on of the armor for battle, the pilgrim's preparation for his journey; and it must be supplemented by action or it amounts to nothing.

ANONYMOUS

Nothing lies beyond the reach of prayer except that which lies outside the will of God.

ANONYMOUS

[About Praying (John) Hyde] He prayed as if God were at his elbow.
ANONYMOUS

Pray for great things, expect great things, work for great things, but above all, pray.
R. A. TORREY

Prayer is not overcoming God's reluctance: it is laying hold of His highest willingness.

RICHARD CHENEVIX, ARCHBISHOP TRENCH

Work as if everything depended upon your work, and pray as if everything depended upon your prayer.
GENERAL WILLIAM BOOTH

And Satan trembles when he sees
The weakest saint upon his knees.
ANONYMOUS

Hurry is the death of prayer.

SAMUEL CHADWICK

Prayer is not conquering God's reluctance, but taking hold of God's willingness.

PHILLIPS BROOKS

I judge that my prayer is more than the devil himself. If it were otherwise I would have fared differently long before this. Yet men will not see and acknowledge the great wonders or miracles God works in my behalf. If I should neglect prayer but a single day, I should lose a great deal of the fire of faith.

MARTIN LUTHER

By one hour's intimate access to the throne of grace, where the Lord causes His glory to pass before the soul that seeks Him you may acquire more true spiritual knowledge and comfort than by a day's or a week's converse with the best of men, or the most studious perusal of many folios.

JOHN NEWTON

I have been driven many times to my knees by the overwhelming conviction that I had nowhere else to go. My own wisdom, and that of all about me seemed insufficient for the day.

ABRAHAM LINCOLN

Any housewife knows that the best way to remember the things she meant to do and forgot is to start praying. They will come to her mind to divert her from prayer.

VANCE HAVNER

Did any of you, parents, ever hear your child wake from sleep with some panic fear and shriek the mother's name through the darkness? Was not that a more powerful appeal than all words? And, depend upon it, that the soul which cries aloud on God, "the God and Father of our Lord Jesus Christ," though it have "no language but a cry," will never call in vain.

ALEXANDER MACLAREN

Trouble and perplexity drive us to prayer, and prayer driveth away trouble and perplexity.

PHILIPP MELANCHTHON

Let us advance upon our knees.

JOHN HARDY NEESIMA

When we become too glib in prayer we are most surely talking to ourselves.

A. W. TOZER, *BORN AFTER MIDNIGHT*

> *When God inclines the heart to pray,*
> *He hath an ear to hear;*
> *To him there's music in a groan,*
> *And beauty in a tear.*
> ANONYMOUS

Since the Holy Spirit makes intercession for the infirmed saints according to God's will, who are we to pray any other way? (Romans 8:22-27).

G. S.

In my thinking, the "prayer of faith" cannot be prayed simply at will. It is given of God in certain cases to serve His purpose and to accomplish His sovereign will.

G. S.

Prayer will make a man cease from sin, or sin will entice a man to cease from prayer.

JOHN BUNYAN

> *We, ignorant of ourselves,*
> *Beg often our own harms, which the wise powers*
> *Deny us for our good; so find we profit*
> *By losing of our prayers.*
> WILLIAM SHAKESPEARE,
> *ANTONY AND CLEOPATRA*

Dwight L. Moody had a practical mind that never let a meeting get out of hand. Long public prayer particularly irritated him. Once he told his song leader, Sankey, "Lead us in a hymn while our brother is finishing his prayer."

G. S.

Good prayers never come creeping home. I am sure I shall receive either what I ask or what I should ask.

JOSEPH HALL

Will petitions that do not move the heart of the suppliant, move the heart of Omnipotence?

ANONYMOUS

Is there any place in any of our rooms where there is a little bit of carpet worn white by our knees?

ALEXANDER MACLAREN

Prayer is the gymnasium of the soul.

SAMUEL M. ZWEMER

The life of prayer shapes the unity of Christian morality.

CARL F. H. HENRY,
CHRISTIAN PERSONAL ETHICS

Whoever only speaks of God, but never or seldom to God, easily leases body and soul to idols. The Christian thus places his whole future in jeopardy by a stunted prayer life.

CARL F. H. HENRY

The very breath of prayer sustains the Christian life.

CARL F. H. HENRY

Yes, there is only one thing that will save us in this hour of desperation, and that is prayer.

STEPHEN OLFORD,
HEART CRY FOR REVIVAL

Prayer without work is like an empty wagon—lots of noise but no load.

ANONYMOUS

There are great drynesses even in the way of meditation; the bread of prayer is often without taste.

FRANÇOIS MALAVAL,
A SIMPLE METHOD OF RAISING THE SOUL TO CONTEMPLATION

The function of prayer is to set God at the center of attention.

ALBERT EDWARD DAY

We must alter our lives in order to alter our hearts, for it is impossible to live one way and pray another.

WILLIAM LAW

Prayer is the world in tune.

HENRY VAUGHAN

We tiptoe around in the throne room of God, afraid to ask what we really want. We don't go to Him on the basis of what He said He would do. We go weakly and fearfully.

CHARLES STANLEY

Prayer begins where human capacity ends.

NORMAN VINCENT PEALE

Prayer moves the Hand which moves the world.

JOHN A. WALLACE

Every time we pray to God, seeking His will, there are two things He wants to show us. He wants to show us Himself, and He wants to show us what He is able to do. Is there anything greater than seeking God and knowing His power?

CHARLES STANLEY

Humanity is never so beautiful as when praying for forgiveness or else forgiving another.

JEAN PAUL RICHTER

It is not preaching, teaching, singing, or organizing; it is the Word of God brought against Satan's lies through prayer. Our prayers build the kingdom of God and destroy the kingdom of Satan. But where there is no prayer, there is no warfare. Where there is no warfare, there is no spiritual reality. Where there is no spiritual reality, there is no victory. Where there is no victory, there is nothing glorifying to God.

CHARLES STANLEY

PREACHING
· ·

A preacher may be wrapped in the robes of learning, and his study walls may be decked with diplomas. His home may be filled with travel souvenirs from many lands, and he may wear all the trappings of ecclesiastical prestige and pageantry. But he cannot function without unction.

VANCE HAVNER

Faith comes from hearing the message, and the message is heard through the word of Christ.

ROMANS 10:17 NIV

I am certain that when I enter the pulpit or stand at the lectern to read, it is not my word, but my tongue is the pen of a ready writer.

MARTIN LUTHER

God . . . deigns to consecrate to Himself the mouths and tongues of men in order that His may resound in them.

JOHN CALVIN

Preaching that costs nothing accomplishes nothing.

JOHN HENRY JOWETT

With preaching, Christianity stands or falls because it is the declaration of a Gospel. Nay, more—far more—it is the Gospel prolonging and declaring itself.

P. T. FORSYTH

The preaching that kills may be, and often is, orthodox—dogmatically, inviolably orthodox. In the Christian system, unction is the anointing of the Holy Ghost, separating a person unto God's work and preparing him for it. This unction is the one divine enablement by which the preacher accomplishes the peculiar and saving ends of preaching. Without this unction there are no true spiritual results accomplished. The results and forces in preaching do not rise above the results of unsanctified speech. Without unction the former is as potent as the pulpit . . . without it the gospel has no more power to propagate itself than any other system of truth. This is the seal of its divinity. Unction in the preacher puts God in the gospel.

CHARLES HADDON SPURGEON

. . . until we have wrestled with God till the break of day, like Jacob: that is, until we have struggled to the utmost limits of our strength, and have known the despair of defeat. . . . [until] we have really understood the actual plight of our contemporaries, when we have heard their cry of anguish, [until] we have shared their suffering, both physical and spiritual, and their despair and desolation . . . then we shall be able to proclaim the word of God—but not till then!

JACQUES ELLUL

Richard Baxter praised those preachers who "preached as never sure to preach again . . . as a dying man to dying men."

G. S.

A homiletics professor said to his seminary class, "Students, when you want an illustration for a sermon, take it out of the Bible. Your people will not be familiar with it."

The hearer's life is the preacher's best commendation.
ANONYMOUS

I heard of a pastor who met one of his delinquent members and said, "Well, I haven't seen you in church lately."

"No," he said, "you know how it's been. The children have been sick, and then it's rained and rained and rained."

The pastor said, "Well, it's always dry at church."

"Yeah," he said, "that's another reason why I haven't been coming."

It ought not be so. We are dealing with divine dynamite, and I believe that everyone who comes to every service ought to get a blessing and go out charged up.
VANCE HAVNER

PREJUDICE
. . . .

Prejudice is the ink with which all history is written.
MARK TWAIN

[Prejudice is] the mistreatment of people without their having done anything to merit such mistreatment. It has been a source of human unhappiness and misunderstanding wherever and whenever it has arisen.
ARNOLD ROSE,
THE ROOTS OF PREJUDICE

To label people as worthy and unworthy, as good and bad, as acceptable and repulsive, is contrary to God's law and thoroughly anti-Christian.
G. S.

The mind of the bigot is like the pupil of the eye; the more light you pour upon it, the more it will contract.
OLIVER WENDELL HOLMES, JR.

I am free of all prejudices. I hate every one equally.
                                    W. C. FIELDS

All looks yellow to a jaundiced eye.
                                    ALEXANDER POPE

Nothing is so firmly believed as that which is least known.
                                    MICHEL DE MONTAIGNE

> *A man convinced against his will*
> *Is of the same opinion still.*
>   SAMUEL BUTLER

No man has a right in America to treat any other man tolerantly, for tolerance is the assumption of superiority.
                                    WENDELL WILLKIE

The real democratic American idea is, not that every man shall be on a level with every other man, but that every man shall have liberty to be what God made him, without hindrance.
                                    HENRY WARD BEECHER

PRIDE

The animals were arguing about who had the biggest litters. Some talked big about their twins or triplets, some bragged of a dozen. Finally they asked the lioness, who rather quietly replied, "Only one—but that one is a lion."
                                    AESOP'S FABLES, ADAPTATION

If you feel or imagine that you are right and suppose that your book, teaching or writing is a great achievement. . . . then, my dear man, feel your ears. If you are doing so properly, you will find that you have a splendid pair of big, long shaggy asses' ears.
                                    MARTIN LUTHER

But too many people now climb onto the cross merely to be seen from a greater distance, even if they have to trample somewhat on the one who has been there so long.

ALBERT CAMUS

He that is proud eats up himself: pride is his own glass, his own trumpet, his own chronicle.

WILLIAM SHAKESPEARE,
TROILUS AND CRESSIDA

In his pride, Moses lost his temper and was kept out of the Promised Land (Numbers 20:1–13). Pride kept Joshua from seeking God's will at Ai, and he lost the battle (Joshua 7). King Nebuchadnezzar's pride turned him into an animal (Daniel 4), and Peter's pride led to his denial of Christ (Luke 22:31–34).

WARREN WIERSBE

God made us, and God is able to empower us to do whatever He calls us to do. Denying that we can accomplish God's work is not humility; it is the worst kind of pride! . . . The proud man is possessed by things; the humble man possesses things and uses them for the good of others and the glory of God.

WARREN WIERSBE, *LIVE LIKE A KING*

A proud man is always looking down on things and people; and, of course, as long as you're looking down, you can't see something that's above you.

C. S. LEWIS

Lord . . . where we are wrong, make us willing to change, and where we are right, make us easy to live with.

PETER MARSHALL

No matter how dear you are to God, if pride is harbored in your spirit, He will whip it out of you. They that go up in their own estimation must come down again by His discipline.

CHARLES HADDON SPURGEON

PROGRESS

Restlessness and discontent are the first necessities of progress.
THOMAS A. EDISON

You can't hold a man down without staying down with him.
BOOKER T. WASHINGTON

> *How does the soul grow? Not all in a minute!*
> *Now it may lose ground, and now it may win it;*
> *Now it resolves, and again the will faileth;*
> *Now it rejoiceth, and now it bewaileth;*
> *Now its hopes fructify, then they are blighted;*
> *Now it walks sullenly, now gropes benighted;*
> *Fed by discouragements, taught by disaster;*
> *So it goes forward, now slower, now faster,*
> *Till all the pain is past, and failure made whole,*
> *It is full grown and the Lord rules the soul.*
> SUSAN COOLIDGE

PURPOSE OF MAN

Man was made to grow, not stop.
ROBERT BROWNING

> *To look up and not down,*
> *To look forward and not back,*
> *To look out and not in, and*
> *To lend a hand.*
> EDWARD EVERETT HALE

Thou hast made us for Thyself, and the heart of man is restless until it finds its rest in Thee.
SAINT AUGUSTINE

Life is a mission. Every other definition is false, and leads all who accept it astray.

GUISEPPE MAZZINI

When God wanted sponges and oysters He made them and put one on a rock and the other in the mud. When He made man He did not make him to be a sponge or an oyster; He made him with feet and hands, and head and heart, and vital blood, and a place to use them and He said to him, "Go work."

HENRY WARD BEECHER

I see no business in life but the work of Christ.

HENRY MARTYN

In the spring of 1871, a young man picked up a book and read twenty-one words that had a profound effect on his future. A medical student at the Montreal General Hospital, he was worried about passing the final examination, worried about what to do, where to go, how to build up a practice, how to make a living.

The twenty-one words that this young medical student read in 1871 helped him to become the most famous physician of his generation. He organized the world-famous John Hopkins School of Medicine. He became Regis Professor of Medicine at Oxford—the highest honor that can be bestowed upon any medical man in the British Empire. He was knighted by the King of England. When he died, two huge volumes containing 1466 pages were required to tell the story of his life.

His name was Sir William Osler. Here are the twenty-one words that he read in the spring of 1871—twenty-one words from Thomas Carlyle that helped him lead a life free from worry: "Our main business is not to see what lies dimly at a distance, but to do what lies clearly at hand."

DALE CARNEGIE,
HOW TO STOP WORRYING AND START LIVING

Lives of great men all remind us
We can make our lives sublime,
And, departing, leave behind us
Footprints on the sands of time.

HENRY WADSWORTH LONGFELLOW

Fear God and work hard.

DAVID LIVINGSTONE

Good morning, God, I love You! What are You up to today? I want to be a part of it.

NORMAN GRUBB, MORNING PRAYER

I have loved to hear my Lord spoken of; and wherever I have seen the print of His shoe in the earth, there I have coveted to set my foot too. His name has been to me as a civet-box; yea, sweeter than all perfumes. . . . And His countenance I have more desired than they that have most desired the light of the sun.

JOHN BUNYAN

RACE

. . . .

Jesus has a family in an interracial neighborhood called heaven.
DECISION

In teaching race pride, it will be disastrous if we teach a false distinction and a false superiority. We do not correct white racism by erecting black racism.
ROY WILKINS

There are no "white" or "colored" signs on the foxholes or graveyards of battle.
JOHN F. KENNEDY

God is color-blind to skin.
G. S.

Race prejudice is not only a shadow over the colored—it is a shadow over all of us, and the shadow is the darkest over those who feel it least and allow its evil effects to go on.
PEARL S. BUCK

For I am my mother's daughter, and the drums of Africa still beat in my heart. They will not let me rest while there is a single Negro boy or girl without a chance to prove his worth.
MARY MCLEOD BETHUNE

All colors will agree in the dark.
FRANCIS BACON

REDEMPTION
· ·

Two small boys were comparing progress in study for the Saturday catechism lesson.

"I've gotten as far as redemption," said one. "How far you got?"
"Oh, I'm way beyond redemption," said the other proudly.
ANONYMOUS

To deliver us from evil is not merely to take us out of hell, it is to take us into heaven.

P. T. FORSYTH, *THE WORK OF CHRIST*

We are God's very own, being redeemed by Him. Every Christian therefore should wear a sign in his heart, "Not for sale!"
ANONYMOUS

But God will redeem my soul from the power of the grave: for he shall receive me.

PSALM 49:15

Let Israel hope in the Lord: for with the Lord there is mercy, and with him is plenteous redemption.

PSALM 130:7

He will swallow up death in victory; and the Lord God will wipe away tears from off all faces; and the rebuke of his people shall he take away from off all the earth: for the Lord hath spoken it.

ISAIAH 25:8

For ye are bought with a price: therefore glorify God in your body, and in your spirit, which are God's.

1 CORINTHIANS 6:20

RELIGION
· ·

Religion . . . is the opium of the people.
KARL MARX

Don't be ashamed of the old-time religion. There is nothing newer. We have a New Testament about a new and living way. We enter that way by new birth. We are new creatures with a new name and a new song, walking in newness of life, living by a new commandment, headed for a new heaven and a new earth and a new Jerusalem. And almost the last word of the New Testament in Revelation 21:5 is, "Behold, I make all things new." No wonder the gospel is good news old time, new time, any time, all the time. God is not running an antique shop.
VANCE HAVNER

Men will wrangle for religion; write for it; fight for it; anything but live for it.
CHARLES CALEB COLTON

We have just enough religion to make us hate, but not enough to make us love one another.
JONATHAN SWIFT

Most men, indeed, play at religion as they play at games, religion itself being of all games the one most universally played.
A. W. TOZER, THE DIVINE CONQUEST

Going to church doesn't make you a Christian any more than going to a garage makes you an automobile.
BILLY SUNDAY

I have treated many hundreds of patients. Among those over thirty-five, there has not been one whose problem in the last resort was not that of finding a religious outlook on life.
CARL JUNG

Our great-grandfathers called it the holy Sabbath; our grandfathers, the Sabbath; our fathers, Sunday, but today we call it the weekend. We have substituted a holiday for the holy day.

WESLEYAN METHODIST

This I know—men without religion are moral cowards. The cause of Europe's miseries was its lack of religion.

GEORGE BERNARD SHAW

REPENTANCE
· ·

Man is born with his back toward God. When he truly repents, he turns right around and faces God. Repentance is a change of mind. . . . Repentance is the tear in the eye of faith.

D. L. MOODY

There is one case of death-bed repentance recorded—the penitent thief —that no one should despair; and only one, that no one should presume.

SAINT AUGUSTINE

He that hath promised pardon on our repentance hath not promised life till we repent.

FRANCIS QUARLES

True repentance has a double aspect; it looks upon things past with a weeping eye, and upon the future with a watchful eye.

ROBERT SMITH

Jesus said, "I came not to call the righteous, but sinners to repentance."

LUKE 5:32

REPUTATION

· ·

> *Who steals my purse steals trash; . . .*
> *But he that filches from me my good name*
> *Robs me of that which not enriches him,*
> *And makes me poor indeed.*
>
> WILLIAM SHAKESPEARE, *OTHELLO*

It is a maxim with me that no man was ever written out of reputation but by himself.

RICHARD BENTLEY

To disregard what the world thinks of us is not only arrogant but utterly shameless.

CICERO

Reputations, like beavers and cloaks, shall last some people twice the time of others.

DOUGLAS JERROLD

A man's virtue is his monument, but forgotten is the man of evil repute.

EGYPTIAN TOMBSTONE INSCRIPTION
(2100 B.C.)

RESPONSIBILITY

· ·

If people concentrated on their responsibilities, others would have their rights.

STUART BRISCOE, *WHAT WORKS*

When they told me yesterday what had happened, I felt like the moon, the stars and all the planets had fallen on me. If you fellows ever pray, pray for me.

HARRY S. TRUMAN,
AFTER HIS ACCESSION TO THE PRESIDENCY,
13 APRIL 1945

Life always gets harder toward the summit—the cold increases, responsibility increases.

FRIEDRICH NIETZSCHE

You can't escape the responsibility of tomorrow by evading it today.

ABRAHAM LINCOLN

Ask not what your country can do for you; ask what you can do for your country.

JOHN F. KENNEDY

If you can't stand the heat, stay out of the kitchen.

HARRY S. TRUMAN

I believe that every right implies a responsibility; every opportunity, an obligation; every possession, a duty.

JOHN D. ROCKEFELLER, JR.

The ability to accept responsibility is the measure of the man.

ROY L. SMITH

RESURRECTION

In the early 1920s, Nikolai Bukharin was sent from Moscow to Kiev to address a vast anti-God rally. For an hour he abused and ridiculed the Christian faith until it seemed as if the whole structure of belief was in ruins. Questions were invited. A priest of the Orthodox church rose and asked leave to speak. He faced the people and gave them the ancient Easter greeting, "Christ is risen." Instantly the whole vast assembly rose to its feet, and the reply came back like a crash of breakers against the cliff, "He is risen indeed."

G. S.

Our Lord has written the promise of the resurrection, not in books alone, but in every leaf of springtime.

MARTIN LUTHER

Germany's Count Bismarck is said to have remarked, "Without the hope of eternal life, this life is not worth the effort of getting dressed in the morning." There is a great deal of truth in that statement. "For what is your life?" asks James, "It is even a vapour, that appeareth for a little time, and then vanisheth away" (James 4:14).

Job knew something of the brevity and futility of life. "My days are swifter than a weaver's shuttle," he said, "and are spent without hope" (Job 7:6). "Man that is born of a woman is of few days, and full of trouble. He cometh forth like a flower, and is cut down: he fleeth also as a shadow, and continueth not" (Job 14:1–2).

Isaiah wrote, "All flesh is grass, and all the goodliness thereof is as the flower of the field: the grass withereth, the flower fadeth" (Isaiah 40:6–7).

Yes, this life is brief and full of sorrows. And if our existence ends with the grave, what is the use? That is what Paul meant when he wrote in 1 Corinthians 15:19, "If in this life only we have hope in Christ, we are of all men most miserable." But the hope that Jesus gives goes beyond the grave, and His resurrection is the proof of it.

Paul goes on to say, "But now is Christ risen from the dead, and become the first fruits of them that slept" (v. 20). He is the first fruits. The harvest is yet to come. All who put their trust in Him will be a part of that great harvest of souls that will rise from the dead.

G. S.

The Result of the Resurrection

1. It guarantees the deity of the Lord Jesus. He is "declared to be the Son of God with power, according to the Spirit of holiness, by the resurrection from the dead" (Romans 1:4).
2. It is essential to our justification. (See Romans 4:25; 8:34.) Because Jesus rose from the dead all who believe in Him are justified "from all things, from which ye could not be justified by the law of Moses" (Acts 13:39).
3. It makes possible the forgiveness of sins. (See 1 Corinthians 15:17.)
4. It makes certain a final judgment "because he hath appointed a day, in the which he will judge the world in righteousness by

*that man who he hath ordained; whereof he hath
given assurance unto all men, in that he hath raised him from
the dead" (Acts 17:31).*

5. *It furnishes every believer with a deathless hope. "But now is
Christ risen from the dead, and become the firstfruits of them that
slept" (1 Corinthians 15:20). As He rose from the dead and liveth
forever, so will the bodies of believers be raised from the tomb.
This is the unshakable confidence of the saints.*

HAROLD LINDSELL AND CHARLES
WOODBRIDGE

*Christianity is in its very essence a resurrection religion. The concept
of the resurrection lies at its heart. If you remove it, Christianity is
destroyed.*

JOHN R. STOTT

*In Glendale, California, at Forest Lawn Cemetery, hundreds of people
each year stand before two huge paintings. One pictures the crucifixion of Christ. The other depicts His resurrection. In the second painting the artist has pictured an empty tomb with an angel near the
entrance. In the foreground stands the figure of the risen Christ. But
the striking feature of that huge canvas is a vast throng of people,
back in the misty background, stretching into the distance and out of
sight, suggesting the multitude who will be raised from the dead
because Jesus first died and rose for them.*

G. S.

RETIREMENT
·····································

To retire is to begin to die.

PABLO CASALS

*When some people retire, it's going to be mighty hard to be able to tell
the difference.*

VIRGINIA GRAHAM

I'm against mandatory retirement. It ought to be left to individuals. It is a shame to assume that all fools are old fools. I've found that there are more young fools than old fools. Nature has a way of getting rid of old fools.

SAM ERVIN

REVIVAL
· ·

The best way to revive a church, is to build a fire in the pulpit.

D. L. MOODY

. . . times of refreshing from the Lord.

J. EDWIN ORR

[Revival is a] new beginning of obedience to God. . . . Just as in the case of a converted sinner, the first step is a deep repentance, a breaking down of heart, a getting down in the dust before God, with deep humility and a forsaking of sin.

CHARLES FINNEY

O that God would teach us that it is just as important to be spiritual as to be sound in our approach to the Bible, just as vital to be obedient as to be orthodox, and that the purpose of revelation is nothing less than transformation of human lives!

STEPHEN OLFORD, *HEART CRY FOR REVIVAL*

The greatest obstacle to the conversion of Nineveh was not to be found in Nineveh. It was not the sin and corruption of the Ninevites, although those were great. It was not the graft-ridden police force or corrupt politicians. It was not the false cults and religions. The biggest obstacle to the salvation of Nineveh was found in the heart of a pious, prejudiced man named Jonah. There was no deceitfulness in all of Nineveh like the deceitfulness in Jonah's heart.

Jonah was the key to the salvation of Nineveh. God's people are the key to the spiritual climate of our nation and world.

G. S.

Seven steps to revival

1. *Develop the desire to know Jesus Christ better. Develop a holy dissatisfaction. The contented Christian is the sterile Christian. Paul said in substance, "Jesus arrested me on the Damascus road. Now I want to lay hold of all that for which I was arrested by God." Be thoroughly dissatisfied with your spiritual posture.*
2. *Pray for a revolutionary change in your life. I think of Jacob wrestling with God. He wanted blessing. He wouldn't be denied. Throw your entire life into the will of God. Seek God's very best.*
3. *Do what you know to do. If we pray for revival and neglect prayer, that's hypocrisy. To pray for growth and neglect the local church is absolute foolishness. To pray that you'll mature and neglect the Word of God is incongruous. Put yourself in the way of blessing.*
4. *Totally repent. "Create in me a clean heart!" David sobbed. For a whole year David was out of fellowship. But he confessed his sin; he turned from that sin, and then he could sing again; he could write again; he could pray again.*
5. *Make the crooked straight. If you owe a debt, pay it. Or have an understanding with the people you owe. Zacchaeus said, "Lord, the half of my goods I give to the poor; and if I have taken anything from any man by false accusation, I restore him fourfold" (Luke 19:8). As much as possible, make the crooked straight.*
6. *Develop a seriousness of purpose. Keep off the detours. Let nothing deflect that magnetic needle of your calling. If there is anything that is a Trojan horse in our day, it is the television set. Beware lest it rob you of your passion and your purpose.*
7. *Major in majors. The Christian life requires specialists. Jesus said in effect, "Be a one-eyed man" (cf. Luke 11:34-36). Paul said, "This one thing I do." Too many of us burn up too much energy without engaging in things that bring us nearer to God.*

Refuse to rust out. Start sharing your faith. Make yourself available. Back your decision with your time and talent and dollars. Finally, ask God for great faith in Him. Begin to expect great things.

G. S.

I can give a prescription that will bring revival . . . revival to any church, or community, or any city on earth.

First: Let a few Christians get thoroughly right with God. If this is not done, the rest will come to nothing.

Second: Let them bind themselves together to pray for revival until God opens the windows of heaven and comes down.

Third: Let them put themselves at the disposal of God for His use as He sees fit in winning others to Christ. That is all. I have given this prescription around the world . . . and in no instance has it failed. It cannot fail.

R. A. TORREY

Revival is absolutely essential to restrain the righteous anger of God, to restore the conscious awareness of God, and to reveal the gracious activity of God.

STEPHEN OLFORD, HEART CRY FOR REVIVAL

RIGHTEOUSNESS
· ·

You can always tell when you are on the road of righteousness—it's uphill.

ERNEST BLEVENS

I greatly longed to understand Paul's Epistle to the Romans, and nothing stood in the way but that one expression, "the righteousness of God," because I took it to mean that righteousness whereby God is righteous and deals righteously in punishing the unrighteous. . . . Night and day I pondered until . . . I grasped the truth that the righteousness of God is that righteousness whereby, through grace and sheer mercy, he justified us by faith. Thereupon I felt myself to be reborn and to have gone through open doors into paradise. The whole of Scripture took on a new meaning, and whereas before "the righteousness of God" had filled with hate, now it became to me inexpressibly sweet in greater love. This passage of Paul became to me a gateway to heaven.

MARTIN LUTHER

SAINTS

A humble saint looks most like a citizen of heaven.

D. L. MOODY

Why, why will we most gladly set days aside to honor the fathers of our nation—Washington, Lincoln, Jefferson—but draw back in dismay from giving honor to the Fathers of our Faith?

THOMAS HOWARD,
EVANGELICAL IS NOT ENOUGH

The saints are the sinners who keep on going.

ROBERT LOUIS STEVENSON

He that falls into sin is a man; that grieves at it, is a saint; that boasteth of it, is a devil.

THOMAS FULLER

SALVATION

It is the rightful heritage of every believer, even the newest in the family of faith, to be absolutely certain that eternal life is his present possession. To look to self is to tremble. To look to Calvary's finished work is to triumph.

LARRY McGUILL

Diverse are the ways by which men come to Christ. And great is the temptation to judge others if they do not have mud put on their eyes and go to Siloam exactly as we did.

VANCE HAVNER

Salvation is . . . bringing back to normal, the Creator-creature relation.

A. W. TOZER, *THE PURSUIT OF GOD*

If I can get a man to think for five minutes about his soul, he is almost certain to be converted.

D. L. MOODY

I've never gotten over the wonder of it all.

GIPSY SMITH

The elect are the "whosoever wills"; the non-elect are the "whosoever won'ts."

D. L. MOODY

One might better try to sail the Atlantic in a paper boat than to get to heaven in good works.

CHARLES HADDON SPURGEON

> *My father is rich in houses and lands,*
> *He holdeth the wealth of the world in His hands.*
> *Of rubies and diamonds, of silver and gold,*
> *His coffers are full,*
> *He has riches untold. . . .*
> *I'm a child of the King, a child of the King*
> *With Jesus my Saviour, I'm a child of the King.*
> HARRIET E. BUELL

No one can make you again but He who made you the first time.
W. Y. FULLERTON

Thank God for that "fine linen, clean and white, the righteousness" with which Christ covers our wounded nakedness. It becomes ours, though no thread of it was wrought in our looms.

ALEXANDER MACLAREN

When Bishop John Taylor Smith, former Chaplain General of the British Army, was in this country at the time of the D. L. Moody Centenary meetings, it was my privilege to hear him one noon hour in Christ Church, Indianapolis. The sanctuary was crowded with eager listeners, to whom the Bishop spoke most solemnly, yet tenderly, upon the necessity of the new birth, using the text quoted above [John 3:7; "Ye must be born again"]. As a telling illustration, he related the following incident:

On one occasion, he told us, he was preaching in a large cathedral on this same text. In order to drive it home, he said: "My dear people, do not substitute anything for the new birth. You may be a member of a church, even the great church of which I am a member, the historic Church of England, but church membership is not new birth and 'except a man be born again he cannot see the kingdom of God.' The rector was sitting at my left. Pointing to him, I said, 'You might be a clergyman like my friend the rector here and not be born again, and "except a man be born again he cannot see the kingdom of God."' On my left sat the archdeacon in his stall. Pointing directly at him, I said, 'You might even be an archdeacon like my friend in his stall and not be born again and "except a man be born again he cannot see the kingdom of God." You might even be a bishop, like myself, and not be born again and "except a man be born again he cannot see the kingdom of God."'"

Then he went on to tell us that a day or so later he received a letter from the archdeacon, in which he wrote: "My dear Bishop: You have found me out. I have been a clergyman for over thirty years, but I had never known anything of the joy that Christians speak of. I never could understand it. Mine has been hard, legal service. I did not know what was the matter with me, but when you pointed directly to me and said, 'You might even be an archdeacon and not be born again,' I realized in a moment what the trouble was. I had never known anything of the new birth."

He went on to say that he was wretched and miserable, had been unable to sleep all night, and begged for a conference, if the bishop could spare the time to talk with him.

"Of course, I could spare the time," said Bishop Smith, "and the

*next day we got together over the Word of God and after some hours
we were both on our knees, the archdeacon taking his place before
God as a poor, lost sinner and telling the Lord Jesus he would trust
Him as his Saviour. From that time on everything has been different."*
H. A. IRONSIDE

*As a man writes his name upon the fly-leaf of his books, or stamps
his initials on his valuables, so Christ gives His name in token of pro-
prietorship, and builds on the fact at once the assurance of protection
and the demand for service.*
ALEXANDER MACLAREN

Absolute candor is an indispensable requisite to salvation.
A. W. TOZER, MAN, THE DWELLING PLACE OF GOD

The recognition of sin is the beginning of salvation.
ANONYMOUS

SANCTIFICATION
· ·

Lord, make me more like Yourself, less like myself.
ANONYMOUS

*Next to the might of God, the serene beauty of a holy life is the most
powerful influence for good in all the world.*
D. L. MOODY

*Thoughtfulness is the beginning of great sanctity. If you learn this art
of being thoughtful, you will become more and more Christlike, for
His heart was meek and He always thought of others.*
MOTHER TERESA

*God never gave a man a thing to do concerning which it were irrever-
ent to ponder how the Son of God would have done it.*
GEORGE MACDONALD

Take up the cross if thou the crown would'st gain.
PAULINUS, BISHOP OF NOLA

SCIENCE
. . . .

Science without religion is lame; religion without science is blind.
ALBERT EINSTEIN

Science increases our power in proportion as it lowers our price.
CLAUDE BERNARD

Science is a first-rate piece of furniture for a man's upper chamber if he has common sense on the ground floor.
OLIVER WENDELL HOLMES, SR.

SEARCH FOR MEANING
. . . .

[Life] bubbles on the rapid stream of time.
EDWARD YOUNG

The Juke-Box

Exiles from themselves,
And with the wrong address,
They drain the raucous songs
To fill their emptiness.

Louder the juke-box cries
To each poor, wandered ghost:
He wonders why he's here
And fears the silence most.
LOUIS GINSBERG

There are no more worlds to conquer.
ALEXANDER THE GREAT

As I see him, the unutterably infinitesimal individual weaves among
the mysteries a floss-like and wholly meaningless course—if course it
be. In short, I catch on meaning from all I have seen and pass quite
as I came, confused and dismayed.

THEODORE DREISER, *WHAT I BELIEVE*

Youth is a blunder; manhood a struggle; old age a regret.

BENJAMIN DISRAELI

Alas how scant the sheaves for all the trouble,
The toil, the pain and the resolve sublime—
A few full ears; the rest but weeds and stubble,
And withered wildflowers plucked before their time.

A. B. BRAGDON

. . . Out, out brief candle!
Life's but a walking shadow, a poor player
That struts and frets his hour upon the stage
And then is heard no more: it is a tale
Told by an idiot, full of sound and fury,
Signifying nothing.

WILLIAM SHAKESPEARE, *MACBETH*

My Quest

We search the world for truth, we cull
The good, the pure, the beautiful,
From graven stone and written scroll,
From the old flower-fields of the soul,
And, weary seekers for the best,
We come back laden from our quest,
To find that all the sages said
Is in the Book our mothers read.

JOHN GREENLEAF WHITTIER

Man is an inhabitant of a thin rind on a negligible blob of matter, belonging to one of the millions of stars, in one among millions of island universes.

H. G. WELLS

. . . what shadows we are, and what shadows we pursue!
EDMUND BURKE

SECOND COMING

I read of a doctor who all his life took a stand on a certain medical issue that brought a laugh from his fellow doctors, until it was discovered that he was right and they were wrong. Somebody said he was wrong so long that he turned out to be right. Some of us have been accustomed to being laughed at by certain swivel chair experts in eschatology, but when God splits the skies and the stars fall, the moon turns to blood and men cry for rocks and mountains to fall on them, it's going to be pretty hard for some of us to keep from saying, "I told you so."

VANCE HAVNER

More than a fourth of the Bible is predictive prophecy. Approximately one-third of it has yet to be fulfilled. Both the Old and New Testaments are full of promises about the return of Jesus Christ. Over 1,800 references appear in the Old Testament, and seventeen Old Testament books give prominence to this theme. Of the 260 chapters in the New Testament, there are more than 300 references to the Lord's return—one out of every thirty verses. Twenty-three of the twenty-seven New Testament books refer to this great event. Three of the four other books are single-chapter letters written to individuals concerning a particular subject, and the fourth is Galatians, which does imply Christ's coming again. For every prophecy on the first coming of Christ, there are eight on Christ's second coming.

G. S.

The great Dwight L. Moody used to say, "I never preach a sermon without thinking that possibly the Lord may come before I preach another." Dr. G. Campbell Morgan, the distinguished British clergyman, said, "I never begin my work in the morning without thinking that perhaps He may interrupt my work and begin His own. I am not looking for death, I am looking for Him." That is the way a Christian should live his life—in the constant anticipation of the return of Jesus Christ! If we could live every day as though it might be the very last one before the final judgment, what a difference it would make here on earth! But we don't like to think that way. We don't like to think that our carefully made plans, our long-range schemes may be interrupted by the trumpet of God. Too many people would rather say, "Oh well, the end of the world hasn't come yet, so why think about it—it's probably a thousand years away."

BILLY GRAHAM

The bloom of beauty of Apostolic Christianity was created by the upward look.

JAMES DENNEY

The apostolic church thought more about the Second Coming of Jesus Christ than about death and heaven. The early Christians were looking, not for a cleft in the ground called a grave but for a cleavage in the sky called Glory."

ALEXANDER MACLAREN

Dr. Reuben A. Torrey, second president of the Moody Bible Institute, stated: "The latter truth [the second coming of Christ] transformed my whole idea of life; it broke the power of the world and its ambition over me, and filled my life with the most radiant optimism even under the most discouraging circumstances." Dr. Torrey was asked, "Is not the doctrine of Christ's personal and near coming one of practical power and helpfulness?" He replied, "It is transforming the lives of more men and women than almost any doctrine I know of."

G. S.

If Christ were coming again tomorrow, I would plant a tree today.
MARTIN LUTHER

The truth of the catching away of the church was important to my father. I remember him calling it to our attention as children. On one occasion after reading I Thessalonians chapter four, he quietly and methodically faced each of his six children with the question, "If Jesus returned tonight, would you be ready?" It was moving to hear each child answer, "Yes, I'm ready." Father then led us in singing the hymn "Will the Circle Be Unbroken When He Comes?" That is a question each individual must answer.
G. S.

Pastor Horatius Bonar lived in the glow of Christ's coming. As he would conclude his day's ministry, he would draw the curtains of his window and utter as he looked upward, "Perhaps tonight, Lord!" In the morning, as he awoke and looked out on the dawn of a new day, he would pray, looking up into the sky, "Perhaps today, Lord!"
G. S.

The doctrine of the second coming has failed, so far as we are concerned, if it does not make us realize that at every moment of every year in our lives Donne's question, "What if this present were the world's last night?" is equally relevant.
C. S. LEWIS

This is the Voice of Freedom, General MacArthur speaking. People of the Philippines: I have returned. By the grace of Almighty God, our forces stand again on Philippine soil. . . . The hour of your redemption is here. . . . Rally to me.
DOUGLAS MACARTHUR,
ON LANDING AT LEYTE ISLAND IN THE PHILIPPINES,
20 OCTOBER 1944

SELFISHNESS
· ·

Whenever you are too selfishly looking out for your own interest, you have only one person working for you—yourself. When you help a dozen other people with their problems, you have a dozen people working with you.

WILLIAM B. GIVEN, JR.

He who lives to benefit himself confers on the world a benefit when he dies.

TERTULLIAN

Recipe for a Miserable Life:

Think about yourself.
Talk about yourself.
Use I as often as possible.
Mirror yourself continually in the opinion of others.
Listen greedily to what people say about you.
Expect to be appreciated.
Be suspicious.
Be jealous and envious.
Be sensitive to slights.
Never forgive a criticism.
Trust nobody but yourself.
Insist on consideration and respect.
Demand agreement with your own views on everything.
Sulk if people are not grateful to you for favors shown them.
Never forget a service you may have rendered.
Be on the lookout for a good time for yourself.
Shirk your duties if you can.
Do as little as possible for others.
Love yourself supremely.
Be selfish.

ANONYMOUS

. . . he who seeks all things, wherever he goes,
Only reaps from the hopes which around him he sows
A harvest of barren regrets.

OWEN MEREDITH (LORD LYTTON)

From the morning to the evening, careless of the sun or of the rain,
the spectators, who sometimes numbered 400,000, remained at eager
attention. . . . The happiness of Rome seemed to hang on the event of
a race.

EDWARD GIBBON

Salvianus . . . assures us that Christians were indulging in the mad-
ness of the theatre, when the arms of the Vandals were ringing round
the walls, and that the applause of the spectators was mingled with
the groans of the dying and the battle cries of the attackers.

SAMUEL DILL,
ROMAN SOCIETY IN THE LAST CENTURY OF THE
WESTERN EMPIRE

SELF-KNOWLEDGE

Search thy own heart; what paineth thee in others in thyself may be.

JOHN GREENLEAF WHITTIER

Do you want to know the man against whom you have most reason
to guard yourself? Your looking-glass will give a very fair likeness of
his face.

RICHARD WHATELY

We are so accustomed to wearing a disguise before others that eventu-
ally we are unable to recognize ourselves.

FRANÇOIS DUC DE LA ROCHEFOUCAULD

It is not only the most difficult thing to know oneself, but the most
inconvenient one, too.

H. W. SHAW

In proportion as our inward life fails, we go more constantly and desperately to the post-office. You may depend on it, that poor fellow who walks away with the greatest number of letters, proud of his extensive correspondence, has not heard from himself this long while.

HENRY DAVID THOREAU

The more faithfully you listen to the voice within you, the better you will hear what is sounding outside. And only he who listens can speak.

DAG HAMMARSKJÖLD

SELF-PITY

> *Milton the blind, who looked on Paradise!*
> *Beethoven, deaf, who heard vast harmonies!*
> *Byron, the lame, who climbed toward Alpine skies!*
> *Who pleads a handicap, remembering these?*
>
> VIOLET A. STOREY,
> *TEA IN AN OLD HOUSE*

Never allow your own sorrow to absorb you, but seek out another to console, and you will find consolation.

J. C. MACAULAY

> *Who lets his feelings run*
> *In soft luxurious flow,*
> *Shrinks when hard service must be done,*
> *And faints at every woe.*
>
> JOHN HENRY NEWMAN

Great souls suffer in silence.

JOHANN VON SCHILLER

Never give way to melancholy; resist it steadily, for the habit will encroach.

SYDNEY SMITH

SERMONS

· ·

All preachers should keep in mind the maxim: The mind cannot retain what the seat cannot endure.

ANONYMOUS

A church attender commended her pastor for his sermon and said, "You'll never know what your sermon meant to me. It was like water to a drowning man."

G. S.

What too many orators want in depth they give you in length.

BARON DE MONTESQUIEU

The minister of a local congregation approached the desk of the city editor. "I just dropped by," he said, "to thank you for the very generous report on my sermon in your morning edition, and also to register a mild protest. In your article you referred to me as 'the reverend' but you spelled it 'neverend.'"

ANONYMOUS

The sermon is the house; the illustrations are the windows that let in the light.

CHARLES HADDON SPURGEON

SERVICE

· ·

The service we render to others is really the rent we pay for our room on this earth. It is obvious that man is himself a traveler; that the purpose of this world is not "to have and to hold" but "to give and to serve." There can be no other meaning.

WILFRED T. GRENFELL

Our opportunities to do good are our talents.

COTTON MATHER

The greatest pleasure I know is to do a good action by stealth and have it found out by accident.

CHARLES LAMB

The quality of mercy is not strain'd,
It droppeth as the gentle rain from heaven
Upon the place beneath. It is twice bless'd:
It blesseth him that gives and him that takes.

WILLIAM SHAKESPEARE,
PORTIA, *THE MERCHANT OF VENICE*

It is high time that the ideal of success should be replaced by the ideal of service.

ALBERT EINSTEIN

Be an opener of doors for such as come after thee, and do not try to make the universe a blind alley.

RALPH WALDO EMERSON

No man or woman of the humblest sort can really be strong, gentle, pure, and good without the world being better for it, without somebody being helped and comforted by the very existence of that goodness.

PHILLIPS BROOKS

Try to forget yourself in the service of others. For when we think too much of ourselves and our own interests, we easily become despondent. But when we work for others, our efforts return to bless us.

SIDNEY POWELL

Service to a just cause rewards the worker with more real happiness and satisfaction than any other venture in life.

CARRIE CHAPMAN CATT

Service can never become slavery to one who loves.

J. L. MASSE

To give real service you must add something which cannot be bought or measured with money, and that is sincerity and integrity.
DONALD A. ADAMS

Only a burdened heart can lead to fruitful service.
ALAN REDPATH

SILENCE
· ·

The best time for you to hold your tongue is the time you feel you must say something or bust.
JOSH BILLINGS

Many a time I have wanted to stop talking and find out what I really believed.
WALTER LIPPMANN

Besser stumm als dumm—Better silent than stupid.
GERMAN PROVERB

If you don't say anything, you won't be called on to repeat it.
CALVIN COOLIDGE

When Calvin Coolidge was Vice-President, Channing N. Cox, who had succeeded him as Governor of Massachusetts, came to Washington and called on his predecessor. Cox noted that Coolidge was able to see long lists of callers daily and finish his work at five o'clock, while Cox found himself held at his desk as late as nine p.m.
"How come the difference?" he asked.
"You talk back," Coolidge explained.
WALTER TROHAN

The most difficult thing in the world is to know how to do a thing and to watch somebody else doing it wrong, without comment.
T. H. WHITE

In times like the present, men should utter nothing for which they would not willingly be responsible through time and eternity.
ABRAHAM LINCOLN

Sign in an office at a Southern Air base: Caution: Be Sure Brain Is Engaged Before Putting Mouth in Gear.
ANONYMOUS

He who knows does not talk; he who talks does not know.
LAO-TZU

SIN
··

The Son of Man came to seek and to save what was lost.
LUKE 19:10 NIV

Sin is not weakness, it is a disease; it is red-handed rebellion against God and the magnitude of that rebellion is expressed by Calvary's cross.
OSWALD CHAMBERS

[Sin is] cosmic treason.
R. C. SPROUL

They can gas me, but I am famous. I have achieved in one day what it took Robert Kennedy all his life to do.
SIRHAN SIRHAN,
SHORTLY AFTER SHOOTING KENNEDY,
JUNE 1968

We have all sinned, some more, some less.
SENECA

There are certain diseases of which a constant symptom is unconsciousness that there is anything the matter. A deep-seated wound does not hurt much.
ALEXANDER MACLAREN

One reason sin flourishes is that it is treated like a cream puff instead of a rattlesnake.

BILLY SUNDAY

Sin is the only thing that God abhors. It brought Christ to the cross, it damns souls, it shuts heaven, it laid the foundations of hell.

THOMAS BROOKS

Looking at the wound of sin will never save anyone. What you must do is look at the remedy.

D. L. MOODY

The instances are exceedingly rare of men immediately passing over a clear marked line from virtue into declared vice and corruption. There are middle tints and shades between the two extremes; there is something uncertain on the confines of the two empires which they must pass through, and which renders the change easy and imperceptible.

EDMUND BURKE

The voice of sin may be loud, but the voice of forgiveness is louder.

D. L. MOODY

The chains of sin can be got off. Christ looses them by His blood. Like a drop of corrosive acid that blood, falling upon the fetters, dissolves them, and the prisoner goes free, emancipated by the Son.

ALEXANDER MACLAREN

Of Man's first disobedience, and the fruit
Of that forbidden tree, whose mortal taste
Brought death into the world, and all our woe,
With loss of Eden, till one greater Man
Restore us, and regain the blissful seat,
Sing, Heavenly Muse.

JOHN MILTON, *PARADISE LOST*

Sin enough and you will soon be unconscious of sin!
OSWALD CHAMBERS

By nature I was too blind to know Him, too proud to trust Him, too obstinate to serve Him, too base-minded to love Him.
JOHN NEWTON

Many a ship has stood the tempest, and then has gone down in the harbour because its timbers have been gnawed to pieces by white ants and many a man can do what is wanted in the trying moments, and yet make shipwreck of his faith in uneventful times.

> *"Like ships that have gone down at sea,*
> *When heaven was all tranquility."*

ALEXANDER MACLAREN,
(VERSE BY THOMAS MOORE)

> *I wander thro' each charter'd street,*
> *Near where the charter'd Thames does flow,*
> *And mark in every face I meet*
> *Marks of weakness, marks of woe.*
>
> *In every cry of every Man,*
> *In every Infant's cry of fear,*
> *In every voice, in every ban*
> *The mind-forg'd manacles I hear . . .*

WILLIAM BLAKE

A man who believes himself a sinner, who feels himself sinful, is already at the gates of the Kingdom of heaven.
FRANÇOIS MAURIAC

Let us not forget that violence does not have its own separate existence and is, in fact, incapable of having it: it is invariably interwoven with the lie. They have the closest of kinship, the most profound natural tie: violence has nothing with which to cover itself except the lie, and the lie has nothing to stand on other than violence.
ALEKSANDR SOLZHENITSYN

*We are too Christian really to enjoy sinning, and too fond of sinning
really to enjoy Christianity. Most of us know perfectly well what we
ought to do; our trouble is that we do not want to do it.*

PETER MARSHALL

What is Sin? The Bible Answers . . .

1. *Sin is transgression of the law—lawlessness (1 John 3:4).*
2. *A grievous malady, contaminating the whole of man's being
   (Isaiah 1:4, 5; Romans 3:10–18).*
3. *An obscuring cloud, which hides the face of God's blessing
   (Isaiah 59:2).*
4. *A binding cord, which holds man in its power (Proverbs 5:22).*
5. *A tyrannical owner, who embitters the lives of his slaves
   (Nehemiah 9:37).*
6. *A disturber of rest, which causes disorder and anxiety (Psalm
   38:3).*
7. *A robber of blessing, which strips and starves the soul (Jeremiah
   5:25).*
8. *A terrible devastation, which brings untold desolation (Micah
   6:13).*
9. *A tripper-up, which continually overthrows the sinner to his hurt
   (Proverbs 13:6).*
10. *A record writer, which leaves its indelible mark upon the
    committer (Jeremiah 17:1).*
11. *A betraying presence, which "will out" no matter what pains are
    taken to hide it (Ezekiel 21:24).*
12. *A sure detective, which turns upon the sinner and finds him out
    (Numbers 32:23).*
13. *An accusing witness, which points its condemning finger at the
    prisoner in the bondage of sin (Isaiah 59:12).*
14. *A sum of addition which accumulates its weight to the
    condemnation of the sinner (Isaiah 30:1).*

ROBERT G. LEE

We have a strange illusion that mere time cancels sin. . . . But mere time does nothing either to the fact or to the guilt of sin. The guilt is washed out not by time but by repentance and the blood of Christ.

C. S. LEWIS

Our nation was shocked some time ago by the mass murder of eight young student nurses in a Chicago hospital dormitory. Corazon Amurao, an exchange nurse from the Philippines, was the only one to escape. Through police photographs, she was able to identify Richard Speck as the killer. Literally thousands of police were mobilized in a massive manhunt to find this twenty-five-year-old man.

After three days on the run, Speck ended up in the Starr Hotel on West Madison Street. There, in cage 584, an eight-by-six-foot wire cubicle costing ninety cents a night, Speck was found.

Speck had drifted through the underbelly of this great city, reading papers, drinking heavily, and hiding out on skid row. The day before he was captured he had spent drinking, trying to find courage to end his life. At 12:30 A.M. Sunday morning, he was rushed to Cook County Hospital bleeding to death, an unknown drifter from skid row.

As Dr. LeRoy Smith washed the blood off his arm, he saw the tattoo, which read, "Born to raise hell." Immediately he realized this was the killer. Within minutes the police arrived, and the manhunt was over.

In a very real sense, modern man is in flight. He wants to live his own life, be his own judge, his own creator, and his own saviour. But the more he makes himself independent, the more lonely and frightened he becomes.

G. S.

I've been asked many times as Sheriff, "Do you think you will ever eliminate crime?" I'm not naive enough to think that crime can ever be eliminated. There were prostitutes and pickpockets in the days of Christ. There was gambling and debauchery in the days of the prophets. There will always be some who submit to the soft, glittery pleasures and it will always be for the spiritually strong to lead those back.

RICHARD OGILVIE

Some time ago, two Indians who had been watching a lighthouse go up came over to see the thing open on the big day. It was all set up with the lights and the bell and the horn; but the day it was due to open, the worst fog of all fogs came in.

One Indian said to the other, "Light shine, bell ring, horn blow, but fog come in just the same."

We've never had more lights shining, and bells ringing, and horns blowing in the church than we have today. We've never had more fog.

VANCE HAVNER

SOLITUDE
. . . .

Unfortunately the world today does not seem to understand, in either man or woman, the need to be alone. Anything else will be accepted as a better excuse. If one sets time aside for a shopping expedition, that time is accepted as inviolable; but if one says, "I cannot come because it is my hour to be alone," one is considered rude, egotistical, or strange.

ANNE MORROW LINDBERGH

The power to stand alone is worth acquiring at the expense of much sorrowful solitude.

GEORGE BERNARD SHAW

Solitude, the safeguard of mediocrity, is to genius the stern friend.

RALPH WALDO EMERSON

I never found the companion that was so companionable as solitude.

HENRY DAVID THOREAU

Solitude is the nurse of enthusiasm, and enthusiasm is the true parent of genius. In all ages solitude has been called for—has been flown to.

ISAAC DISRAELI

Solitude is the furnace of transformation.
HENRI J. M. NOUWEN

We must show a new generation of nervous, almost frantic,
Christians that power lies at the center of the life.
A. W. TOZER, *THE ROOT OF THE RIGHTEOUS*

SORROW

· ·

Sorrow is like a precious treasure,
Shown only to friends.
AFRICAN PROVERB

O for the touch of a vanish'd hand,
And the sound of a voice that is still!
ALFRED, LORD TENNYSON

The sorrows of life do not create problems, they reveal them.
WARREN WIERSBE, *LIVE LIKE A KING*

Christ is the answer to sorrow. When Harry Lauder, the great Scottish
comedian, received word that his son had been killed in France, he
said, "In a time like this, there are three courses open to man: He
may give way to despair and become bitter. He may endeavor to
drown his sorrow in drink or in a life of wickedness. Or he may turn
to God." In your sorrow, turn to God. There are thousands of people
who have turned to God, but you may be still carrying your burdens.
But God begs of you, "Cast all your care on me, for I care for you" (I
Peter 5:7). You who must go through the valley of the shadow of
death, you who must say goodbye to those whom you have loved, you
who suffer privation and misery, you who are unjustly persecuted for
righteousness' sake—take heart, take courage. Our Christ is more
than adequate for sorrow.

BILLY GRAHAM

There is a sweet joy that comes to us through sorrow.

CHARLES HADDON SPURGEON

Every heart hath its own ache.

THOMAS FULLER

Every sorrow is the shadow of God's hand.

I walked a mile with Pleasure,
She chattered all the way;
But left me none the wiser,
For all she had to say.

I walked a mile with Sorrow,
And ne'er a word said she;
But, oh, the things I learned from her
When Sorrow walked with me!

ROBERT BROWNING HAMILTON

Nothing begins, and nothing ends,
That is not paid with moan;
For we are born in others' pain,
And perish in our own.

FRANCIS THOMPSON

Of all the days of the war, there are two especially I can never forget.
Those were the days following the news, in New York and Brooklyn,
of that first Bull Run defeat, and the day of Abraham Lincoln's
death. I was home in Brooklyn on both occasions. The day of the
murder we heard the news very early in the morning. Mother pre-
pared breakfast—and other meals afterward—as usual; but not a
mouthful was eaten all day by either of us. We each drank half a cup
of coffee; that was all. Little was said. We got every newspaper morn-
ing and evening, and the frequent extras of that period, and passed
them silently to each other.

WALT WHITMAN

Our sorrows are never so great that they hide our mercies. The sky is never covered with clouds so that neither sun nor stars appear for many days.

ALEXANDER MACLAREN

Believe me, every heart has its sorrows, which the world knows not; and oftentimes we call a man cold when he is only sad.

HENRY WADSWORTH LONGFELLOW

SPEECH
· ·

It is not sufficient to know what one ought to say, but one must also know how to say it.

ARISTOTLE

Dr. Wernher von Braun, the American space pioneer, made some startling predictions concerning mass communications. In an article appearing in the Astronautics and Aeronautics Journal, *the NASA chief suggested that soon it will be possible to carry out so many different kinds of transactions within the home, that people will be able to live anywhere. Home communication centers will make office buildings, banks, and stores almost obsolete. Direct visual and audio communication will be possible with anyone at any time and anywhere.*

G. S.

One slogan used during World War II was, "a slip of the lip may sink a ship." I have a picture of a South Pacific battle scene in which Marines are storming a beachhead. They are dropping everywhere. One Marine is wounded and bleeding. The picture bears a two-word title: Somebody Talked. It may be that the tongue has slain more than have all the bullets and bombs of battle. The book of Proverbs tells us that "A soft tongue breaketh the bone" (Proverbs 25:15b). And again we read, "He that keepeth his mouth keepeth his life" (Proverbs 13:3).

G. S.

The Tongue Loosed
"And the string of his tongue was loosed, and he spake plain" (Mark 7:35).

Recalling this miracle wrought by Jesus, a Christian friend—
"Sister Ida"—on the other side of the Atlantic has written the following prayer:

> *Loose Thou my tongue, so silent have I been, Lord,*
> *In telling others of Thy love divine;*
> *Loose Thou my tongue, and use it for Thy glory,*
> *That straying lambs, back to Thy fold may come.*
>
> *Loose Thou my tongue, that Thou canst always help me*
> *To strengthen those by storm and tempest tossed;*
> *Loose Thou my tongue, to guide the sad and lonely*
> *To find in Thee, their refuge and their rock.*
>
> *Loose Thou my tongue, for Thee, O blessed Master,*
> *That I may speak Thy words of truth divine;*
> *Loose Thou my tongue, that I may tell the story*
> *Of all the wondrous things that Thou hast done.*
>
> *Loose Thou my tongue, baptize with love and fire, Lord,*
> *To teach Thy Cross and resurrection power;*
> *Loose Thou my tongue, and fill me with Thy fullness*
> *Till others, too, shall crown Thee Lord of all.*

This prayer, if prayed from clean hearts and lives submissive to God's will, would put tongues of fire where there are now tongues draped in icicles—would melt the frozen fountains of testimony and start refreshing streams in dry gardens—would give us the plain language of truth where there is now evasive stammering and beclouding bombast.

ROBERT G. LEE

> *Take my lips, and let them be*
> *Filled with messages for Thee.*
> FRANCES RIDLEY HAVERGAL

*A young man had cancer of the tongue. Before the operation the doc-
tor told him that he would never speak again. The young man
paused and then said, "Thank God for Jesus Christ." What beautiful
last words.*

G. S.

*Silent Cal Coolidge was famous for his brevity of speech. One day
Mrs. Coolidge surprised him with a presidential portrait hung in the
library of the White House. Coolidge first saw it when he walked in
with a senator. For a long moment the two men looked at the portrait
without saying a word. At last Coolidge said, "I think so, too."*

G. S.

*Edward Everett Hale in his story "The Man Without a Country" tells
of the young naval officer, Philip Nolan, who with some others was
on trial for being false to the service.*

*As the court session dragged on and the trial came to a close,
Nolan was asked if he wished to say anything to show that he had
always been faithful to the United States. In a fit of temper he cursed
and said, "I wish that I may never hear of the United States again!"*

*The judge and the jury were shocked! In fifteen minutes they
issued the verdict: "The Court decides, subject to the approval of the
President, that you shall never hear the name of the United States
again." Nolan laughed, but no one else laughed, and he became the
man without a country.*

G. S.

*Bernard of Clairvaux spoke, and thousands left all their earthly
goods for the Second Crusade. Patrick Henry's immortal words, "Give
me liberty, or give me death!" inspired a nation to fight furiously for
liberty. Young William Jennings Bryan came to the 1896 Democratic
National Convention simply as an alternate delegate. As he spoke to
the great throng of delegates there, he lifted them out of their seats
with his oratory and was acclaimed their nominee for the presidency
of the United States. The tongue is powerful.*

G. S.

STEWARDSHIP

Every charitable act is a stepping-stone toward heaven.
HENRY WARD BEECHER

The problem with our giving is that we give the widow's mite, but not with the widow's spirit.
ANONYMOUS

Where your pleasure is, there is your treasure.
Where your treasure is, there is your heart.
Where your heart is, there is your happiness.
SAINT AUGUSTINE

STORIES

They say I tell a great many stories, I reckon I do, but I have found in the course of a long experience that common people, take them as they run, are more easily informed through the medium of a broad illustration than in any other way, and as to what the hypercritical few may think, I care not.
ABRAHAM LINCOLN

Anecdotes are stories with points. They are tools—nail sinkers to drive home arguments firmly. They are the origin of all teaching.
EDMUND FULLER

[The art of the novel] does not simply consist in the author's telling a story about the adventures of some other person. . . . It happens because the storyteller's own experience of men and things, whether for good or ill . . . has moved him to an emotion so passionate that he can no longer keep it shut up in his heart.
MURASAKI SHIKIBU

411

I love to tell the story
Of unseen things above,
Of Jesus and His glory,
Of Jesus and His love.

I love to tell the story,
Because I know 'tis true;
It satisfies my longings
As nothing else can do.

KATHERINE HANKEY

Jesus spoke to them again in parables, saying . . .
MATTHEW 22:1 NIV

SUBMISSION

· ·

Supreme authority in both church and home has been divinely vested in the male as the representative of Christ, who is Head of the church. It is in willing submission rather than grudging capitulation that the woman in the church (whether married or single) and the wife in the home find their fulfillment.

ELISABETH ELLIOT

The purpose of life is not to find your freedom, but your master.
P. T. FORSYTH

Contemporary society . . . does not value personal submission. Rather, it teaches that the ideal, the highest position a human being can attain, is that of personal autonomy.

STEPHEN B. CLARK,
MAN AND WOMAN IN CHRIST

A Christian man is the most free lord of all, and subject to none; a Christian man is the most dutiful servant of all, and subject to everyone.
MARTIN LUTHER

412

Make me a captive, Lord,
And then I shall be free;
Force me to render up my sword,
And I shall conqueror be.

I sink in life's alarms
When by myself I stand;
Imprison me within Thine arms,
And strong shall be my hand.

GEORGE MATHESON

As Thou wilt; what Thou wilt; when Thou wilt.

THOMAS À KEMPIS

SUCCESS

Success is neither fame, wealth, nor power; rather it is seeking, knowing, loving, and obeying God.

CHARLES HABIB MALIK

Six essential qualities that are the key to success: Sincerity, personal integrity, humility, courtesy, wisdom, charity.

WILLIAM MENNINGER

Nothing is particularly hard if you divide it into small jobs.

HENRY FORD

The common idea that success spoils people by making them vain, egotistic, and self-complacent is erroneous; on the contrary, it makes them, for the most part, humble, tolerant, and kind. Failure makes people cruel and bitter.

W. SOMERSET MAUGHAM

Sum up the life of Jesus by any other standard than God's, and it is an anticlimax of failure.

OSWALD CHAMBERS

Our Lord died an apparent failure, discredited by the leaders of established religion, rejected by society and forsaken by his friends. It took the resurrection to demonstrate how gloriously Christ had triumphed. Yet today the professed church seems to have learned nothing. How much eager-beaver religious work is done out of a carnal desire to make good.

A. W. TOZER, *BORN AFTER MIDNIGHT*

Speaking of Frederick the Great, the historian said: "Frederick the Great won Rossbach by his miraculous marching on the lightest possible equipment."

Another historian, speaking of General Grant, said: "When Grant started out to capture Vicksburg, he took nothing with him but a gun, coat and a toothpick."

What are the historians saying? That we must not give too much attention to baggage.

ROBERT G. LEE

If one advances confidently in the direction of his dreams, and endeavors to live the life which he has imagined, he will meet with a success unexpected in common hours. . . . Why should we be in such desperate haste to succeed, and in such desperate enterprises? If a man does not keep pace with his companions, perhaps it is because he hears a different drummer. Let him step to the music which he hears, however measured or far away.

HENRY DAVID THOREAU

*Success is counted sweetest
By those who ne'er succeed.*

EMILY DICKINSON

SUFFERING
· ·

He who fears to suffer cannot be His who suffered.

TERTULLIAN

We are not at our best perched at the summit; we are climbers, at our best when the way is steep.

JOHN W. GARDNER

The real problem is not why some pious, humble, believing people suffer, but why some do not.

C. S. LEWIS

You must submit to supreme suffering in order to discover the completion of joy.

JOHN CALVIN

I do not believe that sheer suffering teaches. If suffering alone taught, then all the world would be wise, since everyone suffers. To suffering must be added mourning, understanding, patience, love, openness and the willingness to remain vulnerable.

ANNE MORROW LINDBERGH

Your pain has a purpose. I can't tell you what that purpose is—that is something you will discover in your own walk with God. It may be a marvelous discovery, a grace, like Paul's, which once received makes you glad you went down the road of suffering with God at your side.

JOHN HAGGAI

Suffering, although it is a burden, is a useful burden, like the splints used in orthopedic treatment.

SØREN KIERKEGAARD

TACT
. . . .

Tact is like a girdle. It enables you to organize the awkward truth more attractively.

ANONYMOUS

Tact comes as much from goodness of heart as from fineness of taste.

ENDYMION

Tact is the unsaid part of what you think; its opposite, the unthought part which you say.

HENRY VAN DYKE

Tact is the art of making a point without making an enemy.

HOWARD W. NEWTON

Tact consists in knowing how far to go too far.

JEAN COCTEAU

Tact is the ability to describe others as they see themselves.

ABRAHAM LINCOLN

Tact has been defined as the right touch rather than the wrong touch. We are instructed in Scripture to let our lights shine, but remember— not like a blow torch! J. Oswald Sanders defines tact as "an intuitive perception of what is proper or fitting; the mental ability of saying and doing the right thing at the right time, so as not to unnecessarily offend or anger. This qualification is sadly often conspicuous by its absence and the worker spoils the very work about which he is so concerned."

G.S.

We have a head on us for the same reason a pin has: to keep us from going too far.

G.S.

Do not use a hatchet to remove a fly from your friend's forehead.

CHINESE PROVERB

Some people are so tactful that they never make contact.

G.S.

Cultivate tact, for it is the mark of culture . . . the lubricant of human relationships, softening contacts and minimizing friction.

BALTASAR GRACIÁN

Recently I was flying to Washington, D.C. The businessman sitting next to me offered me a drink of vodka. In a friendly, natural way I simply said, "No, thank you."

A few minutes later he noticed my Bible and said, "You seem to be a religious person, and I guess you think I'm ugly."

"No," I responded, "I think you're a very generous person." Immediately he was receptive, and I tactfully shared the gospel with him.

I could easily have answered, "No, thank you, I'm a Christian." In all likelihood he would have felt I was putting him down, and the door of opportunity would have been closed.

G.S.

TEACHING
· ·

If the teacher be corrupt, the world will be corrupt.

PERSIAN PROVERB

To teach is to learn twice.

JOSEPH JOUBERT

Not only is there an art in knowing a thing, but also a certain art in teaching it.

CICERO

Instruction does not prevent waste of time or mistakes; and mistakes themselves are often the best teachers of all.

JAMES A. FROUDE

TELEVISION
· ·

Our broadcasts have not improved. If anything, their quality has declined. The tube has become a trip, a national opiate, a baby-sitter who charges nothing, something to iron by, and to shave to, and to doze over.

ROGER MUDD

I don't think that television has corrupted man. But I do think that man has invented it to flee from reality.

MALCOLM MUGGERIDGE

A TV set is only a machine—glass, metal, wires, and little gadgets— until you place it in your home. . . . In some homes, TV becomes a baby-sitter, for babies of all ages. In other homes, TV is a narcotic, an escape from reality. Or it may be a thief, stealing time, thoughts, friendships, creativity, and opportunities for much-needed recreation and companionship. In too few homes, TV is a servant, providing information, insight, commentary on life, news, laughter, music, and worthwhile entertainment.

What TV becomes depends on you, the user. If you accept it as a tool, use it sparingly, wisely, and purposefully, it can become a servant. If you accept it as a friend, watch and listen continuously, it will become your master.

DAVID AUGSBURGER

TEMPTATIONS
· · · · · · · · · · · · · · · ·

We prayed a lot. . . . I'm a free man now. . . . Every once in a while I meet a youngster who knows I used to be a drug addict, as he is now. He asks what he can do to kick the habit. I tell him what I've learned: "Give God's temple, your body, back to Him. The alternative is death."

JOHNNY CASH

Temptations discover what we are.

THOMAS À KEMPIS

The long, dull monotonous years of middle-aged prosperity or middle-aged adversity are excellent campaigning weather [for the devil].

C. S. LEWIS, SCREWTAPE LETTERS

No one knows how bad he is until he has tried to be good. There is a silly idea about that good people don't know what temptation means.

C. S. LEWIS, SCREWTAPE LETTERS

Oscar Wilde, the well-known British writer, summed up the attitude of millions of people when he said, "I can resist anything except temptation."

Unfortunately, "resisting temptation" has gone out of style and "doing what comes naturally" has become the "in" thing.

Once Jesus told His disciples to "Watch and pray, that ye enter not into temptation" (Matthew 26:41).

G.S.

When Christians find themselves exposed to temptation they should pray to God to uphold them, and when they are tempted they should not be discouraged. It is not a sin to be tempted; the sin is to fall into temptation.

D. L. MOODY

The temptation once yielded to gains power. The crack in the embankment which lets a drop or two ooze through is soon a hole which lets out a flood.

ALEXANDER MACLAREN

If you would master temptation, you must first let Christ master you.

ANONYMOUS

THANKS AND PRAISE

Let us, with a gladsome mind,
Praise the Lord, for He is kind:
For His mercies aye endure,
Ever faithful, ever sure.

JOHN MILTON, PSALM 136

Get Guiterman's wisdom:
Though right it is to give thanks,
True gratitude will live thanks!

ROBERT G. LEE

Thou who hast given so much to me, give one thing more—a grateful heart!

GEORGE HERBERT

The worst moment for the atheist is when he is really thankful and has nobody to thank.

DANTE GABRIEL ROSSETTI

Thanksgiving Proclamation

We have been a most favored people.
We ought to be a most grateful people.
We have been most blessed people.
We ought to be most thankful people.

CALVIN COOLIDGE

> *O Lord, that lends me life,*
> *Lend me a heart replete with thankfulness.*
> WILLIAM SHAKESPEARE

THINKING

Thinking is the talking of the soul with itself.
PLATO

Thinking is the hardest work there is, which is probably the reason why so few engage in it.
HENRY FORD

Few people think more than two or three times a year. I have made an international reputation by thinking once or twice a week.
GEORGE BERNARD SHAW

There's nothing either good or bad but thinking makes it so.
WILLIAM SHAKESPEARE, *HAMLET*

When my gasoline tank registers empty, I know it is full—that is, it is full of air. But the automobile was not built to run on air. To displace the air, I must fill it with gasoline.
God's cure for evil thinking is to fill our minds with that which is good. "Finally, brethren, whatsoever things are true, whatsoever things are honest, whatsoever things are just, whatsoever things are pure, whatsoever things are lovely, whatsoever things are of good report; if there be any virtue, and if there be any praise, think on these things" (Philippians 4:8).
G.S.

THIRST FOR GOD
· ·

If we care anything about Christ at all, our hearts will turn to Him as naturally as, when the winter begins to pinch, the migrating birds seek the sunny south, turning by an instinct that they do not themselves understand.

ALEXANDER MACLAREN

Once a man is united to God how could he not live forever? Once a man is separated from God, what can he do but wither and die?

C. S. LEWIS

Almost every day of my life I am praying that "a jubilant pining and longing for God" might come back on the evangelical churches. We don't need to have our doctrine straightened out; we are as orthodox as the Pharisees of old. But this longing for God that brings spiritual torrents and whirlwinds of seeking and self-denial—this is almost gone from our midst.

A. W. TOZER, MAN, THE DWELLING PLACE OF GOD

If we traverse the world, it is possible to find cities without walls, without letters, without kings, without wealth, without coin, without schools and theatres; but a city without a temple, or that practiseth not worship, prayers, and the like, no one ever saw.

PLUTARCH

I thirst for Thee, O God; when shall I meet Thee? Is there a friend, a saint, a God's-Own who'll take me to the Lord? Without Him I'm comforted not.

THE *GRANTH*,
SACRED BOOK OF THE SIKHS

TIME
. . . .

Lost, yesterday, somewhere between sunrise and sunset, two golden hours, each set with sixty diamond minutes. No reward is offered, for they are gone forever.

HORACE MANN

Our greatest danger in life is in permitting the urgent things to crowd out the important.

CHARLES E. HUMMEL

How completely satisfying to turn from our limitations to a God who has none. Eternal years lie in His heart. For Him time does not pass, it remains; and those who are in Christ share with Him all the riches of limitless time and endless years. God never hurries. There are no deadlines against which He must work. Only to know this is to quiet our spirits and relax our nerves. For those out of Christ, time is a devouring beast.

A. W. TOZER, *THE KNOWLEDGE OF THE HOLY*

God has not bowed to our nervous haste nor embraced the methods of our machine age. The man who would know God must give time to Him.

A. W. TOZER, *THE DIVINE CONQUEST*

Unfinished Cathedral

The query comes: How long is Life?
Threescore and ten, the Good Book reads,
Is time enough for men to write
The record of his life in deeds.

Threescore and ten—how fast they fly!
Threescore and ten—they're almost gone!
And I, who dreamed of castles high,
Have only laid the cornerstone.

S/SGT. JARVIS D. ANDERSON

Asked what he would do if he knew Christ would return in three days, George Whitefield replied, "I would do just what I have scheduled to do."

G.S.

The chief value of an anniversary is to call us to greater faithfulness in the time that is left.

WILLIAM MANNING

A converted Hindu who had been given a Bible and a clock said, "The clock will tell me how time goes, and the Bible will tell me how to spend it."

ANONYMOUS

Most time is wasted, not in hours, but in minutes. A bucket with a small hole in the bottom gets just as empty as a bucket that is deliberately kicked over.

PAUL J. MEYER

I am wondering what would have happened to me if . . . some fluent talker had converted me to the theory of the eight-hour day, and convinced me that it was not fair to my fellow workers to put forth my best efforts in my work. I am glad that the eight-hour day had not been invented when I was a young man. If my life had been made up of eight-hour days I do not believe I could have accomplished a great deal. This country would not amount to as much as it does . . . if the young men had been afraid that they might earn more than they were paid.

THOMAS A. EDISON

To "kill time" is—by definition—to murder it.

ANONYMOUS

If there's a job to be done, I always ask the busiest men in my parish to take it on and it gets done.

HENRY WARD BEECHER

Will a man rob God? Everyone receives an equal supply of time. The only difference between us is in the way we spend it. Each week brings us 168 golden hours. We spend approximately 56 hours for sleep and recuperation. We spend approximately 28 hours for eating and personal duties. We spend approximately 40 to 50 hours for earning a living.

We have 30 to 40 hours left to spend just as we wish. But how do we spend them? How many hours for recreation? How many hours for family fellowship? How many hours for the regular worship of God? How many hours for personal service in the name of Christ?

Will a man rob God? He can; and he does. Perhaps we may be very busy with good things, yet be too busy for the best things. The great question is: Have we made wise use of our time as good stewards of Christ?

ANONYMOUS

A Tiny Little Minute

Just a tiny little minute.
Sixty seconds in it.
Forced upon me;
Didn't ask it, didn't choose it.
Yet, it's up to me to use it;
Must give account if I abuse it.
Just a little minute.

ANONYMOUS

An Indian chief made a wiser reply than any philosopher to someone complaining that he had not enough time. "Well," said the Indian, "I suppose you have all the time there is."

RALPH WALDO EMERSON

Tomorrow is the day when idlers work, and fools reform, and mortal men lay hold on heaven.

ANONYMOUS

Don't Tell Me

Don't tell me what you will do
When you have time to spare;
Tell me what you did today
To ease a load of care.

Don't tell me what you will give,
When your ship comes in from sea,
Tell me what you gave today
A fettered soul to free.

GRENVILLE KLEISER

TODAY

Each morning puts a man on trial, and each evening passes judgment.

ROY L. SMITH

Much may be done in those little shreds and patches of time which
every day produces and most men throw away.

CHARLES CALEB COLTON

Men spend their lives in anticipations, in determining to be vastly
happy at some period or other, when they have time. But the present
time has one advantage over every other: it is our time.

CHARLES CALEB COLTON

Here, Lord, is my life.
I place it on the altar today.
Use it as You will.

ALBERT SCHWEITZER, *MORNING PRAYER*

Starting afresh patiently and in good cheer and hope is the mark of
the Christian. One of the helpful definitions of Christianity is this: the
Christian life is a series of new beginnings.

JOHN B. COBURN

Today is, for all that we know, the opportunity and occasion of our lives. On what we do or say today may depend the success and completeness of our entire life-struggle. It is for us, therefore, to use every moment of today as if our very eternity were dependent on its words and deeds.

HENRY CLAY TRUMBELL

The future that we study and plan for begins today.

CHESTER O. FISCHER

Your attitude toward life in general is reflected in your response to the dawn of a new day.

J. N. GEHMAN

TRUST
· ·

The fact of the matter is that I take refuge in the Lord. Unashamedly I run to Him. In fact, if it were not for the ready access I have to Him, I would never survive the ministry. The pressures would be more than I could take. I hide myself away with Him. I crawl into a corner and talk to Him. When the pressure is on, I pull the drapes and commune with Him. I take refuge in Him.

STUART BRISCOE, *WHAT WORKS*

Woe to the man whose heart has not learned while young to hope, to love and to put its trust in life!

JOSEPH CONRAD

The statement that God is in control is either true or it's not true. If it's not true, we'd better forget about God. But if it is true and we accept God's revelation of Himself, our faith enables us to enjoy and rest in the certainty of His providence.

PAUL LITTLE,
HOW TO GIVE AWAY YOUR FAITH

It is a greater compliment to be trusted than to be loved.

GEORGE MACDONALD

You may be deceived if you trust too much, but you will live in torment if you do not trust enough.

FRANK CRANE, M.D.

This is a sane, wholesome, practical, working faith: first, that it is a man's business to do the will of God; second, that God takes on Himself the special care of that man; and third, that therefore that man ought never to be afraid of anything.

GEORGE MACDONALD

Where there is faith, there is love;
Where there is love, there is peace;
Where there is peace, there is God;
And where there is God, there is no need.

LEO TOLSTOY

Man is not to question, but to adore.

EDWARD YOUNG

TRUTH

When Leo Durocher was manager of the Dodgers, he was booed for pulling a pitcher out in the eighth inning of a close game. A reporter later asked him how he felt about the crowd's reaction. He replied, "Baseball is like church. Many attend. Few understand."

LEO DUROCHER

True genius resides in the capacity for evaluation of uncertain, hazardous, and conflicting information.

WINSTON CHURCHILL

Whatever is only almost true is quite false, and among the most dangerous of errors, because being so near truth, it is the more likely to lead astray.

HENRY WARD BEECHER

The truth is so simple that it is regarded as pretentious banality.

DAG HAMMARSKJÖLD

The best way to show that a stick is crooked is not to argue about it or to spend time denouncing it, but to lay a straight stick alongside it.

D. L. MOODY

Apart from blunt truth, our lives sink decadently amid the perfume of hints and suggestions.

ALFRED N. WHITEHEAD

Those are weaklings who know the truth and uphold it as long as it suits their purpose, and then abandon it.

BLAISE PASCAL

Integrity is the glue that holds our way of life together. What our young people want to see in their elders is integrity, honesty, truthfulness, and faith. What they hate most of all is hypocrisy and phoniness. That is why it is important for us to go to church, to read the Bible, and to say grace at the table. Let them see us doing what we would like to see them do.

BILLY GRAHAM

Of all work done under the sun religious work should be the most open to examination. There is positively no place in the church for sleight of hand or double talk. Everything done by the churches should be completely above suspicion. The true church will have nothing to hide.

A. W. TOZER, *OF GOD AND MEN*

Mr. Lely, I desire you would use all your skill to paint my picture truly like me, and not flatter me at all; but remark all these roughnesses, pimples, warts, and everything as you see me, otherwise I will never pay a farthing for it.

OLIVER CROMWELL

Accuracy is the twin brother of honesty; inaccuracy is a near kin to falsehood.

TRYON SCHWARDS

Some people live their whole lives just around the corner from the world of truth.

CARL F. H. HENRY

For the word of the Lord is right; and all his works are done in truth.
PSALM 33:4

Behold, thou desirest truth in the inward parts: and in the hidden part thou shalt make me to know wisdom.
PSALM 51:6

For the Lord is good; his mercy is everlasting; and his truth endureth to all generations.
PSALM 100:5

Thy righteousness is an everlasting righteousness, and thy law is the truth.
PSALM 119:142

He that speaketh truth sheweth forth righteousness: but a false witness deceit.
PROVERBS 12:17

Howbeit when he, the Spirit of truth, is come, he will guide you into all truth: for he shall not speak of himself; but whatsoever he shall hear, that shall he speak: and he will shew you things to come.
JOHN 16:13

Pilate therefore said unto him, Art thou a king then? Jesus answered, Thou sayest that I am a king. To this end was I born, and for this cause came I into the world, that I should bear witness unto the truth. Every one that is of the truth heareth my voice.
JOHN 18:37

URGENCY

. . . .

As long as it is day, we must do the work of him who sent me. Night is coming, when no one can work.

JOHN 9:4 NIV

Samuel Zwemer once addressed a student convention on the needs of the Islamic world, and closed his appeal by walking over to a great map of the Muslim lands. Spreading his arms over it, he said, "Thou O Christ, art all I need; and Thou, O Christ, art all they need."

    He is our urgency.

LEIGHTON FORD, *THE CHRISTIAN PERSUADER*

I believe that if an angel were to wing his way from earth up to Heaven, and were to say that there was one poor, ragged boy, without father or mother, with no one to care for him and teach him the way of life; and if God were to ask who among them were willing to come down to this earth and live here for fifty years and lead that one to Jesus Christ, every angel in Heaven would volunteer to go. Even Gabriel, who stands in the presence of the Almighty, would say, "Let me leave my high and lofty position, and let me have the luxury of leading one soul to Jesus Christ." There is no greater honor than to be the instrument of God's hands of leading one person out of the kingdom of Satan into the glorious light of Heaven.

D. L. MOODY

I speak to every responsible citizen of the world. I speak especially to everyone who claims a personal relationship with Jesus Christ. There is no time to lose. The lost are dying, and the world is headed for chaos, apart from divine intervention. Let us join hands! Let us walk together after lost men.

JOHN HAGGAI

Whatever we may believe about election, the fact remains that men without Christ are lost, and going to hell. . . . "Except ye repent," said our Lord to the crowd, "ye shall all . . . perish." And we who are Christ's are sent to tell them of the One—the only One—who can save them from perishing. Is not their need urgent? . . . Does that not make evangelism a matter of urgency for us?

J. I. PACKER

Every old-time circus had a barker who promoted each attraction. He would call out, "Hurry! Hurry! Hurry!" And people would rush to some trivial sideshow.

At times in my subconscious I seem to hear the voice of God calling, "Hurry! Hurry! Hurry; for those I love die so fast." The call is not to some passing earthly side show, but to the main issue of time and eternity. Even now the Spirit of God is calling, "Stir up your gift. Redeem the time. Work while it is day. Hurry! Hurry! Hurry!"

G. S.

VANITY
. . . .

Some people are so intractably vain that when they admit they are wrong they want as much credit for admitting it as if they were right.
SYDNEY HARRIS

Oh wad some power the giftie gie us
To see oursels as others see us!
It wad frae monie a blunder free us,
An' foolish notion.
ROBERT BURNS

That which makes the vanity of others unbearable to us is that which wounds our own.
FRANÇOIS DUC DE LA ROCHEFOUCAULD

VICTORY
. . . .

The strength for our conquering and our victory is drawn continually from Christ. The Bible does not teach that sin is completely eradicated from the Christian in this life, but it does teach that sin shall no longer reign over you. The strength and power of sin have been broken. The Christian now has resources available to live above and beyond this world. The Bible teaches that whosoever is born of God does not practice sin. It is like the little girl who said that when the devil came knocking with a temptation, she just sent Jesus to the door.
BILLY GRAHAM

One on God's side is a majority.
WENDELL PHILLIPS

We often rebel against the strenuousness and chaos of our time. But historically it has always been in such time that man won his great inner victories.

E. M. McKEE

I have full confidence in your courage, devotion to duty and skill in battle. We will accept nothing less than full victory.

DWIGHT D. EISENHOWER,
ORDER TO HIS TROOPS
D-DAY, 6 JUNE 1944

The triumphant Christian does not fight for victory; he celebrates a victory already won.

REGINALD WALLIS

VIRTUE
. . . .

If rascals knew the advantages of virtue, they would become honest men out of rascality.

BENJAMIN FRANKLIN

The virtue of a man ought to be measured, not by his extra-ordinary exertions, but by his everyday conduct.

BLAISE PASCAL

Industry, economy, honesty, and kindness form a quartet of virtue that will never be improved upon.

JAMES OLIVER

There is but one virtue—the eternal sacrifice of self.

HENRY GEORGE

WALKING

Of a certain man's walking, George Ada said: "He walks like he had gravel in his shoes." Of a certain woman, Balzac wrote: "She walked with a proud, defiant step, like a martyr to the Coliseum." Of a woman, also, Byron wrote: "She walks in beauty like the night of cloudless climes and starry skies." And Shakespeare wrote: "Walk like sprites to countenance this horror."

But Edward Payson Weston, in 1861, without writing anything, walked four hundred and forty-three miles in two hundred and eight hours to attend the inauguration of Abraham Lincoln.

Would that the spirit that possessed him to be at the inauguration would possess multitudes today as to attendance of the sanctuary of God.

ROBERT G. LEE

Who seeks for Heaven alone to save his soul
May keep the path, but will not reach the goal;
While he who walks in love may wander far,
Yet God will bring him where the blessed are.

HENRY VAN DYKE

Does the pilgrim count the miles
When he travels to some distant shrine?

JOHANN VON SCHILLER

WAR

A man who is at war with himself will be at war with others.

DAG HAMMARSKJÖLD

[War is] the needy bankrupt's last resort.

NICOLAS ROWE

Military alliance, balances of power, the League of Nations—all in turn have failed. We have had our last chance. If we do not devise some greater and more equitable system, Armageddon will be at our door. The problem, basically, is theological and involves a spiritual recrudescence and improvement of human character that will synchronize with our almost matchless advance in science, art, literature, and all material and cultural developments of the past two thousand years. It must be of the spirit if we are to save flesh.

DOUGLAS MACARTHUR

[War is] the chief pursuit of ambitious minds.

EDWARD GIBBON

[War] gratifies . . . the combative instinct of mankind, but it gratifies also the love of plunder, destruction, cruel discipline and arbitrary power.

CHARLES ELIOT

War is hell.

GENERAL WILLIAM T. SHERMAN

The world will never have lasting peace so long as men reserve for war the finest human qualities. Peace, no less than war, requires idealism and self-sacrifice and a righteous and dynamic faith.

JOHN FOSTER DULLES

There never was a good war or a bad peace.

BENJAMIN FRANKLIN, LETTER TO QUINCY

War is kinder than a Godless peace.

G. A. STUDDERT-KENNEDY,
THE UNUTTERABLE BEAUTY

It is well that war is so terrible, or we should grow too fond of it.

ROBERT E. LEE

Yesterday, December 7, 1941—a date which will live in infamy—the United States of America was suddenly and deliberately attacked by naval and air forces of the Empire of Japan.

FRANKLIN DELANO ROOSEVELT

Not long ago a Norwegian statistician computerized every war that had ever been fought. His study quickly indicated that during 5,560 years of recorded history there have been 14,531 wars, averaging a little over 2.6 wars each year. In this history of 185 generations, only 10 of those generations have witnessed unbroken peace.

G. S.

Nicholas Rowe suggested that war is "the needy bankrupt's last resort." Thomas Hobbes said there are three principal causes of war: "competition, diffidence, and glory." But the ancient philosopher, Plato, was probably the closest to the truth when he said, "Wars and factions and fightings have no other source than the body and its lusts. For it is for the getting of wealth that all our wars arise; and we are compelled to get wealth because of our body, to whose service we are slaves."

G. S.

WEATHER
. . . .

Sunshine is delicious, rain is refreshing, wind braces up, snow is exhilarating; there is no such thing as bad weather, only different kinds of weather.

JOHN RUSKIN

*At Christmas I no more desire a rose,
Than wish a snow in May's newfangled mirth;
But like of each thing that in season grow.*

WILLIAM SHAKESPEARE,
LOVE'S LABOUR'S LOST

439

The only faith that wears well and holds its color in all weathers is that which is woven of conviction and set with the sharp mordant of experience.

JAMES RUSSELL LOWELL

Accuse not Nature, she hath done her part;
Do thou but thine!

JOHN MILTON

No one finds fault with the defects which are the results of nature.
ARISTOTLE

I was born with a chronic anxiety about the weather.
JOHN BURROUGHS

Weather is a literary specialty, and no untrained hand can turn out a good article on it.

MARK TWAIN

WISDOM
· ·

Wisdom is seeing things from God's perspective.
BILL GOTHARD

Wisdom is the right use of knowledge. To know is not to be wise. Many men know a great deal, and are all the greater fools for it. There is no fool so great a fool as a knowing fool. But to know how to use knowledge is to have wisdom.

CHARLES HADDON SPURGEON

You have letters but no learning that understand so many languages, turn over so many volumes, and yet are but asleep when all is done.
JOHN MILTON

A wise man sees as much as he ought, not as much as he can.
MICHEL DE MONTAIGNE

Not all the Capitol chaplains were perfunctory. The Rev. Byron Sunderland, one day in April, 1864, invoked:
"O Lord, give us that Thou wilt in Thine infinite wisdom vouchsafe to our rulers and legislators in this Congress assembled more brains—more brains, Lord."
NOAH BROOKS

Wise men learn more from fools than fools from the wise.
CATO

For the Lord giveth wisdom: out of his mouth cometh knowledge and understanding.
PROVERBS 2:6

A reproof entereth more into a wise man than an hundred stripes into a fool.
PROVERBS 17:10

For God giveth to a man that is good in his sight wisdom, and knowledge, and joy: but to the sinner he giveth travail, to gather and to heap up, that he may give to him that is good before God. This also is vanity and vexation of spirit.
ECCLESIATES 2:26

Woe unto them that are wise in their own eyes, and prudent in their own sight!
ISAIAH 5:21

But the wisdom that is from above is first pure, then peaceable, gentle, and easy to be intreated, full of mercy and good fruits, without partiality, and without hypocrisy.
JAMES 3:17

WITNESS
· ·

The real question is not, "Is this the best time for a personal word for Christ?" but it is, "Am I willing to improve this time for Christ, and for a precious soul, whether it is the best time or not?" If the Christian waits until the sinner gives sign of a desire for help, or until the Christian thinks that a loving word to the sinner will be most timely, he is not likely to begin at all. The only safe rule for his guidance—if indeed a Christian needs a specific rule as a guide—is to speak lovingly of Christ and of Christ's love for the individual whenever one has an opportunity of choosing his subject of conversation in an interview with an individual who may be in special need, yet who has given no special indication of it.

HENRY CLAY TRUMBULL,
INDIVIDUAL WORK FOR INDIVIDUALS

Samuel Zwemer once addressed a student convention on the needs of the Islamic world, and closed his appeal by walking over to a great map of the Muslim lands. Spreading his arms over it, he said, "Thou O Christ, art all I need; and Thou, O Christ, art all they need."

He is our urgency.

LEIGHTON FORD, *THE CHRISTIAN PERSUADER*

> *Love this world through me, Lord*
> *This world of broken men,*
> *Thou didst love through death, Lord*
> *Oh, love in me again!*
> *Souls are in despair, Lord.*
> *Oh, make me know and care;*
> *When my life they see,*
> *May they behold Thee,*
> *Oh, love the world through me.*

WILL HOUGHTON

Lord, give me Scotland or else I die!

JOHN KNOX

I believe that if an angel were to wing his way from earth up to Heaven, and were to say that there was one poor, ragged boy, without father or mother, with no one to care for him and teach him the way of life; and if God were to ask who among them were willing to come down to this earth and live here for fifty years and lead that one to Jesus Christ, every angel in Heaven would volunteer to go. Even Gabriel, who stands in the presence of the Almighty, would say, "Let me leave my high and lofty position, and let me have the luxury of leading one soul to Jesus Christ." There is no greater honor than to be the instrument in God's hands of leading one person out of the kingdom of Satan into the glorious light of Heaven.

D. L. MOODY

I saw that it were better to make a mistake in one's first effort at personal religious conversation, and correct that mistake afterwards, than not to make any effort. There can be no mistake so bad, in working for an individual soul for Christ, as the fatal mistake of not making an honest endeavor. How many persons refrain from doing anything lest they possibly should do the wrong thing just now! Not doing is the worst of doing.

HENRY CLAY TRUMBULL,
INDIVIDUAL WORK FOR INDIVIDUALS

Jesus Christ didn't commit the gospel to an advertising agency; He commissioned disciples. And He didn't command them to put up signs and pass out tracts; He said that they would be His witnesses.

JOE BAYLY, *THE GOSPEL BLIMP*

What the world expects of Christians is that Christians should speak out, loud and clear . . . in such a way that never a doubt, never the slightest doubt, could rise in the heart of the simplest man.

ALBERT CAMUS

No man at one and the same time can show that he himself is clever—and that Jesus Christ is mighty to save.

JAMES DENNEY

Non-Christians first need to detect the reality of genuine Christian experience in our lives. Then they will be attracted by our words about Jesus Christ and what it means to know Him personally. After I have spoken to a group, students often approach me with personal questions: "How does it work?" "How can I have the kind of life you've been talking about?" "Is there any hope for me?" It's always a privilege to sit down and explain how forgiveness, cleansing, and power can be individually ours in and through the Lord Jesus Christ.

PAUL LITTLE, *HOW TO GIVE AWAY YOUR FAITH*

Always use your Bible in personal dealing. Do not trust to memory, but make the person read the verse for himself. Do not use printed slips or books. Hence, if convenient, always carry a Bible or New Testament with you. . . .

Sometimes a few minutes in prayer have done more for a man than two hours in talk. . . .

Urge an immediate decision, but never tell a man he is converted. . . . Let the Holy Spirit reveal that to him. . . .

Always be prepared to do personal work. . . .

Do the work boldly. Don't take those in a position in life above your own, but, as a rule, take those on the same footing. Don't deal with a person of the opposite sex if it can be otherwise arranged. Bend all your endeavors to answer for the poor, struggling souls that question of such importance to them, "What must I do to be saved?"

D. L. MOODY

We know what it is to lose health and wealth and reputation . . . but what is the loss of all these things compared with the loss of the soul?

D. L. MOODY

When Dwight L. Moody was asked why he had organized the school that later became Moody Bible Institute, he said that besides training students in the knowledge and the use of the Bible and in gospel music, he wanted to train them in everything that will give them access practically to the souls of people, especially the neglected classes.

G. S.

Never underestimate what God can do through you as an individual. But you must begin by letting Him make you a Christ-like person, a man or woman with a quality of holy life that cannot go unnoticed.

This was the characteristic which Woodrow Wilson noted in the great evangelist, D. L. Moody. Speaking at Princeton University before he became President of the United States, Mr. Wilson said of Moody:

> I was in a very plebeian place. I was in a barber's shop, sitting in a chair, when I became aware that a personality had entered the room. A man had come quietly in upon the same errand as myself and sat in the next chair to me. Every word he uttered, though it was not in the least didactic, showed a personal and vital interest in the man who was serving him; and before I got through with what was being done to me, I was aware that I had attended an evangelistic service, because Mr. Moody was in the next chair. I purposely lingered in the room after he left and noted the singular effect his visit had upon the barbers in that shop. They talked in undertones. They did not know his name, but they knew that something had elevated their thought. And I felt that I left that place as I should have left a place of worship.

God can do great things through consecrated individuals, through yielded lives.

G. S.

A tramp, obviously under the influence of alcohol, approached evangelist D. L. Moody. "Mr. Moody," said he, "you're the man who saved me."

As the great evangelist observed the bearded face, bloodshot eyes, unkempt hair, and torn clothes, he replied, "Yes, it looks as if I did save you. If the Lord had, you wouldn't be in this condition."

G. S.

To be glad instruments of God's love in this imperfect world is the service to which man is called.

ALBERT SCHWEITZER

The wayside pool reflects the fleeting cloud as exactly as does the mighty ocean.

ANONYMOUS

No doctrine of the Christian religion is worth preserving which cannot be verified in daily life.

JOHN T. WATSON

Whatever God gives you to do, do it as well as you can. This is the best possible preparation for what He may want you to do next.

GEORGE MACDONALD

WORDS

The difference between the right word and the almost right word is the difference between lightning—and the lightning bug.

MARK TWAIN

All my life I've looked at words as though I were seeing them for the first time.

ERNEST HEMINGWAY

A writer lives in awe of words, for they can be cruel or kind, and they can change their meanings right in front of you. They pick up flavors and odors like butter in a refrigerator.

JOHN STEINBECK

It's a very excruciating life facing that blank piece of paper every day and having to reach up somewhere into the clouds and bring something down out of them.

TRUMAN CAPOTE

A man's command of the language is most important. Next to kissing, it's the most exciting form of communication mankind has evolved.

OREN ARNOLD

Words are loaded pistols.
JEAN-PAUL SARTRE

All words are pegs to hang ideas on.
HENRY WARD BEECHER

When words fail, wars begin. When wars finally end, we settle our dispute with words.
WILFRED FUNK

Sir Joshua Reynolds once asked Dr. Johnson by what means he had attained his extraordinary accuracy and flow of language. He told him that he had early laid it down as a fixed rule to do his best on every occasion, and in every company; to impart whatever he knew in the most forcible language he could put it in; and that by constant practice and never suffering any careless expressions to escape him or attempting to deliver his thoughts without arranging them in the clearest manner, it became habitual to him.
JAMES BOSWELL

Colors fade, temples crumble, but wise words endure.
EDWARD L. THORNDIKE

Dr. George W. Crane, author and social psychologist, has written a pamphlet called "The Compliment Club" (The Hopkins Syndicate). To qualify for membership in this club, one must pay three sincere compliments a day, one to each of three different persons, for a month. The aspiring member is encouraged to compliment even complete strangers.

Crane's belief is that love cannot replace dislike or indifference at a moment's notice; it requires development of a definite technique and skill in approaching people. Love grows through showing appreciation and dies without it. "You can sincerely compliment your worst enemy, for no human being is totally lacking in merits," says Crane.
G. S.

Words—so innocent and powerful as they are, standing in a dictionary, how potent for good and evil they become, in the hands of one who knows how to combine them!

NATHANIEL HAWTHORNE

America has suffered from a fever of words. We cannot learn from one another until we stop shouting at one another—until we speak quietly enough so that our words can be heard as well as our voices.

RICHARD M. NIXON,
1969 INAUGURAL ADDRESS

Channing Cox, who succeeded Calvin Coolidge as governor of Massachusetts, visited the vice-president. Cox asked him how he could see his visitors every day and manage to leave his office at five, while Cox could rarely leave before nine P.M. Coolidge replied, "You talk back."

CALVIN COOLIDGE

Most of us cannot remember learning our first word, but Helen Keller recalled that event in her life with a flashing vividness. She remembered because she was deaf, mute, and blind from the age of nineteen months and did not learn her first word until she was seven.

When Helen was six, an extraordinary teacher named Anne Mansfield Sullivan entered her life. Miss Sullivan was poor, ill, and nearly blind herself, but she possessed a tenacious vitality that was to force her pupil's unwilling mind from the dark, silent prison in which it lived: "Before my teacher came to me, I lived in a world that was a no-world. I cannot hope to describe adequately that unconscious yet conscious time of nothingness. I did not know that I knew aught, or that I lived or acted or desired."

In his play The Miracle Worker, *William Gibson shows us what happened when Anne Sullivan first met Helen's mother:*

MRS. KELLER: What will you try to teach her first?

ANNE SULLIVAN: First, last, and in between, language.

MRS. KELLER: Language.

ANNE SULLIVAN: Language is to the mind more than light is to the eye.

The miracle that Anne Sullivan worked was to give Helen Keller language, for only language could transform a small animal that looked like a child, a kuntu, *into a human being, a* muntu. *Day after day, month after month, Anne Sullivan spelled words into Helen's hand. Finally, when Helen was seven years old and working with her teacher in the presence of water, she spoke her first word. Years later she described that moment in* The Story of My Life *(1902):*

> *Somehow the mystery of language was revealed to me. I knew then that "w-a-t-e-r" meant that wonderful cool something that was flowing over my hand. That living word awakened my soul, gave it light, hope, joy, set it free! . . . I left the well-house eager to learn. Everything had a name and each name gave birth to a new thought.*

Not only did Helen Keller learn to speak, write, and understand the English language. She graduated cum laude *from Radcliffe College and went on to become a distinguished lecturer and writer. But perhaps the most poignant moment in her life came when, at the age of nine, she was able to say to Anne Sullivan, "I am not dumb now."*

RICHARD LEDERER, THE MIRACLE OF LANGUAGE

Richard Wright spent his childhood in the Jim Crow South—a prison of poverty, fear, and racism. He was born on a farm near Natchez, Mississippi, and, when he was five, his sharecropper father deserted the family. Richard, his mother, and his brother had to move from one community to another throughout the South so that he seldom remained in one school for an entire year. Yet somehow Richard Wright escaped the prison of hunger and hatred to become the most significant black writer in America, the author of Native Son *(1940) and* Black Boy *(1945), two watershed books in American literature.*

In Black Boy, *Wright's unsparing autobiography, he describes his liberation at the age of eighteen. Because black people were not allowed library privileges, Wright used the card of a friendly white man. . . . He obtained a copy of Mencken's* A Book of Prefaces, *and all at once the sun of great literature burst through the window of his prison:*

> *That night in my rented room, while letting the hot water run over my pork and beans in the sink, I opened A Book of Prefaces and began to read. I was jarred and shocked by the style, the clear, clean, sweeping sentences. Why did he write like that? And how did one write like that?. . . I stood up, trying to realize what reality lay behind the meaning of the words. Yes, this man was fighting with words. He was using words as a weapon, using them as one would use a club. . . . Then, maybe, perhaps, I could use them as a weapon. . . .*
>
> *What strange world was this? I concluded the book with the conviction that I had somehow overlooked something terribly important in life. I had once tried to write, had once reveled in feeling, had let my crude imagination roam, but the impulse to dream had been slowly beaten out of me by experience. Now it surged up again and I hungered for books, new ways of looking and seeing.*
>
> RICHARD LEDERER, THE MIRACLE OF LANGUAGE

In the Autobiography of Malcolm X *(1964), Malcolm tells how he rose from a world of thieving, pimping, and drug peddling to become one of the most articulate and dynamic leaders of the black revolution in America. . . .*

Frustrated by his inability to express himself in writing, Malcolm borrowed a dictionary from the prison school and slowly, painstakingly, began to copy—word by word and page by page—the entire dictionary onto his tablet: "With every succeeding page, I also learned of people and places and events from history. Actually, the dictionary is like a miniature encyclopedia." As his vocabulary expanded, an already powerful speaker experienced a new empowerment through literacy. He read all day and even at night, in the faint glow of a corridor light:

> *Anyone who has read a great deal can imagine the new world that opened up. Let me tell you something: from then until I left*

that prison, in every free moment I had, if I was not reading in the library, I was reading in my bunk. You couldn't have gotten me out of books with a wedge. Months passed without my even thinking about being imprisoned. In fact, up to then, I had never been so truly free in my life.

RICHARD LEDERER, THE MIRACLE OF LANGUAGE

Cold words freeze people, and hot words scorch them, and bitter words make them bitter, and wrathful words make them wrathful. Kind words also produce their image on men's souls; and a beautiful image it is. They smooth, and quiet, and comfort the hearer.

BLAISE PASCAL

I would rather play with forked lightning, or take in my hand living wires with their fiery current, than speak a reckless word against any servant of Christ, or idly repeat the slanderous darts which thousands of Christians are hurling on others, to the hurt of their own souls and bodies.

A. B. SIMPSON

You cannot stop people's tongues, and therefore the best thing to do is to stop your own ears and never mind what is spoken.

CHARLES SPURGEON

Colors fade, temples crumble, empires fall, but wise words endure.

EDWARD L. THORNDIKE

We have all been guilty, not of fifteen idle words, but of fifteen million idle words. And we must beg God's forgiveness!

G. S.

A gossip is someone who can give you all the details without knowing any of the facts.

WORK AND DUTY
· ·

If you have a job without aggravations, you don't have a job.
MALCOLM FORBES

The only thing which is of lasting benefit to a man is that which he does for himself. Money which comes to him without effort on his part is seldom a benefit and often a curse . . . And so with regard to money or other things which are given by one person to another. It is only in the exceptional case that the receiver is really benefited. But if we can help people to help themselves, then there is a permanent blessing conferred.
JOHN D. ROCKEFELLER, SR.

No man is born into the world, whose work
Is not born with him; there is always work,
And tools to work withal, for those who will,
And blessed are the horny hands of toil!
JAMES RUSSELL LOWELL

Don't learn the tricks of the trade—learn the trade.
ANONYMOUS

Let men laugh when you sacrifice desire to duty, if they will. You have time and eternity to rejoice in.
THEODORE PARKER

The average human being in any line of work could double his productive capacity overnight if he began right now to do all the things he knows he should do, and to stop doing all the things he knows he should not do.
ELMER G. LETTERMAN

When man loses the sacred significance of work and of himself as worker, he soon loses the sacred meaning of time and of life.
CARL F. H. HENRY,
ASPECTS OF CHRISTIAN SOCIAL ETHICS

As God's fellow worker he [man] is to reflect God's creative activity on Monday in the factory no less than on Sunday when commemorating the day of rest and worship.

CARL F. H. HENRY,
ASPECTS OF CHRISTIAN SOCIAL ETHICS

Few men ever drop dead from overwork, but many quietly curl up and die because of under-satisfaction.

SYDNEY HARRIS

Keep us Lord so awake in the duties of our callings that we may sleep in peace and awake in glory.

JOHN DONNE

God give me work till my life shall end and life till my work is done.

WINEFRED HOLTBY

These things, good Lord, that we pray for, give us Thy grace to labour for.

SIR THOMAS MORE

O Lord, let us not live to be useless, for Christ's sake.

JOHN WESLEY

O Lord, thou givest us everything, at the price of an effort.

LEONARDO DA VINCI

God gives the birds their food, but He does not throw it into their nests.

GERMAN PROVERB

To find one's work is to find one's place in the world.

RICHARD C. CABOT

Unless a man undertakes more than he possibly can do he will never do all he can do.

HENRY DRUMMOND

WORLD

· ·

Better keep yourself clean and bright; you are the window through which you must see the world.

GEORGE BERNARD SHAW

Most church members live so far below the standard, you'd have to backslide to be in fellowship. We are so subnormal that if we were to become normal, people would think we were abnormal.

VANCE HAVNER

Some interesting statistics appear in the book titled American Averages *(Fiensiber and Mead, Doubleday, 1980). Some of the happenings were intriguing and amusing, while others were tragic. For example, on an average day in America—*

- *438 immigrants become United States citizens;*
- *41 million people go to school, kindergarten through graduate school;*
- *28 mailmen are bitten by dogs;*
- *motorists pay $4,036,000 in tolls;*
- *10,930,000 cows are milked;*
- *8 children swallow toys and are taken to emergency rooms;*
- *4,109 people parachute from airplanes for the fun of it;*
- *each of us, on average, produces nearly 6 pounds of garbage;*
- *people drink 90 million cans of beer;*
- *people smoke 1.6 billion cigarettes;*
- *2,740 children run away from home;*
- *88 million people watch prime time television programs;*
- *2,740 teenagers become pregnant;*
- *5,962 couples wed, and before the sun sets, 2,986 divorce;*
- *someone is raped every 8 minutes, someone is murdered every 27 minutes, and someone is robbed every 78 seconds;*
- *a burglar strikes every 10 seconds, and a car is stolen every 33 seconds.*

That is the kind of world we live in.

G. S.

We live in a world of invertebrate theology, jellyfish morality, see-saw religion, India-rubber convictions, somersault philosophy, and a psychology that tells us what we already know in words we don't understand.

ROBERT G. LEE

WORLDLINESS

Jesus sets before us a bold, unvarnished question: are you a bride or a whore? The two possibilities are related: it is only possible to become a whore because God has called us to be a bride. The call to love God creates the alternative, that we squander our love faithlessly. Jesus looks to us for the love of a bride. Any other love which possesses our heart brings us into the state of spiritual adultery.

M. BASILEA SCHLINK

Sophistication is the Spirit's foe.

GEORGE SANTAYANA

When we become a friend of the world, we take our stand in defiance of God. And, God views it as an act of an enemy, an act of espionage against Him. It is as if we were conducting guerrilla warfare against the Lord. We are aiding and abetting the enemy—the same sin committed by Judas. We ask, "How could a man be so black-hearted as to betray Jesus with a kiss of brotherhood?" We are aghast at this most infamous deed in human history. But is that deed any more treacherous than for us to name the name of Jesus Christ but to serve the camp of the enemy?

B. J. CHITWOOD, *A FAITH THAT WORKS*

Worldliness is a spirit, a temperament, an attitude of the soul. It is a life without high callings, life devoid of lofty ideals. It is a gaze always horizontal and never vertical.

JOHN HENRY JOWETT

For centuries the Church stood solidly against every form of worldly entertainment, recognizing it for what it was—a device for wasting time, a refuge from the disturbing voice of conscience, a scheme to divert attention from moral accountability. But of late she appears to have decided that if she cannot conquer the great god Entertainment she may as well join forces with him and make what use she can of his powers.

A. W. TOZER, *THE ROOT OF THE RIGHTEOUS*

A whole new generation of Christians has come up believing that it is possible to "accept" Christ without forsaking the world.

A. W. TOZER, *MAN: THE DWELLING PLACE OF GOD*

Exhalation is as necessary to life as inhalation. To accept Christ it is necessary that we reject whatever is contrary to Him.

A. W. TOZER, *THAT INCREDIBLE CHRISTIAN*

It is right for the Church to be in the world; it is wrong for the world to be in the Church. A boat in water is good; that is what boats are for. However, water inside the boat causes it to sink.

HAROLD LINDSELL,
THE WORLD, THE FLESH, AND THE DEVIL

We are safe at sea, safer in the storm God sends us, than when we are befriended by the world.

JEREMY TAYLOR

He that loveth pleasure shall be a poor man: he that loveth wine and oil shall not be rich.

PROVERBS 21:17

Dearly beloved, I beseech you as strangers and pilgrims, abstain from fleshly lusts, which war against the soul.

1 PETER 2:11

And be not conformed to this world: but be ye transformed by the renewing of your mind, that ye may prove what is that good, and acceptable, and perfect, will of God.

ROMANS 12:2

WORRY
. . . .

Worry is the interest paid by those who borrow trouble.
GEORGE LYONS

It is not work that kills men. It is worry. Work is healthy. . . . Worry rusts upon the blade.
HENRY WARD BEECHER

People who do not know how to fight worry, die young.
ALEXIS CARROLL

Charles Haddon Spurgeon, the great nineteenth-century preacher, once said that he worried for weeks before a speaking engagement, even to the extent of hoping he would break a leg and miss the event. When he finally entered the pulpit to give the speech, he was exhausted!

Then Spurgeon faced up to his fear. He asked himself, What is the worst thing that could happen to me during my sermon? *Whatever it was, he decided, the heavens would not collapse. He knew that he had been magnifying his fears. Once he faced his worries for what they were, he relaxed, simply because his mind was no longer divided.*

G. S.

Bishop William Quayle, awake at night because of fruitless worrying, heard God say to him, "Quayle, you go to bed; I'll sit up the rest of the night." Whimsically put, that experience symbolizes a matter of major importance in the cure of worry.

G. S.

Our English word worry *is equivalent to the Greek word* merimnao. *It is a combination of two words:* merizo, *meaning "to divide," and* nous, *meaning "mind." Worry really means "to divide the mind." It means we are double-minded rather than single-minded. The apostle James warned, "A double-minded man [is] unstable in all his ways" (James 1:8).*

When we are double-minded, we resemble a monster with two heads facing in opposite directions, or we are like rudderless boats, unable to steer straight, "driven and tossed by the wind" (James 1:6 NKJV).

G. S.

There are two days in the week about which I never worry. Two carefree days kept sacredly free from fear and apprehension. One of these days is yesterday—and the other day I do not worry about is tomorrow.

ROBERT BURDETTE

Worry is a thin stream of fear trickling through the mind. If encouraged, it cuts a channel into which all other thoughts are drained.

ARTHUR SOMERS ROCHE

Worry is ravaging societies worldwide. . . . In America at least, it has virtually become part of the national culture. You could write on countless American gravestones the epitaph: Hurried, Worried, Buried.

JOHN HAGGAI

WORSHIP
· ·

We read in the Gospels concerning Jesus that "as He was praying, the fashion of His countenance was altered." Worship evidently did something for Jesus.

ALBERT W. PALMER

We're here to be worshippers first and workers only second. We take a convert and immediately make a worker out of him. God never meant it to be so. God meant that a convert should learn to be a worshiper, and after that he can learn to be a worker. . . . The work done by a worshiper will have eternity in it.

A. W. TOZER,
"WORSHIP: THE MISSING JEWELL OF EVANGELISM"

The glory of God is a living man; and the life of man consists in beholding God.

SAINT IRENAEUS, *AGAINST HERESIES*

Worship is giving to God the best He has given us.

OSWALD CHAMBERS

The one essential condition of human existence is that man should always be able to bow down before something infinitely great. If men are deprived of the infinitely great, they will not go on living and will die of despair. The Infinite and the Eternal are as essential for man as the little planet on which he dwells.

FYODOR DOSTOYEVSKY

Worship is the provision which the spiritual constitution has made for its own perpetual amendment.

WILLIAM E. HOCKING

Give unto the Lord the glory due unto his name; worship the Lord in the beauty of holiness.

PSALM 29:2

O come, let us worship and bow down: let us kneel before the Lord our maker.

PSALM 95:6

Exalt ye the Lord our God, and worship at his footstool; for he is holy.

PSALM 99:5

I will worship toward thy holy temple, and praise thy name for thy lovingkindness and for thy truth: for thou hast magnified thy word above all thy name.

PSALM 138:2

WRITING
·····································

The role of the writer is not to say what we can all say, but what we are unable to say.

ANAÏS NIN

I have kept a hotel room in every town I've ever lived in. I rent a hotel room for a few months, leave my home at six, and try to be at work by 6:30. To write, I lie across the bed, so that this elbow is absolutely encrusted at the end, just so rough with callouses. I never allow the hotel people to change the bed, because I never sleep there. I stay until 12:30 or 1:30 in the afternoon, and then I go home and try to breathe; I look at the work around five; I have an orderly dinner: proper, quiet, lovely dinner; and then I go back to work the next morning. Sometimes in hotels I'll go into the room, and there'll be a note on the floor which says, "Dear Miss Angelou, let us change the sheets. We think they are moldy." But I only allow them to come in and empty wastebaskets. I insist that all things are taken off the walls. I don't want anything in there. I go into the room, and I feel as if all my beliefs are suspended. Nothing holds me to anything. No milkmaids, no flowers, nothing. I just want to feel and then when I start to work I'll remember. I'll read something, maybe the Psalms, maybe, again, something from Mr. Dunbar, James Weldon Johnson. And I'll remember how beautiful, how pliable the language is, how it will lend itself. If you pull it, it says, "Okay." I remember that, and I start to write.

MAYA ANGELOU

Writing a book or a manifesto, is the nearest a man gets to having a baby.

JOHN R. STOTT

460

In writing, your audience is one single reader. I have found that sometimes it helps to pick out one person—a real person you know, or an imagined person—and write to that one.
JOHN STEINBECK

I think of my books not as sermons or directives in a war of ideas but as objects, with different shapes and textures and the mysteriousness of anything that exists. My first thought about art, as a child, was that the artist brings something into the world that didn't exist before, and that he does it without destroying something else. A kind of refutation of the conservation of matter. That still seems to me its central magic, its core of joy.
JOHN UPDIKE

INDEX OF AUTHORS

Charnin, Martin, 256
Chekhov, Anton, 116
Chenevix, Richard (Archbishop Trench), 360
Chevalier, Maurice, 31
Chesterton, G. K., 39, 49, 120, 122, 128, 240, 255, 256, 280, 321, 331, 338, 349
Chitwood, B. J., 455
Choate, Rufus, 284
Christie, Agatha, 31
Chrysler, Walter P., 342
Chrysostom, Saint John, 204
Churchill, Sir Winston, 24, 29, 31, 55, 75, 77, 124, 126, 127, 143, 244, 300, 356, 357, 429
Cicero, 17, 223, 296, 377, 419
Clark, Frank A., 121
Clark, Glenn, 54
Clark, Stephen B., 412
Clarkson, Margaret, 346
Claudian, 128
Clement of Alexandria, 89
Coburn, James B., 427
Cocteau, Jean, 417
Coder, S. Maxwell, 63, 96, 210
Coffin, Carlyn, 263
Coleridge, Samuel T., 107, 249, 303, 314
Colson, Charles, 151, 152, 192, 284
Colton, Charles Caleb, 395, 427
Conrad, A. Z., 69
Conrad, Joseph, 172, 428
Constable, John, 336
Cook, Captain James, 38
Cook, Robert A., 96, 159
Cook, Ted, 195
Cooke, Alistair, 282
Coolidge, Calvin, 354, 356, 399, 421, 448
Coolidge, Susan, 222, 370
Corot, Jean-Baptiste, 50
Cosby, Bill, 257
Coulson, L. A., 130
Cousins, Norman, 250, 253
Cowper, William, 78, 86
Craig, A. C., 287
Craig, Mary Francis Shura, 37

Crane, Frank, M.D., 429
Crane, George, 50, 220
Cromwell, Oliver, 430
Crowell, Grace Noll, 89, 103
Crowninshield, Frank, 259
Culbertson, William, 282
Cyprian, Saint, 95

Dale, R. W., 219
Dana, Bill, 29
Dante. See Aligieri
Darrow, Clarence S., 331
Dashiell, 208
da Vinci, Leonardo, 140, 234, 453
Day, Albert Edward, 364
de Caussade, J. P., 130
Deeping, Warwick, 71
de Gaulle, Charles. See Gaulle, Charles de
De Haan, M. R., 205
Demosthenes, 342
Denny, James, 392, 443
Dewey, John, 348
Dickens, Charles, 85, 281
Dickinson, Emily, 291
Dill, Samuel, 395
Disraeli, Benjamin, 20, 71, 169, 248, 390
Disraeli, Isaac, 405
Dixon, A. C., 236
Dobson, James C. , 86
Donne, John, 197, 453
Dostoyevsky, Fyodor, 92, 240, 459
Dreiser, Theodore, 390
Dressler, Marie, 30
Drummond, Henry, 45, 90, 308, 453
Dryden, John, 140, 145
Dulles, John Foster, 438
Dumas, Alexander, 264
Durant, Will, 233, 329
Durant, Will and Ariel, 113
Durocher, Leo, 429

Eastman, Max, 256
Edison, Thomas A., 370, 425
Edman, V. Raymond, 72, 165, 177
Edwards, Jonathan, 20, 122, 149, 221, 339

Gothard, Bill, 440
Gracián, Baltasar, 418
Graham, Billy, 42, 63, 72, 80, 89, 100,
105, 113, 121, 127, 138, 169, 193,
205, 213, 229, 277, 304, 313, 316,
337, 350, 392, 406, 430, 435
Graham, Virginia, 380
Greenbaum, William A., II, 194
Gregory, Dick, 250
Gregory, Saint, 295
Grenfell, Wilfred T., 397
Grounds, Vernon, 58
Grubb, Norman, 307, 372
Guder, Eileen, 306, 307, 329
Guthrie, Thomas, 161

Haggai, John, 190, 209, 210, 325, 415,
433, 458
Hale, Edward Everett, 81, 126, 370
Haliburton, Thomas Chandler, 81
Hall, Joseph, 363
Halverson, Richard, 99
Hamilton, Robert Browning, 407
Hammarskjöld, Dag, 302, 304, 322, 396,
430, 437
Hand, Learned, 232
Hankey, Katherine, 412
Hanson, R. P. C., 221
Hardwick, Elizabeth, 71
Harnack, Adolph, 228
Harrelson, Woody, 258
Harrington, Bob, 105
Harris, Everett, 64
Harris, Sydney, 156, 352, 435, 453
Hartswick, Gregory, 264
Havergal, Frances Ridley, 114, 409
Havner, Vance, 22, 33, 37, 38, 46, 71,
103, 104, 107, 113, 117, 141, 157,
188, 218, 229, 231, 235, 278, 299,
347, 361, 365, 367, 375, 385, 391,
405, 454
Hawkins, O. S., 66, 94, 106, 108, 190
Hawn, Goldie, 248
Hawthorne, Nathaniel, 23, 250, 448
Hayes, Rutherford B., 356
Hazlitt, William, 82, 324
Heber, Reginald, 101

Hecht, Andrew B., 267
Hemingway, Ernest, 446
Henry, Carl F. H., 273, 277, 283, 363,
431, 452, 453
Henry, O., 48, 291, 299
Henry, Matthew, 245, 359
Henry V (king of England), 67
Henry, Patrick, 93
Heraclitus, , 79
Herbert, George, 74, 160, 172, 197, 313,
421
Herbert, Willie D., 265
Hershfield, Henry, 28
Hesburgh, Theodore, 180
Hesiod, 300
Heskett, Adnelle, 260
Hill, Rowland, 333
Hilton, Conrad, 168
Hitchcock, Raymond, 292
Hitler, Adolf, 118
Hobbes, Thomas, 291
Hobbs, Herschel, 207
Hocking, William E., 459
Hodges, H. A., 60
Hodges, Leigh Mitchell, 264
Hoff, 266
Hoffa, James Riddle, 328
Hoffman, Oswald C. J., 178, 210
Hofstadter, Richard, 329
Holland, J. G., 18
Holmes, Ernest, 000
Holmes, Oliver Wendell, Jr., 234, 269,
367
Holmes, Oliver Wendell, Sr., 42, 108,
143, 389
Holtby, Winefred, 453
Homer, 49, 170
Hoover, J. Edgar, 329
Hope, Bob, 33, 254
Horace, 200
Hough, Lynn Harold, 94, 95
Houghton, Will, 442
Howard, Thomas, 231, 385
Howe, E. W., 24
Howe, Reuel, 310
Howells, W. D., 194
Hubbard, Elbert, 115, 323, 324, 330

Miller, Henry, 51
Miller, J. R., 146
Milton, John, 43, 116, 301, 401, 421, 440
Mizner, Wilson, 169
Moffat, Robert, 176
Moffatt, James, 331
Monroe, James, 335
Montagu, Ashley, 175
Montaigne, Michel de, 271, 297, 368, 441
Montesquieu, Baron de, 397
Moody, D. L., 33, 37, 53, 61, 62, 69, 84, 95, 96, 105, 107, 109, 118, 137, 147, 187, 188, 192, 222, 228, 235, 238, 270, 281, 306, 307, 309, 310, 327, 360, 376, 381, 385, 386, 388, 401, 420, 430, 433, 443, 444
Moody, Jess, 202, 310
Moore, Thomas, 307
More, Sir Thomas, 453
Morell, Thomas, 180
Morgan, Arthur, 30
Morgan, G. Campbell, 178, 236
Morley, Christopher, 229
Morris, Ida Goldsmith, 171
Morrison, Charles C., 108
Mott, John R., 106, 327
Mudd, Roger, 419
Mueller, George, 97, 190, 217
Muggeridge, Malcolm, 33, 71, 179, 227, 255, 339, 419
Munger, Robert, 178
Murray, Andrew, 65, 158, 161, 243, 348
Myers, Philip Van Ness, 192, 195

Napoleon I (Napoleon Bonaparte), 92, 193, 271
Nash, L. L., 106
Nash, Ogden, 318, 346
Neesima, John Hardy, 362
Newman, Ernest, 353
Newman, John Henry, 128, 224, 396
Newton, Howard W., 149, 265, 417
Newton, John, 211, 361, 402
Newton, Joseph Fort, 301
Newton, Richard, 359

Niebuhr, Reinhold, 248, 356
Nielen, A., 85
Niemöeller, Martin, 48
Nietzsche, Friedrich, 200, 324, 333, 378
Nightingale, Earl, 343
Nightingale, Florence, 299
Niles, D. T., 178
Nin, Anaïs, 460
Nixon, Richard M., 448
Nock, A. J., 324
Nofziger, Ed, 263
Nouwen, Henri J., 406

Oatman, Johnson, Jr., 114
Ockenga, Harold, 234
Ogilvie, Richard, 404
Olford, Stephen, 363, 381, 383
Oliver, James, 436
Ormont, Jules, 295
Orr, J. Edwin, 381
Osborn, Alex, 269
Osler, Sir William, 235
Oursler, Fulton, 66, 228
Oursler, Grace Perkins, 262
Overstreet, H. A., 196
Owen, Robert, 351
Oxenham, John, 123, 188, 205

Packer, J. I., 178, 434
Paine, Thomas, 67
Palmer, Albert W., 458
Panin, N. J., 311
Parker, Theodore, 166, 452
Pascal, Blaise, 60, 92, 123, 218, 273, 300, 302, 315, 316, 430, 436, 451
Pasteur, Louis, 199
Paul, Leslie, 210
Paulinas (bishop of Nola), 389
Payne, John Howard, 195
Payson, Russell, 193
Peale, Norman Vincent, 44, 103, 241, 364
Penn, William, 86
Pepper, Claude, 28, 29, 30, 297
Perry, Ralph Barton, 31
Peter the Great, 82
Peterson, Eugene, 154

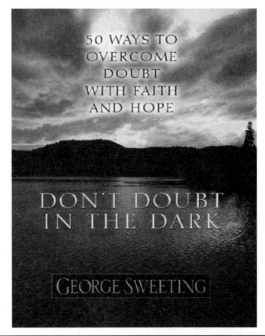

Don't Doubt in the Dark
50 Ways to Overcome Doubt With Faith and Hope

The Christian life can be tough. We often face circumstances beyond our control which can tempt us to doubt God's promises. This book asserts that while we may never know the mysteries of God, we can cling to His promises with confidence.

Quality Paperback 0-8024-8334-8

MOODY
The Name You Can Trust

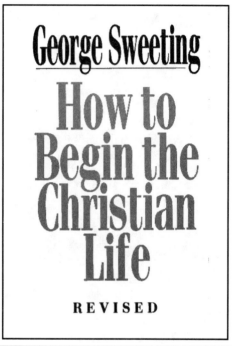

George Sweeting

How to
Begin the
Christian
Life

REVISED

How to Begin the Christian Life

This modern classic which has helped thousands get a strong start
in their Christian lives can do the same for you. Few men are better equipped than George Sweeting to explain how to begin the
most excellent adventure of your life.

Quality Paperback 0-8024-3581-5

MOODY
The Name You Can Trust

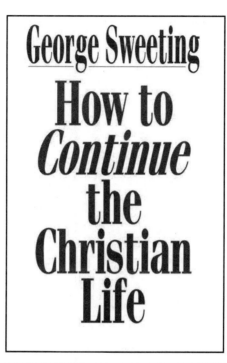

George Sweeting

How to *Continue* the Christian Life

How to *Continue* the Christian Life

By studying the Scriptures, Bible teacher George Sweeting has identified key areas that will enable you to crucial steps toward Christian maturity.

Quality Paperback 0-8024-3587-4

MOODY
The Name You Can Trust

Learn More about the Author.....
George Sweeting

With love as the hallmark of his decades of ministry, Dr.
Sweeting has a story that stands as a beacon to young people
willing to totally commit themselves to Christ. This is the story
of his upbringing in a godly Scottish-American home, his
conversion to Christ and call to the ministry as a young person,
his teenage love, his battle against a life threatening disease, his
emergence as an evangelist, pastor and finally head of one of the
leading Christian Institutions in the world.

ISBN: 0-8024-4024-X, Paperback - BIOGRAPHY